the
Good House Book

A NATURAL
HOME BOOK

The Good House Book

A Common-Sense
Guide to Alternative
Homebuilding

Clarke Snell

SOLAR • STRAW BALE • COB • ADOBE • EARTH PLASTER • & MORE

LARK BOOKS
A Division of Sterling Publishing Co., Inc.
New York

EDITOR: Terry Krautwurst
ART DIRECTOR: Kathleen Holmes
COVER DESIGNER: Barbara Zaretsky
COVER PHOTOGRAPHY: LOWER RIGHT, Don Gurewitz; ALL OTHERS, Clarke Snell
ILLUSTRATOR: Olivier Rollin
ASSISTANT EDITORS: Veronika Alice Gunter, Nathalie Mornu, Rain Newcomb
ASSOCIATE ART DIRECTOR: Shannon Yokeley
EDITORIAL ASSISTANCE: Delores Gosnell
PRODUCTION ASSISTANCE: Jeffrey Hamilton

The author and publisher wish to specially thank photographer Don Gurewitz, whose photographs of traditional buildings around the world add beauty and dimension to this book and celebrate the concept that housing is truly a shared human endeavor. All photos by Don Gurewitz are copyright Don Gurewitz.

Library of Congress Cataloging-in-Publication Data

Snell, Clarke.
    The good house book : a common-sense guide to alternative homebuilding
/ by Clarke Snell.— 1st ed.
       p.   cm.
    Includes index.
    ISBN 1-57990-281-2 (pbk.)
    1. Ecological houses. 2. Sustainable buildings—Design and construction. I. Title.
TH4860.S64 2004
690'.837—dc21

2003011724

10 9 8 7 6 5 4 3 2 1

First Edition

Published by Lark Books, a division of Sterling Publishing Co., Inc.
387 Park Avenue South, New York 10016

© 2004, Clarke Snell

Distributed in Canada by Sterling Publishing, c/o Canadian Manda Group, One Atlantic Ave., Suite 105 Toronto, Ontario, Canada M6K 3E7

Distributed in the U.K. by Guild of Master Craftsman Publications Ltd., Castle Place, 166 High Street, Lewes, East Sussex, England BN7 1XU Tel: (+ 44) 1273 477374, Fax: (+ 44) 1273 478606, Email: pubs@thegmcgroup.com, Web: www.gmcpublications.com

Distributed in Australia by Capricorn Link (Australia) Pty Ltd., P.O. Box 704, Windsor, NSW 2756 Australia

If you have questions or comments about this book, please contact:

Lark Books
67 Broadway
Asheville, NC 28801
(828) 253-0467

Printed in China

ISBN 1-57990-281-2

To my parents,
who gave me life
and let me use
their high-speed
Internet connection.

And most of all
to Lisa,
for sharing
all my dreams.

CONTENTS

INTRODUCTION

A NUMBER OF YEARS AGO, I became interested in buildings—and more specifically, in building houses. My reason was simple: I wanted one. Until then, I'd never really given buildings much thought. I didn't know how they were put together. I'd scarcely ever hammered a nail. In short, I was a babe lost in the building woods.

I did know one thing, though. I liked some buildings, and others I didn't. What was the difference? It took me years of research and practical, on-the-job construction experience—including building my own partially bermed,

passive solar house (shown here)—to realize that this simple question is at the heart of each of our individual searches for shelter: what makes a good building good?

That sounds like a question for a wise old sage, but I, a lowly schlub, can answer it for you. *The characteristic that all good buildings share is that they are specific. A good building is specific to its climate, its site, its culture, and its inhabitants. Good buildings are exact.*

Traditional, centuries-old building approaches—those practiced by native cultures—were, by definition, specific. Each developed slowly, over time, in response to a specific climate and in the context of a particular group of people. Modern building has in many ways lost touch with that heritage. Often the result is, quite simply, bad buildings. If you don't know what I'm talking about, take the discount superstore test. Go to the one nearest you and stand in the center. How do you feel? Your answer, I'm confident, will be that you don't feel at ease there. Such stores are examples of nonspecific building, an approach that is peculiar to our modern industrial society.

"Alternative" building (also variously called "natural," green," or "sustainable" building) encompasses a wide spectrum of ideas, techniques, and approaches that are a reaction against this trend. Alternative building, in a nutshell, is an attempt to recreate the specific nature of buildings in a modern context. For you, it is the search for the building that's specific to your local environment and your personal needs. This book's goal is to get you started on the road to finding that building, your good house.

Of course, I don't know you and I don't know where you live. So how can I help you create that specific house? I can identify and explain the issues you'll need to address in order to make a building that works with your local environment. I can introduce you to housing from the alternative building point of view, and start you thinking about how these concepts might apply to you.

To do that, first we'll consider what a house is, or can be, in connection with the planet and human life. Next, we'll explore the full spectrum of possibilities in building materials. Then we'll examine in considerable detail how buildings work. Chapter by chapter, we'll look at each of the four fundamental functions that all buildings—whether alternative or conventional—must provide. And in each case, we'll look for specific solutions that might help you define your good house. We'll consider traditional approaches that reflect a deep understanding of building specific to a climate and culture. We'll look at modern building techniques and discuss their pros and cons. And, of course, we'll carefully explore alternative building methods, contemporary approaches for creating houses that unite their modern inhabitants with their local environments. Along the way, you'll find interesting interviews with experts; sidebars and detailed drawings to help explain concepts; and photos—hundreds of them—that illustrate our discussions and, perhaps most importantly, demonstrate the extraordinary diversity of human housing all over the world.

Finally, we'll look in-depth at six actual homes that reflect popular directions in alternative building, and we'll talk to their builders about their experiences and the solutions that seemed right for them. Why did they make their particular choices? Would they do anything differently? What advice might they have for would-be owner-builders? Also, to close out the book, I'll discuss my own extensive resume of idealism and mistakes, and try to give you some practical tips on what to expect (and not to expect) as you go about the process of finding your good house.

In fact, I'll give you one important tip right now: The real secret to success in this journey is, first and foremost, to have fun. If you slow down and give the process the time it needs, you'll not only find that learning about building alternatives is interesting and enjoyable, but you'll also end up with a home that will change your life for the better. If you take shortcuts, force things, or let yourself get stressed, you'll probably end up thinking fondly of that old cramped apartment with the paper-thin walls and shag carpeting. In the end, as with most endeavors, it's all up to you.

Let's get started.

CHAPTER 1
WHAT IS A HOUSE?

IF YOU'RE NEW to this topic, you probably have little concept of what is holding the roof over your head or what's under your feet right now. Fortunately, all buildings—from straw huts to skyscrapers—are conceptually similar. Each can be conceived as an attempt to provide four basic functions, or elements: structure, stable temperature, separation from the outside, and connection to the outside. The trick for you as a builder isn't in understanding everything there is to know about these areas, but in finding approaches that work specifically for you and your environment. Over the course of this book we'll look at these four functions with the goal of helping you to start asking questions about ways to provide them for your situation.

Before we get down to how buildings work, though, or to choosing the bathroom wallpaper (I prefer duckies over seashells), let's cover some other fundamentals. We'll begin at the beginning, by defining buildings and exploring the ongoing evolution of their connection to the planet and human life.

The Human Connection

Human life is a paradox. On the one hand, it can't be separated from nature. If, for example, we lose access to oxygen for a few minutes, we'll die. On the other hand, we must be separated from nature. The world is full of forces—pathogens, for example—that can do us harm (see figure 1). How are we both protected from and nurtured by nature? The answer is, by the human body. Our bodies maintain a separation from but constant exchange with nature. They create a stable inside in the face of a fluctuating outside.

This is an amazing feat. Our little bodies maintain their own temperature in defiance of the vast volume of air that simultaneously surrounds and passes through them. They welcome air, food, and water into the inner sanctum while filtering out toxins and ruthlessly attacking hitchhiking pathogens. In this way, the body maintains a consistent interior environment, an inside, while continually adjusting to and incorporating nature, the outside.

This balance is made possible because the body isn't truly separate. It's a part of nature. Like everything in nature, the amazing system that is the human body is the result of myriad responses to specific situations and infinite changes, to trials and errors that yielded a particular result. Our world and the human body evolved

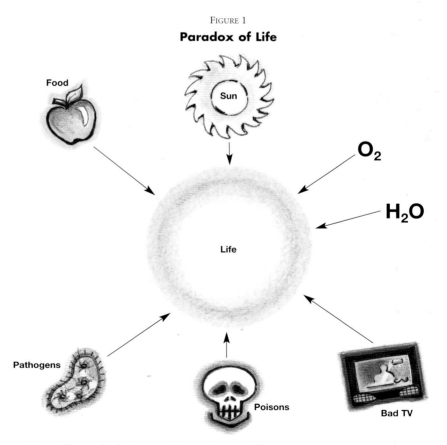

FIGURE 1
Paradox of Life

Food

Sun

O_2

H_2O

Life

Pathogens

Poisons

Bad TV

Human life must be both nurtured by and protected from nature.

> *"A house is a building designed to sustain human life."*

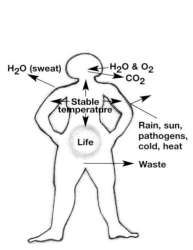

A roof over your head. The line between clothing and buildings is sometimes exceedingly fine. The hats of Balinese rice farmers are portable roofs that protect them from rain and sun.

together; they share a history, a specific story that unfolded slowly. Our inside—our bodies—and our outside—the rest of nature—are made of the same materials, yet are differentiated.

What does this have to do with buildings? A building is defined as a structure that differentiates space, creating an inside and an outside. Sound familiar? We see that the body is a building—the original building. More specifically it is a house, a building designed to sustain human life. As long as nourishment is available year-round, and as long as exterior temperatures remain within a manageable range, the human body is all the house we need. That's how we started out. Like all animals, humans were born into a climate that suited us *au naturel* (French for "butt naked"). As we started to move about the planet, we encountered situations that the body couldn't manage unassisted. Instead of retreating to body-friendly territory, we applied our ingenuity and adapted. Clothing and existing shelters such as caves probably came first, but eventually we started creating our own shelters in response to climate.

Houses, then, are simply an augmentation of the body in response to climate (see figure 2). Like the body, houses must create a stable environment, a separation from nature, while maintaining a constant exchange that nourishes the life within. Also like the body, housing wasn't created in a day; it evolved slowly over time in response to specific needs, specific situations. Long ago some genius was sitting out in the cold rain far from the nearest cave. The clever ancestor gathered some branches together, piled them up, and crawled underneath. The rest, as they say, is history. Housing is not a concept. It is a history. It is a collection of responses to specific stimuli (see figure 3).

FIGURE 2

Housing Is an Extension of the Human Body

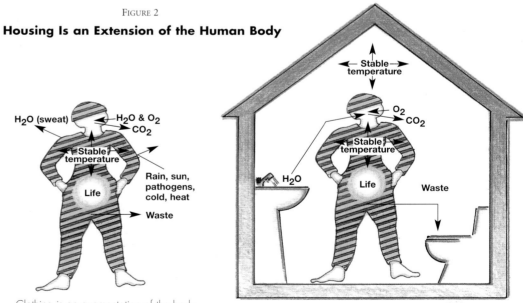

The human body maintains a separation from but constant exchange with nature.

Clothing is an augmentation of the body.

A house is an augmentation of clothing.

Traditional Building

We're still several thousand years from choosing your bathroom wallpaper, but we're closing in fast. Look again at the illustration below of our ancestor figuring out a housing system. No one person is that ingenious. That series of drawings represents the collective problem-solving over time of a group of people. In order for such a system to develop, several conditions must exist: (1) the people have to live in the same climate so that their solutions to specific problems will be useful to others; (2) they have to live there for a long time, so that the same problems can be approached over and over again, allowing for improvement; (3) they need to be able to communicate with one another, so that they can share experience.

What we're talking about is culture. Buildings and culture developed in tandem. In a traditional society, you wouldn't ask what kind of house to build. That'd be like asking

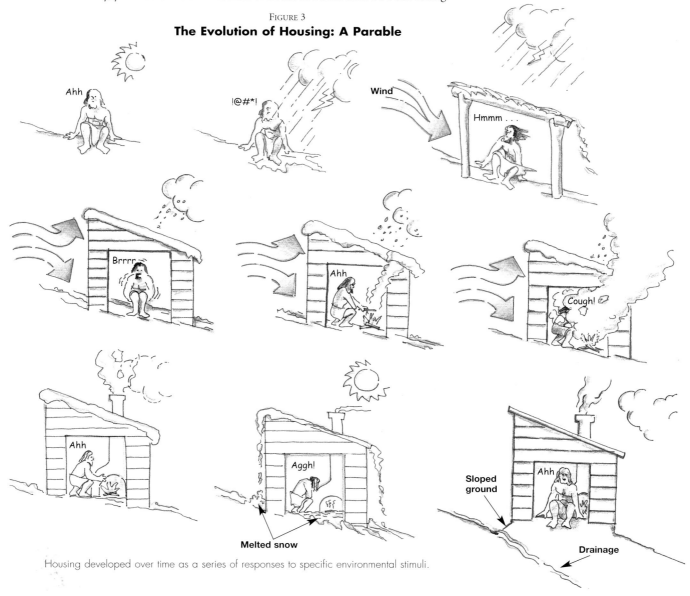

FIGURE 3
The Evolution of Housing: A Parable

Housing developed over time as a series of responses to specific environmental stimuli.

Set in stone. Obviously, this building carved out of solid rock in Petra, Jordan is specific to its local environment. It couldn't be created just anywhere.

Perfect here, but a snowball's chance elsewhere. Igloos are the elegant result of a slow evolution of human interaction with a specific environment.

what color is red. You'd build the same kind of house, with personal adjustments, that your parents built. They built the same house, with slight refinements, as their parents, and so on in a direct lineage back to the guy who crawled under the pile of sticks to get out of the rain. You'd build the kind of house that you had seen being built all your life. Housing would be a part of your culture. It would be specific to you.

An igloo, for example, is specific to the environment in which it evolved. Perfect there, it can't survive elsewhere. You can't build an igloo in Miami. Igloos are the result of specific people, in a specific place, sharing experiences. All over the world, traditional building reflects this localized evolutionary process.

Modern Building

Modern construction has lost contact with the roots of building. The modern world is a melting pot, a global culture defined not by place but by travel, not by the specifics of our environment but by our ability to circumvent those specifics. We aren't local; we're general, and our buildings reflect this.

Of course, in a sense the history of humans is the history of travel, of leaving home. Leaving our comfy original climate was what started our need for buildings. For a long time, this worked fine because we couldn't travel fast enough and shape the world radically enough to outrun our culture. If we moved away too quickly, into a climate that was really at odds with our existing building system, we met with failure (we'd freeze to death, for example), which ended the experiment.

That's not the case any more. We have the ingenuity to survive anywhere on this planet. We've taken buildings out of their environment and boiled them down into modular packages that can be dropped anywhere. This is the hostile-environment, or spaceship, approach: a box with attached life-support systems. You can install this box almost any place—Florida, Minnesota, or the Moon—because it has nothing to do with a specific environment. A general, adjustable environment is provided in the form of mechanical systems such as air conditioning, forced air heating, artificial

Are we having culture yet? Can you tell where this building is located? New York, Miami, San Francisco? No, it's in Hong Kong. Skyscrapers such as this cross climatic and cultural lines. They are replicated ad nauseam worldwide in the urban landscape.

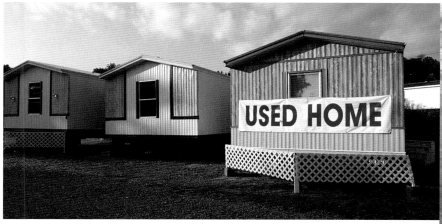

Traditional vs. modern. Top: Most modern housing is specific to an economy, not a climate or people. Right: Traditional housing is tied to its environment and culture.

lighting, pumped water, and flushable sewage. The boxes are the same; only the thermostat settings need be different. Instructions: In Florida, crank up the air conditioning; in Minnesota, crank up the heat.

What's wrong with this approach? Well, remember that the purpose of a house is to sustain human life, and that the paradox of human life is that it must be both separated from and connected to nature. Modern buildings are all *inside*. They're conceived as separate from the outside, as islands. This approach is convenient for an economy tooled to mass production, because it allows the centralized production of housing materials and even housing, as is the case with mobile homes. However, this economic convenience is paid for with a breakdown in the delicate exchange between human life and the environment.

The result is a variety of self-defeating and often destructive practices. We install sewage systems that combine drinking water with human waste, pesticides, and anything

> *"Modern buildings are all inside. They're conceived as separate from the outside, as islands."*
>
> ~

Life support. Like a patient in intensive care, this building is hooked up to the drip: intravenous injections of electric light and forced air circulation.

Outside out. The inoperable windows of modern office buildings turn them into the equivalent of glass-bottom boats. From the comfort and safety of your climate-controlled inside, you can gaze through glass at the strange world outside.

"How does this space make me feel?" How would you feel walking down the corridor above as opposed to the one on the right?

You can't fake it. Top: This dismal mall storefront tries to hide behind a feeble façade. Right: But good building isn't a "look." It can't be faked.

else anyone dumps down a drain, then treat it all with chlorine—a poison itself—and pump the "fresh" water back into our homes. We face our houses away from the sun, then burn polluting fuels to produce heat and light. We seal our houses to keep costly conditioned air in, then fill them with materials that give off dangerous gases. We extract resources from one local environment, digging a huge hole for a quarry or cutting vast tracts of timber, then use energy to transport the materials to another local environment, which we disrupt by bulldozing to make way for the materials.

We'll cover these and other modern-building boners later. My point now is that the general, mass-production, better-living-through-chemicals approach may work okay for manufacturing some products, but it doesn't work for houses. The result is often dangerous for both the inside, the human, and the outside, the environment.

In addition, this approach often fails to create surroundings in which we feel comfortable. Stand in nearly any building constructed in recent decades: your local mall, a high-rise office building, a sprawling high school. Ask yourself how you feel. Does this space make you feel alive? If it does, then you don't need this book. If it doesn't, then you'll be as interested as I am in looking for alternatives.

Alternative Building

I said in the introduction that alternative building is an attempt to re-create the specific nature of buildings in a modern context. How can that be done?

Let's look again at the three things necessary for a group of people to develop a housing system: living in the same climate, living there for a long time, and the ability to communicate. Of the three, modern culture can claim only the third. This is especially true in the United States and other industrial countries. We tend to organize our lives around jobs, not land, so we move frequently. This prevents us from accumulating consistent experience in a single climatic area.

Sustainable? These beautiful rice fields in Bali rival a modern city in the degree to which they've altered their environment. This traditional approach to agriculture is based on relatively small numbers of people supported by large amounts of land and resources. Can it be called "sustainable" on today's crowded planet?

In addition, in many ways we've become an indoor culture. We get our food not from the land, but from a building, a store. Our water is piped into our homes from miles or even hundreds of miles away. Our specific outdoor environment plays little role in our daily lives. Our lifestyle is no longer specific to our environment.

What's more, the activities that used to tie us to our surroundings, like growing food, gathering firewood, and collecting materials for and building houses, have been centralized as part of our economy. We pay to have these things done for us. We are specialists, each choosing one small area on which to concentrate. This focus becomes our career, the proceeds from which we use to pay other specialists to do all the things we don't know how to do. For most of us that includes providing even such basics as food, water, and shelter.

Our loss of self-sufficiency is at the crux of our culture's difficulties in building good buildings. Self-sufficient people had to build housing using their own skills, local materials, and accumulated knowledge of what worked best in their situation. The result was housing specific to and connected with the environment.

But facts are facts: We're no longer self-sufficient. Traditional self-sufficiency was made possible by sparse populations using abundant local resources. It's a whole different game with six billion people, many of whom are concentrated in cities, areas in which local building materials have either been depleted or otherwise made inaccessible. And even when we have the local resources, we no longer know how to use them. Also, we need different things from buildings than traditional people did. We spend more time indoors. We use more technology.

So we can't be self-sufficient in the traditional sense. Yet we've learned that good buildings are specific to their situation and that self-sufficiency allows people to create specific buildings. The key in today's context is to bring the "self" back into the process. We have to start taking responsibility again for our own housing.

Asphalt pasture. Asphalt retires the ground beneath from active duty, isolating it from water, plants, and animals. An asphalt pasture is excellent for grazing cars, but is unable to provide building materials, food, water, or anything else needed to sustain human life.

> *"We each need to create our own personal traditional building system."*
>
> ∼

That doesn't necessarily mean building your own house. It means connecting with your environment, the specific spot where your house will be. It means connecting with yourself, the specific cultural and personal idiosyncrasies that make up your modern tribe, your family. What kind of building will be the intersection of this place and these people?

Our task, then, is to approximate the results of several thousand years of self-sufficient indigenous culture. We each need to build our house as if our family, our ancestors, had been living on our building lot for thousands of years. We each need to create our own personal traditional building system, an approach that is specific to our climate, our site, our culture, our family, and our personality.

You can do this only by being involved in the creation of your home. You are the only expert on the tiny migrating tribe that is settling on your building site. How should a family consisting of a Jewish husband with ties to Eastern Europe and some Swedish blood, a Christian wife with descendants from Nigeria through Cuba, and their two kids who are into rap music and country line dancing, respectively, integrate with the three acres of land they just bought in Arizona? Only they have a prayer of figuring that out because only they are experts on the unique little "tribe" that will live in that three-acre ecosystem.

Traditional builders didn't pick a look, a style, or design for their homes. They built the house they knew and understood based on culture, knowledge, and experience accumulated over a thousand years or more. You are the product of a different thousand years, but that house exists for you, too, hidden within the exactness of who you are and where you live. The process of uncovering that house—your little tribe's indigenous structure—is at the heart of alternative building.

The right house? To my mind, this is a good house not because it uses straw bales to insulate most of the walls, but because it was thoughtfully created by the people who live in it. This house is full of stories, love, and struggle, and that's what makes it work. (To learn more about this house's story, see chapter 7.)

Chapter 2
MATERIALS

"There are no intrinsically good materials for house building."

~

I CAN ALWAYS TELL when I meet an alternative building greenhorn, because the only thing he or she talks about is materials. More than once while I was building my house someone would say, "What kind of house are you building?" I'd ask what they meant and, after getting no clarification, would start explaining my approach; that my site was an old tobacco field, that I was partially earth-sheltering, that I . . . at about that point the person would interrupt me and say, "I'm going to build a straw bale house." Now, as someone interested in straw as a building material, I'd start asking questions about what they had in mind, only to find that they had no real idea. All they knew was that they were going to get some straw bales and build a house and it was going to be better to live in, better for the environment, and cheaper and easier to construct. My friends, that isn't alternative building, or building of any sort. It's delusional thinking, plain and simple.

My first rule of alternative building, and I suggest tattooing this someplace where you'll see it often, is that there are no intrinsically good materials for house building. I agree that there are bad materials (mashed potatoes and plutonium are two that come to mind) but as for good materials, it depends on how, when, and where you use them—in other words (you guessed it) the specifics of your situation. (See the sidebar Defining A "Good" Building Material on page 34 for a discussion of some of the issues you'll want to consider.)

If you're starting out in the world of building, don't let yourself become infatuated with any one material application, like my friends who were "going to build a straw bale house." Get to know all of them, learn all you can, and keep an open mind.

How can you choose the correct materials for your house? You can't, until you know a lot more. Materials are chosen to solve problems, to fulfill particular needs. Until you understand those problems and needs, you can't choose the materials. As you learn about housing and the particular demands of your situation, the roles that various materials might play will slowly fall into place.

Many alternative-building books are organized by materials. There's the straw bale chapter, the cob chapter, the rammed earth chapter, etc. In my opinion, this creates a false perception of difference. Most buildings are more alike than they are different. I choose instead to look at the problems buildings are solving and to lump similar solutions together. Materials will come up again and again in this book in different contexts and grouped together in different ways. This chapter is simply an introduction, a chance for you to get acquainted with the possibilities.

Traditional Building Materials

For most of our history, we've used what was around us to build houses. On the whole, we've been amazingly resourceful in this regard, using only the raw materials at hand. Here's a synopsis of what we've come up with.

EARTH

The most consistently abundant building material on the planet is the ground itself. Put simply (forgive me, geologists), the ground we walk on is made of rock, crushed rock, and rotting dead stuff. *Rock* is a naturally formed aggregate of inorganic materials, mostly minerals. Hunks of rock just lying around are called *stone*. *Dirt* is made of crushed rock (sand and clay) and humus. *Sand* is crushed rock that doesn't absorb water, and *clay* is crushed rock that does. *Humus* is decayed organic matter from dead plants and animals. From this pedestrian mix, we humans have cajoled a cornucopia of varied building materials.

Earth rocks. For eons our planet's generous geology has provided us with building materials such as this stone being worked by a mason in Luxor, Egypt.

Stone

You don't have to be an Einstein to figure out that stone is a good building material. For millennia it has been scattered all over the place virtually shouting, "Hey, I'm stackable!" Remains of simple stone structures in Europe have been dated to before 12,000 B.C. Stone buildings such as the Great Pyramids, probably constructed around 3000 B.C., are mind-boggling even to modern machine-age humans.

> *"The most consistently abundant building material on the planet is the ground itself."*
>
> ∾

Form and function. Stone's strength and versatility are obvious in this entrance to Angkor Thom in Cambodia, the ruined capital city of the ancient Khmer empire.

The Great Pyramids. These stone buildings, astonishing even by modern building standards, were constructed some 5,000 years ago in what is now Giza, Egypt.

Mud (Water and Dirt)

Everybody knows that water plus dirt equals fun (just ask any kid). That's only one of the reasons why mud is such a wonderful building material. Wet dirt is easy to obtain, easy to work with, and dries to a hard, durable substance when the clay in the mix absorbs moisture and acts as a binder for the other materials.

What's more, you can use different soils, and process them in different ways, to produce different results. You can sift out some of the rocks, choose soils with higher or lower clay content, mix in additional ingredients, use more or less water . . . and so on. Humus, for example, is usually removed initially because it will decay, weakening the construction and perhaps attracting pests. But in some applications other organic materials—such as straw—are mixed in later to provide additional strength. Experimentation is a favorite human pastime, and over the eons we've come up with many variations and refinements on using mud. Here are some examples:

MONOLITHIC MUD (COB, RAMMED EARTH)

In this technique, some form of wet soil from which humus has been removed is molded by hand or stuffed into the cavity between temporary partitions, called *forms*, to create thick, self-supporting walls. This approach has been used around the world for thousands of years. Each culture has a different soil and climate to contend with, so many variations have developed. For example, different additives, such as straw, animal dung, blood, or urine, can become the trademark of a local mud mix. Today we usually call this technique *cob*.

Soil, sand, and straw. Here, a heavy clay soil was mixed with water, sand, and straw, then formed by hand into thick earth walls. The next step will be to apply an earthen plaster using mainly the same materials.

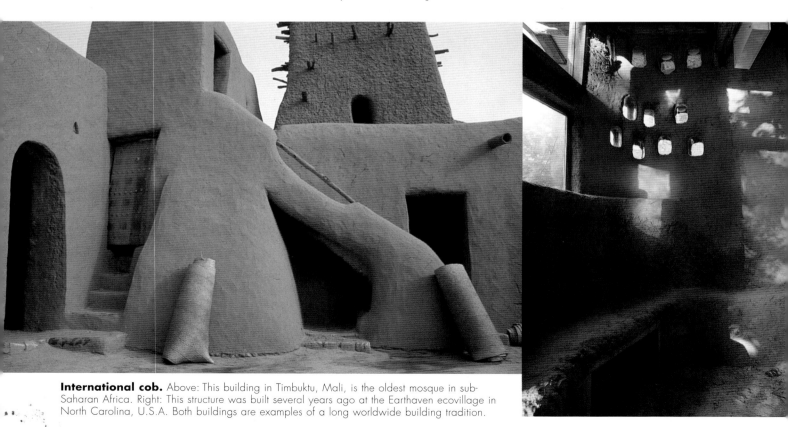

International cob. Above: This building in Timbuktu, Mali, is the oldest mosque in sub-Saharan Africa. Right: This structure was built several years ago at the Earthaven ecovillage in North Carolina, U.S.A. Both buildings are examples of a long worldwide building tradition.

Rammed earth construction is the name sometimes given to a modern adaptation of this method that employs heavy equipment, industrial-strength forms, and small amounts of concrete as a binder.

BLOCK MUD (ADOBE)

Adobe, too, is made from wet soil minus its organic matter. The difference is that the mud is molded into blocks. The blocks are dried in the sun and then stacked in an interlocking fashion to form walls. In the United States adobe is often associated with the arid Southwest, but in fact adobe is used across the continent and throughout the world. Adobe buildings dating to thousands of years B.C. have been found in the Middle East and Africa. The Tower of Babble was reportedly built of sun-dried soil bricks.

FIRED MUD (BRICK)

Fired bricks are made of clay-rich mud. Though perhaps thought of as a modern material, bricks have been made for thousands of years; perfectly intact bricks dating to 5000 B.C. have been excavated. Bricks made today are basically identical to their ancestors. Modern equipment allows greater control in manufacture and, of course, mass production, but the end product is essentially unchanged.

Rammed earth. These rammed earth walls were created by tamping damp soil mixed with a small amount of Portland cement between modular forms.

Adobe blocks. This is a village brickyard in the Tibetan kingdom of Mustang in Nepal. These particular adobe bricks are made of mud and barley straw.

Traditional adobe. This residence in Timbuktu, Mali, is made of adobe blocks. Traditional adobe buildings often are covered with mud plaster for additional protection from the elements. There's little rainfall in Timbuktu, so these blocks can remain unplastered.

"Modern" brick. Bricks made today are essentially the same as those made thousands of years ago.

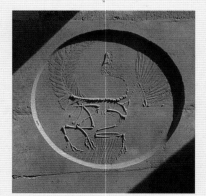

Modern Rammed Earth Wall Construction

by Phillip Van Horn

Here, environmental housing designer Phillip Van Horn describes one technique for using earth as a building material. The house featured was conceived by Phillip Van Horn Design along with the owners, contractor (Terra Firma Builders Ltd), and construction team.

Modern rammed earth wall construction is a variation on an ancient technique. Though much has changed in thousands of years, dirt has remained the same. Now as much as ever, earth walls are an excellent choice for a healthy, comfortable, and sustainable home.

Earth mixes for earthen walls vary based on many factors. Testing of available soils is of paramount importance. In some regions, a mixture of local sand, gravel, and clay soils is adequate. However, in areas where earthquakes or heavy moisture are factors, a small amount of cement powder is added to the soil mixture as a stabilizer. In addition, based on the water content of the soils being used and the temperature and humidity of the air, small, controlled amounts of water may be added to the earth and cement powder mixture in order to achieve the necessary strength of the finished earth walls.

Rammed earth house. This passive solar, partially underground, low-toxicity rammed earth house is located in British Columbia's Southern Gulf Islands. The two-foot-thick earth walls, many of which are completely underground, incorporate an integral, fully insulated cavity-wall system engineered to resist extreme seismic activity. The walls also provide excellent indoor air quality, acoustic control, and thermal storage for geothermal radiant heat and passive solar gain. Nontoxic sealers protect walls exposed to falling or driven rain from erosion.

Preparation for rammed earth wall construction is in many ways similar to that for modern concrete buildings. First, a concrete foundation is poured and strong formwork is erected, along with any required steel reinforcing, mechanical chases, or electrical conduit. Next, the site-mixed earth-and-cement mixture is placed into the formwork about 12 inches at a time and compacted by hand or with pneumatic tampers.

Earth walls are usually very thick, providing excellent thermal mass and a barrier against unwanted outside noise. Differences in soil composition give earth walls distinctive surfaces and color variations. You can get playful with the finished look by adding an assortment of materials, such as crushed oyster and clam shells, cinders, metal fillings, drilling tailings, or iron oxide colorants. A beautiful effect can be achieved by carving reliefs into the forms before adding the soil mixture.

Earth walls are extremely heavy and must be able to carry their own weight as well as that of floors and roofs above them. They also must withstand wind, rain, and earthquakes. In many cases, it's a good idea to have a core sample of a finished wall tested for compressive strength. Every region and site has different characteristics that must be considered. To determine the best materials, ramming techniques, and crucial reinforcement for your situation, consult local building codes and, especially, locally experienced earth builders and engineers.

Rammed art. A bird relief was carved into the formwork before tamping this rammed earth wall.

Rammed earth interior. The beautiful integral skin of these rammed earth walls works equally well as a final finish inside or outside. The floors are made of the same materials as the walls, though more cement and water were added to create a "trowelable" mix.

Wattle and daub. Top: Small branches are used as a substrate for mud and barley straw plaster on this dwelling in Xiahe, China. Right: The intertwined bamboo walls of this Laotian hut are plastered on the inside only.

APPLIED MUD (WATTLE AND DAUB, EARTH PLASTERS)

Mud also is often applied as a coating to a freestanding building. *Wattle and daub* is a technique in which a mud mix is spread over a substructure of woven sticks, branches, or other material. Mud *earth plasters* have long been, and still are, applied to adobe, cob, and other types of wall systems.

CONCRETE

Yes, concrete is a kind of "mud," too. Concrete is defined in my encyclopedia as "a structural material consisting of a hard, chemically inert particulate substance, known as aggregate (usually sand and gravel), that is bonded together by cement and water." Based on this definition, all the muds described above are concretes of a sort, with clay as the "cement," or binding material. Strictly speaking, though, true concrete contains a *hydraulic mortar*, a cement made of fired limestone, clay, and other earth-based materials. Hydraulic mortar doesn't harden by drying out; when mixed with water, the mortar undergoes a chemical reaction and solidifies, even when under water.

Concrete is often mistakenly thought to be a material of modern origins. In fact, it's an ancient technology. Thousands of years ago, the Romans mixed burnt limestone, also called *lime*, with volcanic ash (*pozzolan*), clay (often from crushed bricks), and small stones and other materials to make concrete

Earth plaster. A man replasters his house in Djenne, Mali.

capable of forming structural walls. Roman, or pozzolan, concrete was used to build the Pantheon early in the second century A.D. The Pantheon and other Roman concrete structures such as the Coliseum stand today, their well-preserved structural integrity amazing to modern engineers. Virtually all modern concrete structures are reinforced with steel rod; the Romans' buildings were not (see the sidebar, Roman vs. Modern Concrete).

What we call concrete today is just another in a long line of mixes that have been developed over concrete's illustrious career. Portland cement, the binder in most modern concrete, is a mixture of burnt limestone and clay that was patented in 1824 by a British stonemason who'd created the concoction in his kitchen. Most modern innovations in making concrete, as with those in brick making, involve machines that allow mass production and centralized distribution.

Roman concrete. Roman concrete was pounded, not poured, into place. Layers of a relatively dry mixture of mortar and water were pounded together with aggregate to create a strong material free of weak pockets. The Coliseum in Rome is just one example of the marvel of ancient concrete.

Concrete support. This highway bridge support is made of concrete reinforced with steel rods.

Roman vs. Modern Concrete:
A DISCUSSION WITH DAVID MOORE

Q: Our ancestors were able to do amazing things with concrete without the use of steel reinforcement. Why can't we make concrete as well as the Romans—or can we?

I believe that the incredible longevity of Roman concrete comes not from some magical use of materials, but more likely from the Roman method of mixing and placing concrete. We tend to think of concrete as being "poured," but based on historical evidence it's more likely that the Romans placed the mortar and aggregate of their concrete by hand and then pounded the two together in place. Drier concrete mixes are stronger because they leave fewer air pockets, and hand pounding ensures good contact between the aggregate and the mortar. The Romans had lots of low-cost, often "free," i.e. slave, labor and they had no reinforcing bars that needed to be thoroughly coated and worked around. The result is buildings like the Pantheon, which has a concrete dome that spans 43 meters and still stands today despite almost 2,000 years of weather, earthquakes, floods, wars, and sometimes serious abuse and neglect, all without the use of any metal reinforcement.

On the other hand, despite our technological advances, modern concrete often fails after only a relatively few years of use. This happens fundamentally because of water content. We use more water in our concrete to reduce the cost of placement—a concrete that "pours" is easier to work with, requires less labor, and makes contact with reinforcing bars better. Unfortunately, poured concrete often has too much water or is overworked, which causes pockets of high-water-content material. After the concrete cures, even small amounts of excess water leave voids and pathways for external moisture to enter and freeze and crack the concrete.

We actually do know how to create very strong, long-lasting concrete. A modern approach that employs the same principles as the Romans is roller compacted concrete (RCC), which has been used in the building of dams. In this case, pozzolan, in the form of fly ash from power plants, is mixed with regular Portland cement and aggregate to create a very low-water-content pozzolan concrete that is placed in thin layers and compacted using special vibrating rollers. However, the problems of workability are different in dam building than in most other construction that uses reinforcing bars, so the technology works in this case, where it would not otherwise.

Modern concrete. Modern concrete is often mixed relatively wet, making it easy to pour but structurally more vulnerable. Small amounts of excess water leave openings for external moisture, which can freeze and cause cracks.

David Moore is a civil engineer with more than 45 years of wide-ranging civilian and military work experiences. He has written a book, The Roman Pantheon: The Triumph of Concrete, *and has a website (www.romanconcrete.com) dedicated to the topic.*

Glass is an ancient material.
Ubiquitous in modern construction, glass has been used in buildings for more than 2,000 years.

Metal

Metals make up about 75 percent of known chemical elements and are abundant in the earth's surface. The most common metallic elements are aluminum, iron, calcium, sodium, potassium, and magnesium. Processed metals such as bronze—an alloy of copper and tin—were used by ancient cultures in buildings. The Romans, for example, installed bronze rafters to support a portico roof in the Pantheon, and laid gilded bronze tiles in the building's roof. The Romans also employed lead as a roofing material and for water and sewage pipes (the word *plumbing* comes from a Latin word meaning lead). The Chinese, too, were using metal as a building material thousands of years ago.

Glass

Glass also comes from the earth; it's produced by cooling molten ingredients, usually sand and limestone, rapidly enough to form transparent crystals. Various ancient cultures used glass in their art and, less often, in their buildings. The first known glass factory was created by the Egyptians around 1400 B.C. The first clear window glass was probably produced by the Romans. Glass reportedly was a common sight in public buildings and middle-class housing in Rome 2,000 years ago.

PLANTS

The abundance of plants in our environment and their habit of regenerating made them an obvious choice for building materials right from the start.

Grasses

Grasses are a family of plants with jointed stems and slender leaves. They've been used as building materials for millenia.

Building with grasses. These buildings belonging to migrant Turkana herders in Kenya are made of woven native grass topped with additional grass roofing.

Building with straw. Dirt and millet straw were combined to make the walls of these buildings in Mali. The roofs are covered with mats of woven millet straw.

Roof thatching. Water reed thatching is used on a stable in New York, U.S.A.

Straw is the dried-out, skeletal stalks of grass plants, usually the byproduct remaining after drying and threshing wheat or other cereal grains. It has been used as an additive in adobe bricks for thousands of years in many parts of the world. In addition, bundles of straw stacked in mud mortar have been used for centuries in Asia and Europe.

Straw also has been used for centuries for thatching roofs, a technique—usually used on steeply pitched roofs—in which bundles of straw or wetland grass reeds are laid in overlapping rows. In many parts of the world straw also is a common wall covering, either woven into mats or hung in rows.

Bamboo is an amazing grass with a long history in human housing. Sometimes called tree grasses, there are over 1,000 bamboo species, the tallest of which grows to 130 feet. Bamboo is strong and light, making it suitable for framing walls and roofs. It can also be split to make planks, and smaller types can be woven to make mats. Bamboo has been and still is used extensively as a building material in Africa, Asia, and India.

Living grasses have been used for centuries in buildings. Sod construction, for example, is an ancient technique. Native Inuit living in what is now Newfoundland built sod roofs on simple structures around A.D.1400. Sod building, brought over from Scandinavia and Europe, was popular in the midwestern United States in the nineteenth century. Sod is basically a grass brick cut from the ground; a thick network of roots entrenched in heavy soil holds the brick together. Sod is laid like brick to form walls. In pioneer sod buildings, roofs made of wood timbers or sticks were often covered with more sod.

Bamboo. This building in northern Thailand has a bamboo floor structure, as well as split-bamboo wall and floor coverings.

Sod. Sod houses weren't always tiny pioneer shacks, as is evident from this regal sod building in North Dakota, U.S.A.

Workable wood. Durability, availability, and workability all make wood a popular choice as both a structural and decorative building material.

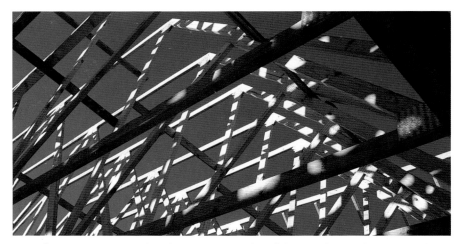

Wood trusses. Trusses utilize the geometric rigidity of the triangle to make strong structural units. These modern trusses are the progeny of a concept that's been around for thousands of years.

Wood

Wood is the hard, fibrous tissue that conducts water and gives structural strength to the roots and stems of trees and shrubs. No one knows when wood construction began, but perhaps among the first wooden structures were the woven frameworks of twigs used in wattle-and-daub buildings, the wooden poles of tents, and the wooden frameworks of yurts. There's evidence of construction using heavy timbers dating from thousands of years B.C. With the advent of metal tools in the Bronze and Iron Ages, less effort was required to fell and work large trees. We began to shape wood to form better connections, paving the way for sophisticated log cabins and timber framing. With metal tools, wood could also be split into planks and shingles for siding and roofing. Wood *trusses* were used as early as 2500 B.C. and were later utilized extensively by the Greeks and Romans.

ANIMAL PRODUCTS

Animal parts and products also are ancient fixtures in human building materials. Animal skins have long been used to cover tents, yurts, and the doors of simple structures. Animal dung, blood, milk, and urine have been mixed in as additives for monolithic mud, adobe, and earth plaster. Resourceful humans have made the most of various other animal-provided materials, too. There's evidence, for example, that the Inuit sometimes used whalebones for roof rafters.

Animal products. The camel dung drying near this house in Rajasthan, India, will be used as fuel; dung is also used as an additive in earth-based building materials.

Modern Building Materials

As you can see, many materials we think of as modern actually have been used for thousands of years. Brick, concrete, glass, metal, and wood all are building materials that remain largely unchanged from their ancient counterparts. Most modern innovations are simply the result of mechanization aimed at quality control and mass production. It can be argued, for example, that modern drywall is really a version of wattle and daub (see figure 1). Other innovations, such as tempered glass, are variations on a theme rather than out-and-out modern concoctions. There are, however, some materials that are genuinely modern in origin and are now used widely in building. Plastics, in particular, are predominant.

PLASTICS

"Plastics" is a catchall term for synthetic polymers, materials made of long strings of carbon and other elements. Plastic polymers are usually derived from petroleum. It is truly mind-boggling how many plastics can be made from this single raw material. They can be molded into an infinite variety of shapes; can be extruded in thin, strong sheets; and for the most part are highly water-resistant. All these qualities make them tempting building materials. Polyethylene sheet plastic is used as a moisture and air infiltration barrier. Polystyrene and polyurethane plastics are used as insulation. Polyvinyl chloride and other plastics are used in water and drain pipes. Many common adhesives and sealants are made from plastics, including the glues used in plywood and other composite lumber products.

Mass production. Many so-called "modern" building materials actually have been used for millennia. Present-day versions are the result of mechanization focused on mass production and uniformity.

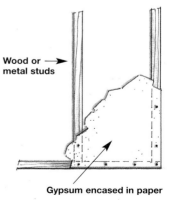

Plastic. Polyvinyl chloride (PVC) pipe is a genuinely modern material.

FIGURE 1

Evolution of a "Modern" Material

The modern material we know as drywall is essentially a mass-produced version of traditional wattle and daub.

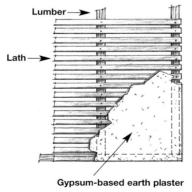

WATTLE AND DAUB

Woven sticks →

Clay-based earth plaster

Wattle and daub consists of a clay-based soil and water mix (the daub) placed over an interlaced stick frame (the wattle).

LATH AND PLASTER

Lumber →

Lath →

Gypsum-based earth plaster

Lath and plaster is a more recent version. Earth-based plaster made from gypsum rock and water is laid over a framework of wooden lath and lumber.

DRYWALL

Wood or metal studs →

Gypsum encased in paper

Drywall is basically lath and plaster in sheet form. It consists of a core of gypsum rock wrapped in paper. The gypsum is crushed, wetted, and allowed to dry, forming a rocklike panel.

Defining a "Good" Building Material

As I've said, there are no intrinsically good building materials—ultimately, the specifics of your situation determine whether a given material is right for your application. Among the factors to weigh, of course, are performance and function. But in today's world other considerations are important, too.

In traditional, self-sufficient cultures there are three questions, or issues, that define a good building material:

1) *Is it easy to get?*
2) *Is it easy to use?*
3) *Does it do its job?*

Easy to get means locally abundant. Easy to use means that it doesn't require a lot of processing before it can be used, and is good to work with. Doing its job means that it fulfills its specific purpose and withstands the test of time.

In the modern world, the same issues apply—but our culture approaches them differently. "Easy to get" is defined by two factors: commercial availability and cost. A building material is "easy to get" if it's sold at the local lumberyard for a price you can afford. In other words, it must be mass-producible to make it inexpensive, and transportable to make it available. "Easy to use" also takes on a different connotation. Products are often geared toward specialists who invest in specialized machinery and tools for installing specialized materials. These materials, then, are easy for the specialists to use, not for most others.

This shift from local craft to centralized mass production has enabled the development of some wonderful materials. For example, double-pane glass, also called *insulated glass,* is an industrial product that allows us to better utilize our oldest heat source, the Sun (see chapter 4 for a discussion of the Sun as a heat source).

But this approach also has led to problems. Many modern production techniques cause pollution and release toxic materials. Often the products themselves are harmful. Numerous synthetic building products, for example, release hazardous compounds into the air, or *off-gas,* long after they've been installed. The combination of a well-insulated house and materials off-gassing results in an unhealthy indoor environment. In addition, the manufacture, transportation, and use of many materials create pollution that damages the outdoor environment.

Waste vs "unwaste." Right: Just a small part of the mountain of trash that will be one new building's contribution to the local dump. Bottom: A shallow pit made of straw bales holds a mixture of clay-rich dirt, sand, straw, and water for forming cob walls. The material isn't modular, so it can be made to fit the job without creating waste. If there's any left over, it can just go back to being dirt. The added straw will decompose and enrich the soil.

Clearcut. Once you start taking resources from one place to use in another, when do you stop?

If a building material contributes to an unhealthy outdoor or indoor environment, it goes against the entire purpose of housing—to help sustain human life—and therefore can't be considered good. This adds a modern criterion to the definition of a good building material:

4) *Does it pollute the indoor or outdoor environment?*

Another complication of mass production is that it tends to deplete local resources. When resources for thousands of buildings are harvested from one area, that area's ecosystem can be severely disrupted. Large-scale logging and stone quarrying are examples of such practices. Interestingly, this isn't strictly a modern phenomenon. For example, both the ancient Greeks and Romans suffered wood shortages several thousand years ago. Wood was in demand as a heating fuel, as an energy source for smelting operations, and as a building material. There simply wasn't enough to meet the demand.

However, our current situation is much more delicate due to the sheer number of people who need to be housed. When the Romans were having their wood shortage, there were around 200 million people on the planet. Today, we have over 30 times that many people and the growth rate is ever on the rise; the world's population doubled in the past 30 years. It is simply a necessity to consider a resource's renewability when assessing its value as a building material. Therefore, we have another addition to the definition of a good building material in the modern world:

5) *Can it be replenished?*

Another trait of mass-produced materials is that they're modular. On the face of it, that sounds great. When you go to buy a piece of plywood, for instance, you know it'll be 4 feet wide by 8 feet long. You know what you're getting. But in actual use modularity is often wasteful because the world doesn't always conform to multiples of a given product's dimensions. If you visit a conventional construction site, much of what you'll see is people cutting modular materials into sizes to fit the job at hand. By the end of the project there'll be a mountain of plywood, dimensional lumber, fiberglass insulation, and other materials that are simply the cut-offs from mass-produced modular units. This heap is headed for the dump. Plywood, fiberglass, plastic sheeting, and other modular materials don't break down, or biodegrade, easily—if at all. As trash in a landfill, they become resources that are for all practical purposes permanently inaccessible.

In a crowded, polluted world, that makes no sense. So there's yet another question to be answered when defining a good building material in today's world:

6) *Does it create waste?*

Alternative Building Materials

We've established (see the sidebar, left) that the ideal building material for today's world is easy to get, easy to use, effective and durable in doing its job, nonpolluting both indoors and out, replenishable, and non-waste-producing. This formula is more complicated than it might seem at first, one that involves some difficult issues (see the sidebar on page 42, Embodied Energy, for one example) that can quickly create simplistic zealots or disheartened idealists. Your specific answers can come only from an understanding of your local environment and the particular problems and challenges it poses.

However, there are basic strategies to alternative building that have made some materials particularly popular. Let's look at these strategies and some of the corresponding materials.

RECYCLED AND "WASTE" MATERIALS

Humans have always found building uses for whatever is abundant around them. But our world is changing rapidly, and once-seemingly infinite resources are dwindling. So what is abundant today? One intriguing answer is trash, the byproducts of industry and contemporary culture.

The new wood? People have always used abundant materials for building. In the modern world, used tires are more abundant than wood.

Earthship. This building's exterior walls are made mostly of used tires stacked and tamped full of dirt.

Used Tires

Used automobile tires are a real problem in our world. The same characteristic that makes them suitable for the grueling job of rolling cars over pavement also makes them terrible garbage: they're almost indestructible. They don't break down easily, and burning them creates plumes of noxious black smoke, so they quickly fill our dumps. By the same token, the property that makes tires terrible trash makes them a great building material. Tires are durable in most situations. They're relatively unaffected by water and sun and are unpalatable to insects.

Michael Reynolds, a Taos, New Mexico architect and visionary, has pioneered the use of waste tires in housing. In his system, tires are tamped full of dirt and used like bricks in earth-sheltered homes that he calls Earthships. (See chapter 7 for a discussion of a house using a hybrid Earthship design.) Far from being a funky anomaly, Earthships have been built, monitored, and steadily improved for the past 30 years. As a result, the use of tires as forms for rammed-earth blocks is catching on with other builders in other parts of the United States and the world.

Byproduct Straw

Straw has been used for thousands of years in buildings, but straw bales are a relatively new development. The first baler was invented in the late 1800s, allowing straw to be packaged in nice tidy blocks. It didn't take people long to realize that you could stack

Pioneer straw bale. You can clearly see how the straw bales were stacked in a staggered pattern, like fuzzy bricks, to create self-supporting walls for this temporary building at a county fair in 1913.

Clay-slip straw. Here, a clay-slip straw mixture, often simply called slipstraw or light straw-clay, was packed by hand into temporary forms attached to a wooden post-and-beam structure. To the right of the wood post, you can see the hardened slipstraw. The slipstraw to the left of the wood has been covered with an earthen plaster.

these blocks like bricks. Soon houses with baled straw walls started appearing on the Nebraska prairie. Some of those late-nineteenth-century buildings still survive.

Today, straw is most often a byproduct of industrial agriculture. After cereal grasses are harvested and processed to extract the grain, the skeletal stalks are left over. This straw is generally viewed as waste and is sometimes burned as such.

But in fact, baled straw can be a superior building material. It's excellent insulation, fire resistant, not particularly interesting as a food source for pests, and can be exceptionally durable. In addition, it's easily renewable. For all these reasons, straw is a popular alternative building material, either baled or used to make other building materials such as straw-filled, paper-covered insulative panels. It's also used with clay to make cob and *clay-slip straw* (also called *straw-clay*) walls. Clay-slip is a mix of fine clay particles and water. This slurry is blended with straw to create a mixture that, when dry, becomes solid.

Wood-based Waste

Many industries create huge amounts of wood-based waste that can be recycled into useful building materials. For example, recycled paper and newsprint are used to create *cellulose insulation*. This material has many of the advantages of straw and is superior to fiberglass insulation in many ways (see chapter 4). Composite blocks made of cellulose and concrete, such as Faswall and Durisol, are another use for industrial wood waste. These blocks are made of recycled wood fibers, nontoxically treated for protection against rot and insect damage, bound together with Portland cement. The result is a strong concrete block with superior insulation value. In addition, chipped waste wood held together by strong glues is fashioned into a variety of products, including I-beams to replace dimensional wood floor joists and sheets to replace conventional plywood. However, many such products use virgin wood and formaldehyde glues, so educate yourself before buying.

Read it and re-use it. Recycled paper is used to make cellulose insulation and other building products.

New block off old chips. Recycled wood chips bonded with concrete make up this building block.

Cellulose insulation. A cellulose product made of recycled paper was blown behind fabric mesh to insulate this wall.

Recycled Plastic

Recycled plastics are being used in increasing quantities to make durable building materials. Among them are composite recycled plastic lumbers that can replace, among other things, "rot resistant" exterior wood products treated with a poisonous solution containing arsenic. The Plastic Lumber Company, for example, uses recycled plastic milk jugs to make decking as a substitute for conventional pressure-treated wood decking. Another company, Carefree Xteriors, makes a similar decking product and estimates that 2,500 milk jugs are diverted from the landfill for every 100 square feet of decking used. They also produce a fiberglass-reinforced recycled-plastic lumber suitable for structural applications.

Recycled plastics also are used to make permanent concrete forms. Rastra foundation forms, for instance, are made of 85 percent recycled polystyrene plastic. The forms are stacked and filled with concrete, then left in place, creating an insulated concrete wall.

Recycled Concrete Ingredients

Many materials are being recycled as replacements for virgin materials in concrete. For example, fly ash, a powder residue that is a byproduct of coal-fired electric generating plants, is a common substitute for some of the Portland cement in concrete mixes. In addition to saving energy and removing a material from the waste stream, using fly ash can improve concrete's quality by reducing the amount of water in the mix, which increases the concrete's strength and reduces corrosion of steel reinforcement. Spent sand from glass production and the steel belts from used tires are two more industrial byproducts that are being used in concrete production.

In addition, the high temperatures required to manufacture cement allow plants to burn many waste products, thus utilizing their energy. Scrap tires, used motor oils, surplus printing inks, dry cleaning solvents, paint thinners, sludge from the petroleum industry, and agricultural wastes such as almond shells are some of the products adding fuel to the fires at cement plants. Of course, the downside of this is that the burning can also create air pollution.

Plastic lumber. These materials, made of recycled plastic milk jugs, are designed to replace wood in many of its common uses in building.

Fly ash concrete. The concrete posts and beams, the bricklike stabilized-earth blocks at left and along the foundation, and the stucco over straw bales at the far end of this wall all contain fly ash.

Recycled plastic forms. This house was built using permanent concrete Rastra forms made of recycled plastic.

LOCAL MATERIALS

Traditional building materials were almost always local. Today, many materials are traditional in origin but no longer local. Cement, bricks, and even wood are often shipped long distances from where they're produced to where they're used. As we've noted, this practice causes pollution in manufacture and transport. Just as significant, it robs builders of materials with site-specific flexibility. Traditional materials were adjustable to local environmental requirements. Plaster, concrete, and mud mixes were developed through experimentation to withstand the particular environment in which they were utilized. Alternative builders are leaning toward local materials in an attempt to regain flexibility, move toward self-sufficiency, and reduce pollution of both the indoor and outdoor environments. Here are a few examples of this trend.

Local materials. These Dogon men are using millet straw to weave baskets. The same straw is used as an additive in local adobe.

Earth

Though many modern building materials originate with natural substances extracted from the earth, they seldom utilize the dirt available on the building site itself. Deservedly, this age-old practice is coming back. Soil-mix "recipes" and guidelines for traditional practices such as adobe and cob have been developed to help people utilize their local dirt. Modern rammed earth building is a relatively technical undertaking requiring substantial formwork and close soil monitoring, but nonetheless also utilizes site-extracted dirt. Basic cob is made by mixing local clay soils with sand, straw, and water. The mixing is usually done with your feet; then the material is placed by hand to create thick, beautiful walls (see the photos below).

Another approach to rammed earth is to use small permanent forms for the packed dirt. We've already discussed one example of this technique, the rammed-earth tire walls of Earthships. Another example is *superadobe,* pioneered by Iranian-born architect Nader Khalili. In this technique, polypropylene or burlap bags are filled with soil and laid in courses like bricks. Each layer must be compacted by hand

Dig a hole, build a house. Building with cob is dirt simple: From this (left) . . . to this (middle) . . . to this (right).

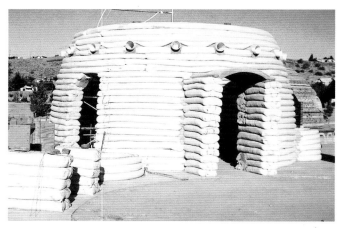

Superadobe construction. This dome at Khalili's Cal-Earth Institute is being constructed of long fabric tubes pumped full of damp dirt, then coiled like a huge coiled-clay pot.

Ceramic construction. The Rumi Dome of Lights at Cal-Earth in Hesperia, California, was designed by Nader Khalili and is made of fired bricks. Khalili also creates similar structures by building domes out of unfired adobe blocks and then firing the entire building from the inside out, creating an integrated ceramic building.

tamping. Reinforcement is provided by barbed wire laid between courses. The resulting wall or dome is then covered with a thick layer of plaster. Superadobe buildings also can be constructed using long fabric tubes instead of bags. These tubes are pumped full of damp soil and coiled into beehive-shaped domes. Khalili also has pioneered a technique for building ceramic houses. An entire dome built of adobe blocks is fired from within, fusing the adobe and creating a solid fired-clay building, like a big ceramic pot.

Plants

Modern-day builders seldom use wood or other plant-based materials from the building site, or even from the immediate area. Often, trees are cleared to make room for a house and then lumber is trucked in, frequently over long distances, to build the house.

Wood can be a sensible building material, especially if it's harvested from the site. *Portable saw mills* can turn felled trees into lumber. Another approach, one that uses smaller diameter trees, is *cordwood masonry* construction. In this technique short pieces of round or split wood, basically firewood, are laid like bricks in a sandwich of mortar and insulation.

We've already mentioned another plant source that's often available locally: baled straw. In addition, straw can be harvested every year, unlike trees, which makes it a more likely candidate as a renewable, local building resource. The same is true of such plants as bamboo when abundant in the region.

Cordwood construction. This wall-building technique makes use of small-diameter trees, which are routinely bulldozed and burned on conventional construction sites.

Living roof. Plants growing in soil atop layers of material providing drainage, waterproofing, and insulation add beauty and energy efficiency to a conventional roof.

Roofs covered in living plants, often called *living* or *green* roofs, are also becoming increasingly popular in alternative building circles. In the modern version, a synthetic waterproof membrane, often made of rubberized asphalt and plastic, is laid over a conventional roof structure. Then layers including rock or synthetic drainage, insulation, and soil are added and topped off with a vegetative layer suitable for the local climate. Living roofs are discussed further in chapter 5.

Split-bamboo fence. Renewable, site-harvested plant materials such as bamboo are useful wherever they're abundant.

NATURAL MATERIALS

"Natural" has to be one of the most abused words in our vernacular. The funniest definition I've seen is, "Natural: anything commercially packaged by the natural products industry." However, there's a useful concept behind the hype. When you use a material that appears naturally on the planet, you get a known quantity. Most building materials have been used for thousands of years. They're the things around us: stone, earth, trees. In the past century, humans have developed technology capable of creating synthetic compounds. The main problem with using synthetics is that you don't know how they will interact with the world. These products really do make guinea pigs out of all of us.

This is one reason why alternative builders have a strong propensity toward natural materials. For example, they often choose earth plasters over those containing industrial lime or Portland cement, and organic paints and stains over their mainstream commercial counterparts. In general this practice reflects a healthy distrust of the newest miracle products and results in efforts to relearn older techniques that may still be of great use. Hence, the renewed interest in adobe, cob, straw, and stone construction.

Is gravel natural? Gravel is a good example of the nebulous character of the word "natural." What could be more natural than rocks? However, "natural" probably isn't the first word you think of when you look at a gravel quarry.

Embodied Energy

Embodied energy is a major buzz term in alternative building circles. Basically, it refers to the total energy expended to produce a material, transport it to the point of use, and install it. This may sound simple, but when you really think about it your head starts to spin. In order to come up with an accurate total you have to consider, for example, all the energy needed to create the machinery used to produce a material; the energy consumed to mine, harvest, process, synthesize, etc. every element used in any given material; even the energy expended to produce the lunches the truck drivers and construction workers eat while they're transporting and installing that material.

Embodied energy numbers are the sort of thing self-confident people at parties throw out to help make their point (if it's a really boring party), but I take them with a grain of salt. The concept is important though, and for that reason I'm including some numbers in the chart shown here. The second column (Joules/kg) compares the materials based on weight. The third column (Joules/m3) makes a comparison based on volume.

Embodied energy figures alone, however, don't provide a complete picture. Once you've determined a material's embodied energy, you then need to factor in how long the material will last in a building and what its energy performance is likely to be.

For example, glass has a high embodied energy. However, a window opening without glass—in other words, a hole—would be a huge energy drain in winter (and in summer if you have air conditioning. . .but if you have AC, the embodied energy of glass is the least of your energy consumption problems). Putting glass in that hole will eventually save more energy than it took to make, transport, and install it. How much energy something saves compared to its embodied energy is a good measure of its value as a building material.

> *"How much energy something saves compared to its embodied energy is a good measure of its value as a building material."*

In other words the real efficiency question is, how much energy will a house consume over its lifetime? Using low-embodied-energy materials to build a house makes little sense if that house then eats a lot of energy in its daily life for heating, cooling, lighting, etc. By the same token, a low-embodied-energy, energy-efficient house isn't of much value if it doesn't last. Cool materials and hip construction approaches do nothing if they lack quality and aren't durable.

Material	Millions of Joules/kg	Millions of Joules/m3
Adobe, straw stabilized	0.5	750
Aluminum, recycled	8.1	21,870
Aluminum, virgin	191.0	515,700
Brick	2.5	5,170
Concrete, ready mix	1.0	2,350
Glass	15.9	40,060
Insulation, cellulose	3.3	112
Insulation, fiberglass	30.3	970
Insulation, polystyrene	117.0	2,340
Lumber, kiln-dried	2.5	1,380
Paper	36.4	33,670
Rammed-earth cement	0.8	
Steel, recycled	10.1	37,210
Steel, virgin	32.0	251,200
Stone, local	0.8	1,890
Straw, baled	0.2	31

Hammering It Home

We've seen that most common materials used in housing have been around for thousands of years and that modern innovations are mainly refinements or the result of mass production. Alternative building is not striking off in wildly experimental directions, nor is it returning to some forgotten, primitive past. There are more similarities than differences between traditional, modern, and alternative building materials. The exception is synthetics, such as plastics, which are new to the scene and relatively untested. Therefore, it's modern conventional construction that's often experimental, while alternative builders tend to be conservative by preferring local, time-tested "natural" materials to the newest innovations.

The challenge for you is to keep an open mind about materials. Until you understand the basic challenges of housing and the specific ways they manifest themselves in your particular situation, you have no criteria with which to choose materials. Identify your problems and challenges first, then choose materials that will solve them.

> *"It's modern conventional construction that's often experimental."*

Chapter 3

STRUCTURE

WHAT IS THE STRUCTURE of the building you live in now? How is it put together? If you're like many people, you know something is holding your house up, keeping the roof from falling on your head, but you're not sure what it is—or worse, what might cause it to fail. If you're apprehensive about taking charge of building your own house, the ominous nature of structure is probably part of the reason why. How can you possibly make decisions about something as crucial as the structure of your home?

Relax; the subject isn't as daunting as you might think. Most buildings are structurally similar. The materials may be different and may be used in different combinations, but the principles are essentially the same. Popular alternative techniques use the same tried-and-true structural concepts as their commercial counterparts. In this chapter, we'll look at these concepts and at the structural components of popular approaches in alternative building.

Loads

Everything in our world has some form of self-supporting structure, the function of which is to withstand physical pressures. The basic pressure that everything must endure is that of its own weight, the force of gravity.

The pressures exerted on buildings are called *loads* (see figure 1). There are two types: *dead* and *live*. Dead loads are forces exerted by the building itself. These include the weight of the building's structure and outer covering, plus that of permanent fixtures such as fireplaces. Live loads are the forces exerted by everything that isn't part of the building, such as wind, earthquakes, people, furniture—and maybe the occasional meteor. All buildings deal with these loads via a self-supporting structure made up primarily of three structural elements: foundation, walls, and roof.

FIGURE 1

Forces on a Building

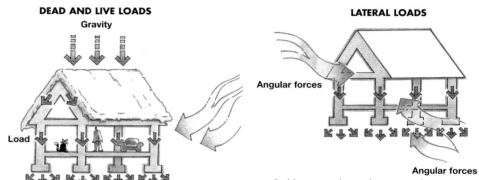

DEAD AND LIVE LOADS

A *load* is any force on a structure. *Dead loads* are permanent forces on a structure: the weight of the building and permanent fixtures. *Live loads* are transient or moving forces: occupants, furniture, snow, wind, etc.

LATERAL LOADS

Buildings must have *shear strength* to resist wind, earth tremors, and other forces, called *lateral loads*, that come at angles to the structure. This strength is accomplished by redirecting lateral loads to the ground.

COMPRESSION AND TENSION

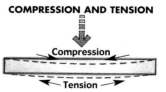

Compression is a pressing force that squeezes a material together. *Tension* is a stretching force. *Bending* occurs when one side of a material squeezes in compression as the other side stretches in tension in response to a force.

A spring toy has excellent *compressive strength* . . . but horrible *tensile strength*.

Foundations

Ultimately, the support structure for every house is the earth. The job of the foundation is to transfer all loads exerted on the house to the earth. All foundations accomplish this by (1) accessing solid ground, (2) keeping that ground solid, and (3) distributing or spreading out onto the ground loads exerted on the house.

"Solid ground" means undisturbed soil below the frost line (see the sidebar, What Is the Frost Line?, below right). The basic idea is that the ground must be stable, susceptible neither to frost heave nor to moisture. You don't want the ground moving under your house. Wet dirt, frozen or not, moves. Both surface and ground water must be kept off any foundation, a necessity achieved by sloping soil away from the building and by proper drainage (see the sidebar, Foundation Drainage, on the next page).

The foundation's other job, distributing loads from the house evenly to the ground, is a task accomplished best by a monolithic structure (see figure 2). Snowshoes are a good illustration of this concept. A snowshoe is able to distribute weight because it's wide and doesn't bend. If you step in deep snow, you sink. The snow isn't stable enough to support the weight of your body concentrated in an area the size of your foot. The snowshoe distributes the same weight across more area, putting less pressure on each square inch of snow, thus allowing you to be supported (see figure 3). Foundations work on the same principle. They're wide and work as a unit.

> *"Ultimately, the support structure for every house is the earth."*
>
>

A solid foundation. This carved-rock building in Cappadocia, Turkey, not only sits on solid ground—it is part of the ground.

FIGURE 2

Monolithic Structure

Wood plank: monolithic	Spring mattress: not monolithic

Monolithic structures act as a unit and distribute forces throughout their volume. Nonmonolithic structures don't work as a unit and tend to give way to point loads (such as your butt when you lie down). What's good in a mattress is bad in a foundation.

FIGURE 3

A Foundation Works Like a Snowshoe

The snow gives way to body weight distributed through the foot's relatively small surface area.

The snow is stable enough to support the same weight distributed over the snowshoe's larger surface area.

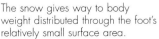

What Is the Frost Line?

The frost line is the depth to which frost penetrates the soil. When water freezes, it expands. If a foundation rests above the frost line, soil moisture can freeze, expand, and push on the foundation. This phenomenon is called *frost heave* and can cause a foundation to shift or even fail. The frost line varies widely in different climates, from more than four feet in wintry northern regions to a level at or just below the surface where freezing seldom occurs.

All foundations, then, are wide units sitting on dry, solid, nonfreezing ground. Because their job is to transfer building loads to the ground, their physical form is dictated by those loads. The most significant load on a foundation is the weight of the building. The heavier the building, the more substantial the foundation must be. Thus, foundations vary from a few stakes for a light tent to huge fortresses of subterranean concrete for a massive skyscraper.

There are two basic types of foundations: *pier* and *continuous*. A *pier* foundation can be seen as a skeletal structure that divides and channels loads to a series of smaller, independent monolithic

Continuous strength. The huge concrete monolith that is the base of a dam is an impressive example of a continuous foundation.

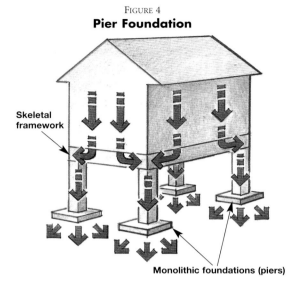

FIGURE 4
Pier Foundation

Skeletal framework

Monolithic foundations (piers)

Pier foundations are made up of a series of small monolithic foundations. Each pier handles the loads from a specific part of the building.

Foundation Drainage

One of the universal laws of building, applying to any hut or skyscraper, is to slope the ground away from a building to keep away surface water. This may sound obvious, but just look around your neighborhood to see how often it's overlooked. In addition, groundwater—water *in* the soil—must be given passage to drain away from the foundation. The system commonly employed for this is called a *French drain* and consists of a passageway for water—usually a perforated pipe set in gravel—and some method to keep dirt out of the passageway, usually filter fabric enclosing the gravel (figure 5).

A recent innovation is the *sheet drain,* a rigid plastic form, similar to a flattened egg carton, wrapped in filter fabric. This simple form replaces the usual gravel and plastic pipe, and requires only a fraction of the filter fabric used in conventional drains.

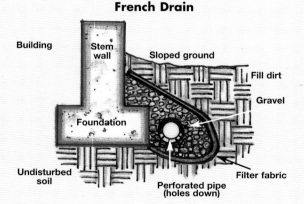

FIGURE 5
French Drain

Building
Stem wall
Sloped ground
Fill dirt
Gravel
Foundation
Undisturbed soil
Filter fabric
Perforated pipe (holes down)

Sloped ground will direct most rainwater away from the building. Water that seeps into the fill dirt will move through the filter and gravel and be carried away by the pipe. For basement applications, other measures such as waterproofing and rigid insulation are added.

Integrated foundation sheet drain. The black sheets being applied to this concrete wall, which later will be backfilled, are rigid plastic forms covered with filter fabric. They create space that directs water that reaches the wall to a perimeter drain at the foundation's base.

foundations spread out beneath the building. Each pier receives the loads of a specific section of the building and distributes them to the ground (see figure 4). Pier foundations require less excavation and far fewer materials; consequently they're much less expensive than continuous foundations. However, pier foundations are appropriate only for certain types of applications, such as pole buildings and porches. *Continuous* foundations are large monolithic units that usually follow the perimeter or floor plan of a building. They can be incredibly strong and absorb the effects of isolated ground movement better than pier foundations.

Both kinds of foundations, regardless of the form they take (see figure 6) work on the same principles: they provide adequate width and distribute the loads to the ground via a rigid monolithic structure. These two foundation types cover the gamut from camping tent to large-scale dam.

Pure pier. A tent's thin poles are a simple example of a pier foundation.

FIGURE 6

Foundation Types and Variations

Pier

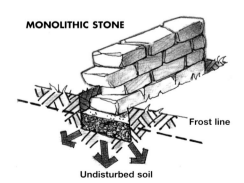

TEPEE

Tepees are light enough that the relatively small diameter of their poles is all the foundation they need. The poles are supported by the ground they rest on. The tepee's structure also is flexible enough to be unaffected by frost heave.

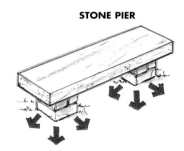

STONE PIER

Wide stones, dry-stacked or mortared, distribute the weight of the building to the ground. Such a foundation can also extend below the surface if frost is a problem.

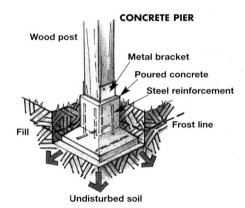

CONCRETE PIER

Wood post
Metal bracket
Poured concrete
Steel reinforcement
Fill
Frost line
Undisturbed soil

The wide base is the pier foundation. The rest of the concrete serves as the beginning of a column that continues as a wood post above ground. Because the wood doesn't contact the ground it's less susceptible to water and insect damage.

Continuous

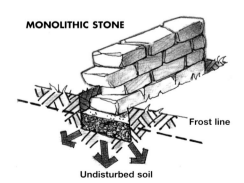

MONOLITHIC STONE

Frost line
Undisturbed soil

This continuous foundation can be built higher to form the building's walls. When monolithic, wide, and made of material that will survive below grade, walls can be their own foundation. The tire walls of Earthships are another example.

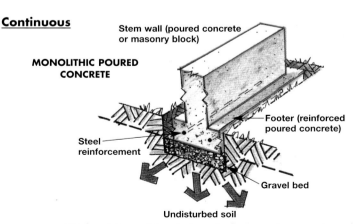

Stem wall (poured concrete or masonry block)

MONOLITHIC POURED CONCRETE

Footer (reinforced poured concrete)
Steel reinforcement
Gravel bed
Undisturbed soil

This foundation and its variants are by far the most common in modern construction. The base is called the footer. The wall built or poured on top and extending above the surface is called the stem wall.

Where does the foundation stop and where do the walls begin? In my definition, the foundation is the wide monolithic unit sitting on the dirt (in conventional construction, this is often called the *footer*; I consider "footer" and "foundation" to be synonymous). Therefore, if a building has a continuous foundation set below *grade* (below the surface of the ground), then the walls of the building start underground. These walls, often called *stem walls* if there's only a crawl space and *basement walls* if they enclose a living space, must be constructed of materials that can stand up to water, insects, and the considerable pressure of the earth pushing against them. Conventional stem and basement walls are made of poured concrete or concrete block. Good alternatives exist in various composite blocks utilizing recycled waste products, such as Faswall, Durisol, and Rastra blocks.

Hydrostatic pressure, the force of trapped water building up against a wall, can be tremendous and, in addition to creating leaks, can cause structural failure. In most climates, underground walls must be carefully waterproofed with some sort of membrane, whether sprayed, painted, or rolled in sheets, to prevent moisture from entering the building. In addition, space must be created outside the walls to allow water to drain away (see page 46). This goes double, or even triple, for underground or bermed buildings where a significant and crucial living space lies on the other side of these walls.

ALTERNATIVE FOUNDATIONS

Foundations for alternative buildings tend to resemble their commercial residential counterparts. In industrialized countries the ready availability of concrete makes that material a tempting choice. Unlike many modern materials, concrete for foundations isn't mass produced in modules, but made in small batches to your specifications. Because it's poured wet into forms or directly into trenches, it's completely adjustable; the foundation can be made as wide and thick as needed for the specific application. As it dries, concrete hardens into a single monolithic mass that, when reinforced with steel, has excellent tensile and compressive strength (see figure 1, page 44). It's like a poured-in-place rock designed to fit your needs.

However, concrete also has its downsides. Its high embodied energy, expense, and pollution in manufacture have fueled a search for alternatives. Many of these options still have concrete as their functional center, but use various approaches to reduce the amount of concrete required. For example, the rubble trench foundation consists of a trench dug below the frost line, filled with compacted stone and usually capped with a concrete foundation. The stones drain away water, preventing frost heave at the footer. The result is a surface foundation, eliminating the need for concrete or other materials that would be needed to build a stem wall from the frost line to the surface.

Another concrete-saving alternative is to install only a shallow footer while taking steps to prevent the ground around it from freezing, effectively raising the frost line. This is accomplished by installing insulation in the dirt that's backfilled over the footer. Such foundations are called *frost-protected shallow foundations* and were used by the well-known architect Frank Lloyd Wright in Chicago in the 30s. Today, this technique is widely used in Europe and Scandinavia and increasingly in the United States.

As we discussed in the previous chapter, concrete can also be spiffed up, ecologically speaking, by replacing some of the Portland cement or aggregate with such

a look at... FOUNDATIONS

TRADITIONAL

Pole to ground, Mali   Stone pier on grade, U.S.A.   Continuous footer and stem wall, Tibet

MODERN

Reinforced concrete, U.S.A.   Integrated foundation and wall, U.S.A.   Concrete pier, U.S.A.

ALTERNATIVE

Earthship tire foundation/wall, U.S.A.   Poured pier on rubble trench, U.S.A.   Pier on grade, U.S.A.

Daylight basement. There is dirt behind this painted concrete wall. The wall across from it has lots of glass and opens out onto a meadow. This potential basement was transformed into comfortable living space by siting the house on a hill, allowing the back of the building to be buried while the front remains exposed, providing natural light and a view to the outside.

Failed stone foundation. This stone stem wall rests directly on a dirt slope instead of a wide stone base. The builder also neglected to lay the stone in overlapping courses, resulting in a structurally weak wall that will eventually collapse.

industrial waste products as fly ash, wood chips, or recycled plastic. Other creative solutions are being tried, too, such as encasing rammed earth tires in concrete. Another approach is to use the area created by the stem wall, a dark basement or crawl space in conventional buildings, as primary living space. Instead of using a lot of expensive materials simply to raise a building from the frost line to the surface, these same materials are now doubling as living-space walls. Partially bermed and underground passive solar houses use this approach to great effect. Earthships, with their rammed earth tire walls, accomplish this with the use of little or no concrete.

Of course, if you have lots of stone on your site all this talk of concrete may not be for you. Stone can make a wonderful, strong foundation. Laying a stone foundation can be a lot of work, but on the other hand there's no hurry—after all, unlike other materials, stone won't be damaged if you leave it out in the weather for months. But stone, too, has its downsides. Creating a solid monolithic unit from a pile of rocks takes real skill. Its irregular surface also makes stone difficult to waterproof, in cases where that's necessary. Making strong connections between stone and other components can be challenging, too (see the discussion of connections on page 62).

"Your foundation is probably the single most critical aspect of your entire house."

Foundations are the first hard lesson in creating self-sufficient buildings in the modern world. Chances are, you won't have the materials on site to build an appropriate foundation. Whether you're using reinforced concrete or some fashionable alternative, you'll probably have to purchase these materials and have them trucked to you. Once materials hit the highway, you've left the traditional, self-sufficient world of our ancestors and landed squarely in the present.

Most innovations in alternative-building foundations are focused not so much on which materials to use as on being smarter in design and thus using fewer of them. More fundamentally, they come from a conscious decision to build smaller, more efficient housing. When it comes to foundations, the main variable you have control over is size. The size and weight of your house determines the size of your foundation. The bigger your foundation, the more materials and resources it will require, the more money it will cost, and the more impact it will have on your building site.

Finally, remember these words of advice: Your foundation is probably the single most critical aspect of your entire house. If you get it wrong, it's difficult to repair after the fact, and the consequences can be as severe as the loss of your entire building. Accept your place in the modern world and don't use your foundation as a place to make a statement. If someone is building your house for you, don't ask them to experiment with foundation techniques with which they're unfamiliar. If you're doing it yourself, be sure you're confident in your methods and design. If you're considering something a little different, run it by an engineer or try it out on the new dog house first. On the other hand, if you find someone who's versed in building in your area and who's confident in an alternative to conventional foundations, listen to what they have to say. Remember, a foundation is conceptually quite simple. If it acts like a unit and is strong enough to withstand the house's loads, it'll make a good foundation.

FIGURE 7

FIGURE 7
Skeletal Structures

The wood-frame members in this building act like the bones in a skeleton, distributing the stucture's weight to the foundation.

Jungle gym. This playground assembly is a beautiful example of a skeletal structure, with walls, roof, and foundation all in one.

Walls

Of any part of a house, we're most familiar with the walls. They hold the windows we look out of and the doors we walk through. We decorate them to reflect our personalities. They're the places where we plug things in and where various pipes disappear. Structurally speaking, these are just fringe benefits of the *real* purpose of walls: to distribute loads to the foundation.

The structure of every house depends on walls that can carry the weight of the roof and floors above them, as well as withstand environmental forces such as wind. There are two structural wall types, with variations, that are employed to accomplish this task: *skeletal* and *monolithic*.

A skeletal wall utilizes a framework of small members to carry the building's loads. The most common skeletal walls use vertical members, called *posts* or *columns*, and horizontal members, called *beams*, to form a self-supporting cage that carries vertical loads, such as the dead weight of the building (see figure 7). Exterior and interior surfaces wrap this skeleton, creating an enclosed space and helping to solidify the structure by resisting lateral loads, such as those imposed by wind.

The layout of a structure's skeleton is determined largely by the materials used. Conventional stick-frame construction uses many small, lightweight wooden sticks, usually 2x4s of pine or fir, to fashion beams and columns. Larger wood members are used in post-and-beam and timber frame construction, allowing for wider spaces between columns. Modern industrial

"The real purpose of walls is to distribute loads to the foundation."

Skeletal walls. Skeletal structure layouts vary according to their materials and the loads they have to carry. Left: a light bamboo framework for a portable chicken coop in Laos. Right: a strong steel skeleton for a large hospital addition in the U.S.

Monolithic walls. Built to distribute loads throughout their volume, monolithic walls must be sufficiently wide for their height. Left: a traditional monolithic mud, or adobe, wall. Right: a modern monolithic concrete wall.

FIGURE 8
Monolithic Wall Structures

COLUMN   WALL

LINTEL
REINFORCEMENT   STACKED BLOCK
WALL

A downward force on a monolithic wall spreads out through the wall's volume. A column is a tall, compact monolithic wall. When elongated, the "column" becomes what we think of as a wall. An opening in a wall must be reinforced above, so that forces can flow around it. The reinforcement is called a lintel. Building blocks stacked in an interlocking pattern also form a monolithic wall.

construction often uses incredibly strong steel members that permit huge spans between them.

A monolithic wall functions as a unit, with its entire volume contributing to the transfer of loads to the foundation (see figure 8). Monolithic walls can either be poured, tamped, or molded as a whole or constructed from interlaced building blocks that function together as a unit. The wider a monolithic wall is in relation to its height, the stronger it will be. For this reason, monolithic walls tend to be thick.

ALTERNATIVE WALLS

To the popular mind, alternative building is defined by its wall systems. Walls made of straw, earth, and old tires are both the brunt of jokes by skeptics and the altar at which many initiates worship, looking for salvation from the modern world's problems.

When viewed from the point of view of structure, we can see that these innovations are simply materials filling slots in the archetypal composition of a house. In a load-bearing wall, for example, straw bales or tires simply replace bricks, concrete blocks, or stones as the building blocks interlocked to form the functional unit. These materials are not revolutionary or even necessarily valuable in and of themselves. Straw and tires are exciting materials not because of any intrinsic worth but because they're both industrial byproducts with properties that make them useful in building. By the same token, there's nothing crazy, far-fetched, or mysterious about using them in construction. They're simply materials of more or less value to you based on the specifics of your situation. Let's group the popular alternative building approaches to wall construction in terms of their structural configuration: monolithic and skeletal.

Alternative Monolithic Walls

Monolithic walls made from adobe, rammed earth, cob, straw bale (see the sidebar, Two Types of Straw Bale Construction, below) tires, cordwood, logs, composite blocks, and earthbags are all structurally the same in concept. All these materials can form a monolithic wall that transfers building loads as a unit to the foundation. The differences in this diverse array of materials lie most importantly in how each addresses the other functions that a house is meant to provide: separation from the outside, connection to the outside, and a stable temperature. Other differences deal with ease and cost of construction as well as the specific details of working with each material. We'll discuss many of these issues in upcoming chapters. For now, we're focusing on their similarity. They all perform the same structural function.

Two Types of Straw Bale Construction

Straw bales can be used to build both monolithic (load-bearing) and skeletal walls. In *skeletal straw bale walls*, bales are used as infill for insulation. The bales carry no weight and have no structural function. *Monolithic, load-bearing straw bale walls* are often called "Nebraska style" because the first such walls in the U.S. were built in the late 1800s in Nebraska. In this system, straw bales are stacked in an interlocking pattern like bricks. The bales are mortared or, more often, pinned together using steel rebar.

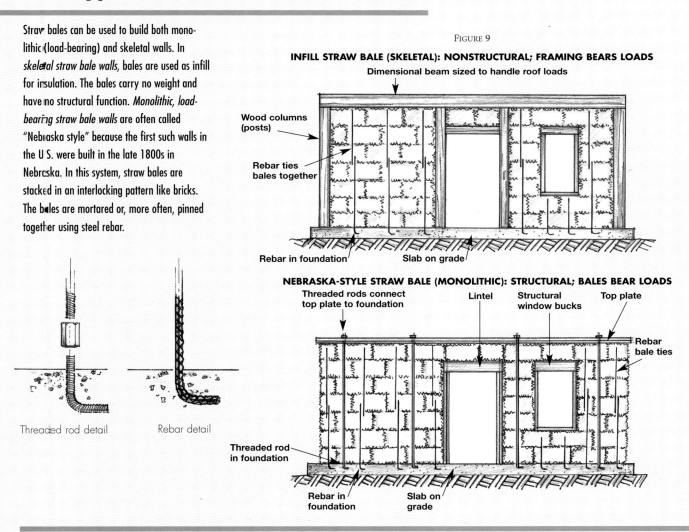

FIGURE 9

INFILL STRAW BALE (SKELETAL): NONSTRUCTURAL; FRAMING BEARS LOADS
Dimensional beam sized to handle roof loads
Wood columns (posts)
Rebar ties bales together
Rebar in foundation
Slab on grade

NEBRASKA-STYLE STRAW BALE (MONOLITHIC): STRUCTURAL; BALES BEAR LOADS
Threaded rods connect top plate to foundation
Lintel
Structural window bucks
Top plate
Rebar bale ties
Threaded rod in foundation
Rebar in foundation
Slab on grade

Threaded rod detail

Rebar detail

Monolithic wall reinforcement. Above: Steel rebar is tied together as reinforcement in poured-concrete footers and walls. Below: Long, thin shafts of straw can reinforce mud mixes such as this unplastered cob.

Alternative monolithic wall. This strong, attractive wall is made of wood chip/concrete block covered with stucco.

Keep in mind, too, that many materials—whether conventional or alternative—need reinforcement in order to be useful in monolithic walls. Unreinforced concrete, for example, is strong in compression, but weak in tension (see page 44). Steel mesh or rebar rods are used in conventional concrete reinforcement. Bamboo is used for this purpose in some other parts of the world and, to a much lesser degree, in the United States. Similarly, cob construction is made possible by reinforcing the dense, clumpy clay with long, thin, fibrous straw. Walls made of interlocked units, such as concrete blocks or straw bales, also are reinforced.

Alternative Skeletal Walls

Alternative skeletal walls are usually variations on post-and-beam construction infilled with insulation using—and here's the alternative part—something other than conventional fiberglass or foam insulation (for a discussion of insulation, see chapter 4). Whether the framework is constructed of large timbers, common dimensional lumber such as 2x4s, or something else—for example, Faswall blocks filled with concrete—the structural result is the same: a skeleton of individual members transferring building loads to the foundation.

Alternative skeletal wall. Beneath this handsome home's plaster skin is a post-and-beam and split-bamboo-lath wall.

a look at... WALLS

TRADITIONAL

SKELETAL

Tudor post and beam, France

Bamboo house, northern Thailand

MONOLITHIC

Dogon granary, Mali

Stone house, Mali

MODERN

SKELETAL

Steel pole porch, U.S.A.

Stick-built wood frame, U.S.A.

MONOLITHIC

Poured concrete wall, U.S.A.

Concrete block wall, U.S.A.

ALTERNATIVE

SKELETAL

Post and beam, U.S.A.

Timber frame, U.S.A.

Ladder truss and scrap-lumber lath, U.S.A.

MONOLITHIC

Cordwood with cob, U.S.A.

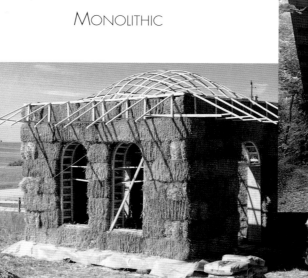

Load-bearing straw bale, U.S.A.

Cob, U.S.A.

Roofs

The roof is the archetypal symbol for house. When you have "a roof over your head" you have a home. A building can have only dirt for a foundation and a few poles for walls, but it must have a roof to be a shelter. The roof of a building takes more abuse than any other component. It's baked in the sun, pounded by rain, tugged on by wind, and—in many regions—blanketed by snow. A well-built house will last only as long as its roof. Even tiny passages for water in a roof can begin the slow decay of the entire house.

Structurally, however, a roof's job is simple. The roof needs to carry its own weight and that of live loads, such as snow, ice, and rain, and withstand lateral and uplift loads such as those caused by wind or earthquakes. The roof's structure must transfer these loads to the walls below. Though roofs come in many shapes and sizes, they all perform this function. They're conceptually the same: self-supporting structures sloped to provide drainage. Even "flat" roofs are sloped slightly.

As with walls, the structure of roofs may be either skeletal or monolithic. *Skeletal roof systems* come in many variations, including flat, shed, gable, and hip (see figure 10). Skeletal roofs can be constructed of a variety of materials. The members of the basic framework, depending on their configuration, are

Archetypal roof. A turtle's shell is strong and sloped for drainage, making it an excellent roof.

FIGURE 10

Skeletal Roof Types

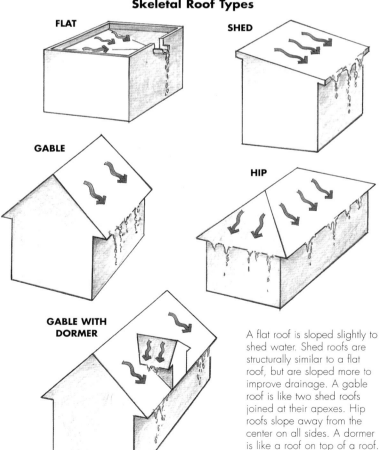

FLAT

SHED

GABLE

HIP

GABLE WITH DORMER

A flat roof is sloped slightly to shed water. Shed roofs are structurally similar to a flat roof, but are sloped more to improve drainage. A gable roof is like two shed roofs joined at their apexes. Hip roofs slope away from the center on all sides. A dormer is like a roof on top of a roof.

Skeletal roof structure. Three trusses, one at each end and another in the center, form this roof's structural core. Each truss consists of a pair of right triangles defined by a piece of milled lumber at their base, a round pole in the center to create the right angles, and a length of bamboo on each side, thus forming the slope of the roof. Thin bamboo rafters connected by horizontal bamboo purlins and a bamboo ridge beam are attached to the trusses. Diagonal bamboo braces further solidify the structure. Tying thin, lightweight members together in this way creates a strong structural unit.

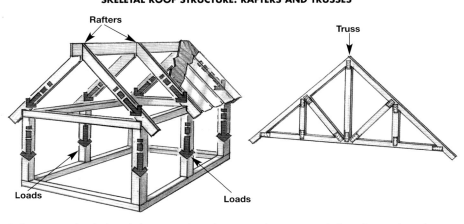

FIGURE 11

SKELETAL ROOF STRUCTURE: RAFTERS AND TRUSSES

Rafters

Truss

Loads

Loads

Rafters are made of relatively large members. A *truss* can be constructed of smaller members than corresponding rafters accepting the same loads. Only the walls that support the rafters carry any appreciable load. For buildings with flat, shed, and gable roofs, this means that some walls bear a lot of weight while others bear almost none. Thus, there's no reason why all the walls must be built with the same structural strength or even out of the same materials.

Corbelling. Students at a Cal-Earth workshop demonstrate the strength of a simple corbelled arch made of stacked earthbags.

"The roof of a building takes more abuse than any other component."

∼

called *rafters* or *trusses* (see figure 11). As with skeletal walls, this framework is then covered with an exterior surface such as plywood sheathing or wood planking (called *purlins*), to help solidify the structure. This surface is in turn covered with a weather-resistant material such as shingles, metal sheeting, thatch, or the multiple layers of a living roof (see chapter 5).

Monolithic roofs can be either flat or domed. The Celts were using large stone lintels to function as small, flat monolithic roofs as early as 3,000 B.C. However, flat monolithic roofs as applied today to modern homes are, to my knowledge, made only of poured concrete reinforced with steel, and are strictly a product of the Industrial Age. Some modern underground homes utilize such a roofing system. Domed monolithic roofs can be made by pouring lightweight concrete onto a formwork or by *corbelling* building materials. If you lay materials in rows directly on top of one another, as in a brick wall, the result is a vertical structure. However, if you slightly offset each course, or corbel them, the result is a structure that leans in. In arches and domes, the result is a structure that forms its own roof. Monolithic domes are covered, if necessary, with some form of weatherproof coating, such as stucco. An igloo is an example of a monolithic dome that forms its own covering. The traditional tepee is something of a hybrid; though structurally its walls are skeletal, they lean inward and create a roof, much like a dome (see figure 12, left).

FIGURE 12

Domes and Tepees

Structures such as domes and tepees are interesting structural hybrids. Their inward-leaning walls become roofs, too.

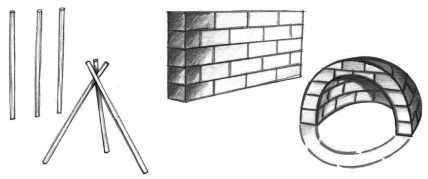

The wall structure of a tepee (left) leans in to form the roof's framework (right).

The wall structure of a monolithic dome (left) leans in to form its own roof (right).

ALTERNATIVE ROOFS

The roofs of most alternative buildings today are skeletal and resemble their conventional counterparts. Their structure is most often supplied by some sort of wood framing and sheathing. Wood is strong in compression and tension (see figure 1 on page 44) and is easy to cut and fasten. These are all qualities that make it useful for roof framing. Interestingly, wood roof framing is one case in which alternative builders turn to industry for solutions. Factory-built trusses, which are inexpensive and can be built to your specifications, are often made of small-dimension lumber cut from small trees, thus saving old-growth forests.

Alternative skeletal roofs. Left: Although this green roof system looks much like someone's backyard, it's supported by a conventional metal-and-concrete flat roof. Right: This thatched roof is supported by wood framing.

The structures of some of the most visually alternative roofs, such as thatched, living, and earth-sheltered, also are usually supplied by some form of wood or other conventional framing. Even geodesic domes, though often constructed of metal, are sometimes framed with wood. So again we see that things can look very different on the outside while being made up of the same structural elements on the inside.

Monolithic roofs such as domes and vaults are an ancient answer to the problem of roof structure. Many historical buildings in the Middle East, Europe and the United States have structural domed roofs or vaulted interior ceilings. Though not as popular in modern housing, monolithic domes and vaults are making a mark in the world of alternative building. As I mentioned on page 40, architect Nader Khalili has developed domed houses built of adobe blocks that are fired from within. The adobe fuses together, creating a strong monolithic structure much like a clay pot. Domes also are being constructed of earth-filled bags, rammed earth tires, straw bales, and even ice.

In addition, hybrid buildings combining the structural properties of a dome with other innovative elements and materials are being developed. Among them are structures such as the Yome, discussed in the sidebar on page 65.

As with foundations, roofs are a rude awakening for us dreamy idealists. Most of you will probably put a conventional roof on your building. If you end up going that route, don't feel bad. A roof has to be strong and, in most climates, must be absolutely impervious to water. Water is incredibly sneaky and can find its way into the smallest imperfections. Through capillary action, water can even climb uphill! Just a tiny leak can cause serious structural damage if left unchecked. When it comes to roofing, boring fine points such as flashing (see chapter 5) are just as important as the materials you use because they largely determine how long a roof will last. Modern roofing systems, if correctly installed, are long-lasting with little maintenance. Even if you opt for an alternative, such as a living roof, the structural demands may be best fulfilled with some form of conventional framing. There are other answers, however, and they also may be right for you.

Monolithic ice roof. This igloo was constructed using an "IceBox," a commercial portable tool for building snow shelters.

TRADITIONAL

SKELETAL

MONOLITHIC

Mud dome, Dogon granary, Mali

External bamboo roof frame, northern Vietnam

Marble masonry dome, Jain temple, India

Tile roof on wood framing, Buddhist temple, Miyajima, Japan

MODERN

SKELETAL

MONOLITHIC

Wood framing, conventional home, U.S.A.

Poured concrete stairwell roof, parking garage, U.S.A.

ALTERNATIVE
SKELETAL

Earthship wood roof, U.S.A.

Pole and bamboo roof, Earthaven community building, U.S.A.

MONOLITHIC

Papercrete dome, pumice-filled bags covered with paper/concrete stucco, U.S.A.

Superadobe dome, fabric tube filled with damp earth, U.S.A.

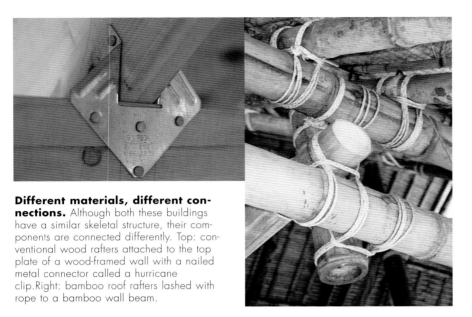

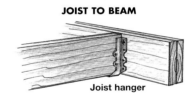

Connections

No matter what specific form a building takes, its structure must work together as a unit. Wind can easily blow a strong roof off strong walls if the two aren't properly fastened together. A building's foundation, walls, and roof are commonly constructed separately and of different materials. This approach causes breaks in the structure that must be remedied by strong connections.

As we've seen, the structural frameworks of different alternative and conventional buildings are often similar, and sometimes identical. One area of significant difference, however, lies in

Different materials, different connections. Although both these buildings have a similar skeletal structure, their components are connected differently. Top: conventional wood rafters attached to the top plate of a wood-framed wall with a nailed metal connector called a hurricane clip. Right: bamboo roof rafters lashed with rope to a bamboo wall beam.

FIGURE 14

Material Connections

Conventional mass-produced connections

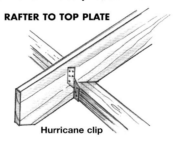

POST TO CONCRETE

Concrete anchor

RAFTER TO TOP PLATE

Hurricane clip

JOIST TO BEAM

Joist hanger

Alternative building connections

CONCRETE SLAB TO STRAW BALE WALL

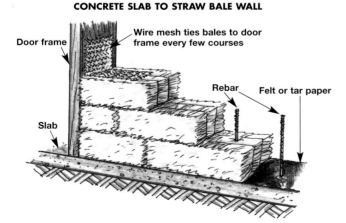

Door frame

Wire mesh ties bales to door frame every few courses

Rebar   Felt or tar paper

Slab

COB WALL TO FRAMED ROOF

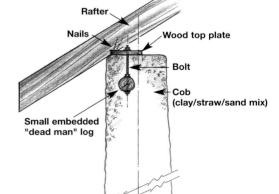

Rafter

Nails   Wood top plate

Bolt

Cob (clay/straw/sand mix)

Small embedded "dead man" log

the materials and techniques used to make structural connections. Connecting a concrete foundation to a load-bearing straw bale wall is much different than connecting the same foundation to a stick-framed wall. Likewise, connecting bamboo structural members is different than connecting conventional dimensioned lumber.

These seemingly small details are absolutely crucial and if overlooked can cause nightmares for the builder. Remember, the breaks between materials are probably the weakest structural links in your building. So take connections very seriously. As you learn about different approaches to construction, ask yourself how the structural components of the buildings are connected. The illustrations in figure 14 show just a few examples of conventional and alternative material connections.

Wall to foundation connections. Left: For straw walls, bales will be impaled on the long rebar pins being set in the wet concrete of this recently poured slab. Above: For wood framing, a board called a sill plate will be drilled, placed over the bolts, and attached to the concrete stem wall with nuts and washers.

Floors

Why haven't we talked about floors as structural elements? Well, floors are definitely structural. They carry the weight of the people, furniture, and all the other stuff moved into a building. These loads must in turn be transferred to the walls below, to the foundation, or directly to the ground, as with a slab-on-grade for instance. In addition, floors are often important components of the structural integrity of a building, its ability to stand on its own two feet, so to speak. In multistory buildings, floors often lock all the walls together, thus making the building act more like a unit and greatly increasing its ability to handle lateral and compression loads (see figure 13).

However, the floors of many buildings have a negligible effect on a building's overall structural integrity. Many barns and single-story slab-on-grade buildings are examples. In fact, in many conventional single-story wood-framed buildings the floor could be taken out without significant structural effect. Put simply, buildings can be built to stand without the structural assistance of a floor. When floors do contribute to the overall structure, they generally enhance the structural characteristics of the walls of the building.

In short, the structural role of floors varies widely from building to building. Make an engineer's day the next time you find yourself standing next to one at the buffet table. Ask him or her if and how the floor you're standing on contributes to the structure of that particular building.

FIGURE 13

Floor as Bracing

In some multistory buildings, intermediate floors can serve to lock the walls together, increasing a building's strength against lateral and compression loads.

Hammering It Home

Structure is the most basic element of a house. It's what everything else is added to or surrounded by. Understanding how materials should come together to create a solid structure is crucial to your ability to get involved in making decisions about your house. Structural knowledge builds your confidence, enables you to discuss matters with builders and other professionals, and gives you a clearer overall picture of your house.

One of this chapter's main lessons is that alternative building approaches offer few innovations in their basic approach to structure. Far from an indictment of these techniques, this realization only takes away some of the mystery. Though the structural combination of foundation, walls, and roof has taken many shapes and sizes all over the world for thousands of years, most buildings are fundamentally much more alike than different. Alternative techniques are based on age-old structural concepts, the same ones inherited by modern commercial building. This is good news. You don't want mystery and magic holding your house together.

"The key to structural success or failure is in the execution."

In the end, the key to structural success or failure is in the execution. As one expert put it, "It's not the differences in materials, but in the way they're put together." A poorly constructed alternative building can suffer structural failure as easily as a conventional one, and vice-versa.

One of the best things you can do at this stage is to start examining and thinking about the structural components of the buildings around you. Crawl under your house or visit the basement of your apartment building and look carefully at the foundation. You'll be amazed at how much you can learn. If you don't yet own a place to build, be conscious of the importance of foundations as you're looking for land. That steep lot with a beautiful view might be a foundation nightmare requiring lots of excavation and even blasting if you hit rock. If you already know where you're going to build, start looking at it in terms of important foundation issues such as solid soil structure and good drainage.

Likewise, check out the walls in the buildings you come in contact with every day. Can you tell what they're made of? Are they monolithic or skeletal? How are they attached to the foundation? What do you like or dislike about them? Find older buildings in your area and inspect their roofing systems. Climb into your attic and study the framing.

Also, look for alternative buildings near you and see what kinds of structural techniques were used. Are there any homes with straw bale or cob walls, domes, or living roofs in your area? Most people who've chosen an alternative approach are proud of and passionate about their homes. Call them and ask for a tour.

Above all, don't be too quick to choose a given technique. Only after you take your time, learn as much as you can, and reserve judgment for as long as possible will the structural approaches that are right for your situation become clear.

Yomes and Tensile Fabric Structures:
A Discussion with Peter Belt

Q What is a tensile fabric structure and how does it differ from more common structural building approaches?

Conventional structures rely upon two main principles, gravity and internal rigidity, to achieve stability and carry loads. Tensile fabric architecture uses neither of these principles, but instead relies on a flexible, lightweight fabric membrane stretched between a fixed set of support points. These structures, consisting of elements that have little or no sheer stiffness, rely on their form and internal tension alone to carry their loads. They work because they're flexible. This flexibility means that the entire fabric membrane will carry the load applied to any part of it.

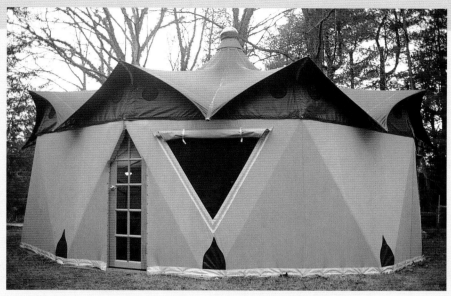

Tensile fabric roof. The Tensile-Yome combines elements of yurts, domes, and tensile architecture in one whimsical, portable building.

As structural elements, tensile members are more efficient than compression members such as metal columns or wood studs. Unless they have a certain minimal thickness, compression members will bend out of shape and fail regardless of their direct material strength. Structures made of tensile members, on the other hand, become more stable with increasing stress levels. The stress pulls each member into line, making the structure taut.

Keeping the curved surface in tension while carrying upward loads of wind and downward loads of snow requires a careful balance of curvature in opposite directions. This curvature represents the minimal surface area possible for the flexible membrane given a certain fixed set of endpoints. The more the endpoints stretch the membrane away from a two-dimensional plane, the greater the load-carrying capacity. Consequently, the shape of the structure is not arbitrary, but derives from structural function. Form and function, art and engineering become one.

Yome. The walls of this little building use the same structural geometry of Buckminster Fuller's geodesic domes, yet are covered with a fabric shell much like a yurt.

Q What is a Yome?

A Yome is a portable living shelter that combines the features of the modern yurt with the geodesic dome pioneered by Buckminster Fuller. As with a geodesic dome, a framework is created using triangulation based upon an icosahedron, one of the most stable of the geometric solids. However, this wooden framework is covered with a fabric shell much like modern yurts. Taking advantage of cutting-edge developments in fabric technology, this shell provides a waterproof, durable, and long-lasting shelter.

Yomes are designed to provide a functional shelter quickly and at an affordable price. They're often used as a temporary dwelling for people who have bought land and need a shelter while they're building their home. Insulation can keep the Yome warm in the winter and cool in the summer. A stovepipe vent allows a wood stove or vented heater to be installed.

Q How are you now using tensile roof structures to expand the possibilities of your original Yome design?

I'm passionate about creating functional yet affordable portable living shelters, and have been refining the Yome design over the past several years. At the same time, I've been fascinated with the concept of tensile architecture and have built several open-sided tension canopies. The time came to integrate the two concepts. The standard Yome can't get any bigger than the largest model, 19 feet in diameter, without adding a lot of extra roof supports. Using a roof based upon tensile principles not only allows for a larger shelter; it also pushes the envelope to see how lightweight such a structure can get and still be stable.

The strength of triangles. Top: A Yome's triangular structure is strong, yet light. Bottom: Hardware connects two intersecting wall triangles on the floor platform.

Q Your work is a wonderful example of the symbiosis of traditional and modern concepts and materials. What is your main inspiration from the past and what excites you most about current developments?

Actually, the earliest known housing structure, dating back 400,000 years, was a dome. In southern France evidence was found where circles of saplings were placed into the ground and likely tied at the top and covered to form a shelter. This type of shelter remained in use in Africa, Asia and the Americas into the 20th century. These structures were covered in available materials such as leaves, grass, straw, reeds, animal skins, bark, reinforced clay, and eventually woven textiles.

Frei Otto, the pioneer of tensile architecture, has been a source of inspiration for me. In 1964 Otto formed The Institute for Lightweight Surface Structures in Germany. By studying indigenous building practices along with the structures found in nature such as spider webs, soap bubbles and tree branches, Frei Otto and the institute published volumes of innovative ideas for lighter, more efficient, mobile and adaptable structures. However, Otto's tensile structure prototypes were made in the 1960s out of cotton and didn't last too long. Now there are fabric membranes such as PTFE-coated fiberglass that will surpass the lifespan of most commonly used roofing materials today. I'm excited about the developments in silicone-coated fabric as a roofing material. I feel that modern building practices have become wasteful, compartmentalized, and stagnant. People are stuck into squares. If we're going to meet the challenges of sheltering ourselves through the new millennium, we need to start looking for smarter, more flexible and efficient structures.

Peter Belt is the creator of the portable structure he calls the Yome, which his company, Red Sky Shelters, manufactures.

CHAPTER 4
TEMPERATURE

As we discussed in chapter 1, the human body was once all the house we needed. Originally, we were born into climates in which the body was able to maintain a stable interior environment in the face of constant external change. One of the main features of this environment is an incredibly stable temperature somewhere in the neighborhood of 37°C (98.6°F). As we started our migratory adventure across this planet, we began to find ourselves in new climates, places where our bodies could no longer maintain this interior temperature without help. Housing was a response to this problem. Housing was created to help the body maintain its stable temperature.

How Do Houses Create a Stable Temperature?

Temperature fluctuations on Earth are due to changes in the amount of sun hitting the planet's surface in any given place at any given time. The temperature inside a building without mechanical life support such as air conditioning is determined by the extent to which the building is connected to or separated from the temperature outside. Our normal body temperature is at the high end of outdoor temperatures on the planet. Our bodies struggle to maintain this healthy temperature, however, when outdoor temperatures rise even higher. This is because the body creates a lot of heat, through the metabolism of food, that must be dissipated. If the temperature outside slows that dissipation, we become uncomfortable.

This is also why we experience air temperatures in a certain range *below* body temperature as "comfortable." Exactly what temperatures fall within this comfort range is a question complicated by such factors as humidity, air movement, the temperature of nearby surfaces (*mean radiant temperature*), clothing, and cultural norms. However, the range commonly mentioned as the human comfort zone is between 68 and 78°F (20 and 25.5° C). One important goal of housing is to raise or lower the indoor temperature relative to the outdoor temperature to produce this ideal or something close to it. In order to accomplish this, you have to do two things: produce a desired temperature and then maintain it.

HEATING

Comfortable temperatures for human life are often closer to summer highs than winter lows. This fact tends to make heating a building more important and more difficult than cooling it. The source of heat for our planet, the Sun, is also almost always the source of heat for our houses. Wood and fossil fuels are all forms of solar energy

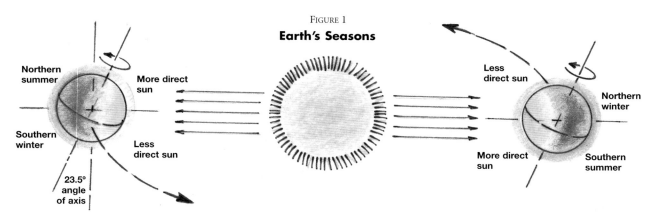

FIGURE 1

Earth's Seasons

Northern summer

More direct sun

Southern winter

Less direct sun

23.5° angle of axis

Less direct sun

Northern winter

More direct sun

Southern summer

Because of the tilt of Earth's axis as it orbits the Sun, different parts of the planet lean toward or away from the Sun at different times of the year. The resulting changes in the angle at which the Sun's energy strikes a given portion of the globe determine seasons. When the Northern Hemisphere is leaning toward the Sun in June, the Sun's rays strike at a high angle, focusing their energy on a relatively small area and creating warmer temperatures: summer. Meanwhile, the Sun's rays strike the Southern Hemisphere at a lower angle, diffusing their energy over a wider area and causing lower temperatures: winter. Six months later, when the planet has orbited 180 degrees, the scenario reverses.

stored by way of photosynthesis in plant tissue. Fossil fuels are dead plants and plant-eating animals converted by time, heat, and pressure into energy-rich glop, gas, or rock. When we burn any of these materials for heat, whether as wood in a stove, gas in a furnace, or coal to generate the electricity that runs a baseboard heater, we're simply recycling the solar energy converted by photosynthesis into food energy and stored in plant tissue.

We can also use sunlight directly to create heat for our homes. This approach is called *passive solar heating.*

Passive Solar

Earth is in constant movement, continually spinning on its tilted axis while revolving around the Sun. These factors combine to produce life as we know it on the planet. Earth's spin creates day and night—the apparent rising of the Sun in the east, movement across the sky during the day, and setting to the west. The planet's tilt as it orbits the Sun creates the seasons (see figure 1).

One specific physical effect of all this, from our perspective on Earth, is that the Sun follows a lower path through the sky in winter than it does in summer. This phenomenon can be used to great effect in housing design. If a building is oriented to the south, the sun will penetrate deeper through south glass-covered openings as it gets lower in the sky (see figure 2). This means that more sunlight will enter the house during the colder months of the year. Conversely, the Sun will be higher in the sky during warmer months, causing more sun to fall on the roof and less, if any, to come through southern openings.

The Sun is the most predictable natural element for any given building site. If you have an exact place to build in mind, you can say with certainty where the Sun will be on any given day at any given hour in relation to that building. Thus, you can plan your building to utilize the sun.

The use of building orientation with the Sun to affect temperature is called *passive solar design.* It's called "passive" to distinguish it from *active solar* approaches, in which solar energy is collected in one place and used in another (see figure 3). The most common active solar technique is the conversion of sunlight into electricity. This process is called *photovoltaics* and is discussed in chapter 6.

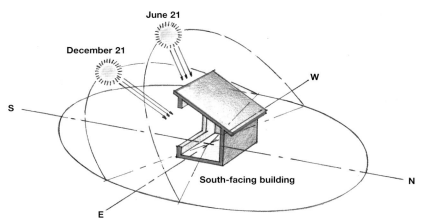

FIGURE 2

The Sun's Changing Path

Throughout the year, the Sun's elevation in the sky changes. In the Northern Hemisphere, the Sun moves across the southern sky. It reaches its highest path on the summer solstice, June 21, then follows an increasingly lower path until it reaches its lowest point on the winter solstice, December 21. Facing a building south takes full advantage of the Sun's light and heat. In winter, the low sun penetrates deep into the building. In summer, roof and window overhangs keep the high sun from entering.

"The Sun is the most predictable natural element for any given building site. "

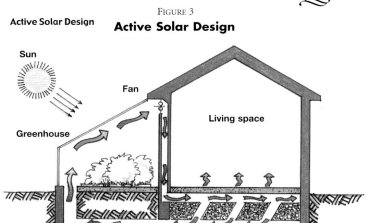

FIGURE 3

Active Solar Design

On a sunny day in winter, this greenhouse receives much more solar heat than it needs. The heat rises and is pulled by a fan through vents high in the greenhouse wall, then into beds of rock in the home's crawl space. The rock absorbs the heat and slowly radiates it back to the house. Cooled air flows back toward the greenhouse to continue the cycle.

COOLING

As we've seen, hot summer temperatures are often closer to our ideal than cold winter temperatures. In most parts of the world, lying down under a shady tree with a gentle breeze blowing will allow you to survive the harshest summer heat. The shade blocks the sun, lowering the ambient temperature, and the breeze allows your body to dissipate heat.

Most strategies for cooling a building are a variation on this archetype. For example, trees and shrubs lower the temperature of the air around a building, and windows allow circulation through the building to dissipate heat. Again, passive solar design is the most basic step that can be taken. A house facing south with east and west windows shaded by vegetation and appropriate roof overhangs can severely limit the amount of sun entering the building during the hottest part of the year. On the other side of the spectrum is the modern invention of air conditioning, in which fuels are burned to run equipment that mechanically cools indoor air.

MAINTAINING TEMPERATURE

So far we've established that heating and cooling basically comes down to manipulating the sun. To create heat, you capture the sun either directly through orienting your building to let it in, or through burning stored solar heat in the form of fuels. To create cool, you either isolate your house from sunlight and encourage ventilation, or close your house up and burn stored solar heat to mechanically cool the air.

Once you've produced heat or cool, the next step is to maintain it. There are two basic strategies for reaching this goal: *thermal mass* and *insulation*.

Thermal Mass

All materials have the ability to store heat, though some are able to hold more heat per unit of weight or, more technically correct, *mass* than others. A *thermal mass* is any mass used to collect and hold heat. *Specific heat* is the measure of a material's capacity to hold heat. Water has a very high specific heat. Our bodies are mostly water and are able to keep their stable temperature partially due to the thermal mass of that water. Among building materials, adobe, brick, concrete, and stone share similar specific heats and are often used as thermal mass.

Thermal mass can be used to keep a building warm or cool. To keep a building warm, the heat of the sun, either directly or through burning fuels, is allowed inside. A thermal mass such as adobe or brick walls or a concrete floor absorbs the heat, collecting it slowly throughout its exposure. Later when the Sun goes down or the stove

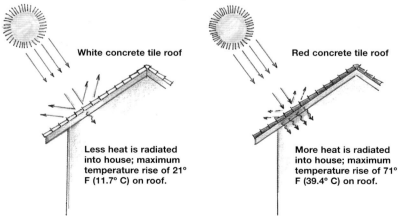

FIGURE 4

Color Can Help Control Radiant Heat

White concrete tile roof

Red concrete tile roof

Less heat is radiated into house; maximum temperature rise of 21° F (11.7° C) on roof.

More heat is radiated into house; maximum temperature rise of 71° F (39.4° C) on roof.

Reflective or light-colored materials absorb less heat and therefore help prevent too much heat from radiating into a building.

burns out and the indoor air begins to cool, the thermal mass can help maintain a stable temperature as it slowly radiates stored heat into the building. In some situations, this process can be made to work in reverse to keep a building cool. For example, during the relative cool of a summer night, windows are opened to allow cool air into the house. In the morning, windows are closed as the temperature begins to rise. The thermal mass of thick outdoor walls—of cob, concrete, or stone, for example—slowly absorbs the heat of the day. Before this heat makes it to the interior of the house, the Sun goes down and the air begins to cool. The thermal mass slowly lets off its heat to the cooler outside air through the night and is cool and ready to start the process again in the morning.

Insulation

In building, insulation is anything that retards the movement of heat. Heat moves through three possible mechanisms: radiation, convection, and conduction. Different strategies are employed to prevent heat movement depending on the kind of movement involved.

Radiation is the emission of heat energy from warm surfaces through the air to cooler surfaces. The heated thermal mass in the example I just mentioned gave its heat back to the cooling air through radiation. Radiant heat transfer is best prevented through the use of a reflective or light-colored material (see figure 4, left, and Providing Insulation on page 78).

Convection is the movement of warm air to colder air zones. A furnace with ducts moves heat through convection. Unwanted convective heat transfer is prevented by blocking air movement through walls, around windows and doors, and between floors. An air lock or *mudroom*, for example, creates a transition space that prevents warm indoor air from escaping when the door to the outside is opened.

Conduction is the transmission of heat through the mass of a material. Heat passes through a frying pan on a stove by conduction. Conductive heat transfer is slowed by materials that resist the movement of heat through their volume. A material's ability to do this, in other words its thermal resistivity, is expressed as its *R-value*. Materials made up of little units, cells or short strands, tend to have higher R-values because heat can't take a direct route through them. The heat has to move around cell walls or over air spaces and is therefore constructed to a more difficult route and consequently contained. Cellulose, including straw and recycled newspaper, some airy or rigid foam plastics (such as polystyrene), and fiberglass are materials often used to prevent conductive heat loss.

Insulation against convection. The space between these two doors is an air lock, or mudroom.

Insulation against conduction. Heat has no direct passage through this clay-slip straw wall's many strands and air pockets. Of course, the wall will need to be sealed with several coats of plaster before it becomes a truly effective insulator.

Traditional Approaches to Temperature

Designing a building that could maintain a comfortable indoor temperature when exposed to all the extremes of outdoor earthly temperatures would be an amazing and difficult technical feat. Fortunately, there's no reason to undertake such a task. All we need to do is deal with the amount of sun, or lack thereof, where we live.

Dealing with the sun has long been a major motive in human building. People in hot, arid desert climates have, for example, built thick walls and roofs of adobe for thousands of years. As we've already seen, if built sufficiently thick, adobe walls will slow the movement of the sun's heat sufficiently to allow building interiors to remain cooler. Cooler desert nights allow walls to dissipate this heat to the outside by morning. In hot, windy, tropical climates, the focus is usually on shade and encouraging the circulation of cool breezes. Airy huts featuring thatched roofs with large overhangs for shade have long been the norm. These huts have loose thatching or mats as walls that allow the cooling breeze free rein within the building.

Traditional adobe. Thick thermal mass walls absorb solar heat, slowing its movement toward the interior. This building is in Senosa, Mali.

Grass house. Large overhangs for shade, permeable walls, and free ventilation beneath the floor all contribute to keeping this building cool in the hot Laotian jungle.

Climates with both hot summers and cold winters are more challenging. In their excellent book, *A Golden Thread: 2500 Years of Solar Architecture and Technology,* Ken Butti and John Perlin describe how people in different parts of the world who faced such climates often independently discovered passive solar techniques. The ancient Greeks, for example, were using a combination of solar orientation and appropriate building materials to create passive solar buildings 2,500 years ago. Socrates and Aristotle both discuss passive solar building concepts in their writings. The fact that the Greeks worshipped the Sun, were very conscious of its movements due to the use of sundials, and were already experiencing wood shortages in the fifth century B.C. may have contributed to their use of the sun in building.

Whatever the reasons, excavations have uncovered entire cities laid out to give equal solar access to all inhabitants. North Hill, a section of the ancient city of Olynthus, has streets laid out so that all houses face south. Buildings there had foot-and-a-half thick adobe walls on the north to keep out cold winter winds and were open to the south, allowing winter sun to penetrate the building. Earthen floors and adobe walls, serving as excellent thermal mass, collected the winter sun's heat and released it to the house at night. In summer, a covered porch, or portico, shaded the house against the high sun during the hottest part of the day. Contiguous houses and solid walls on the east and west protected the house from early morning and late afternoon sun.

The Romans studied the Greek example and added their own refinements. Most notably, clear glass or mica windows were used by the Romans to cover south windows, thus allowing far greater heat retention from the winter sun. Passive solar design became so important to the Romans that they enacted sun-rights laws guaranteeing a citizen's right to access the sun. The state of New Mexico followed the Roman lead and established solar access rights in 1978.

Other cultures have developed similar solar building techniques. In ancient China, for example, major cities were laid out giving buildings a south face whenever possible. Living quarters on the north of a south-facing courtyard made the layout of these buildings strikingly similar to those of Olynthus. In the eleventh and twelfth centuries A.D., the Anasazi people, living in what is now the southwestern U.S., built communities of adobe buildings that faced south and were tiered to give all dwellings access to southern sun. In these buildings, most of the door and window openings are to the south, allowing winter solar heating. Heavy timber and adobe roofs and thick adobe walls protect the interiors from hot summer sun.

An ancient technique for cooling uses the fact that turning liquid water into water vapor requires energy in the form of heat. Plants, for example, often create cooler air in their vicinity because they are constantly giving off water vapor, in a process called *transpiration*, which pulls heat from the surrounding air. Similarly, as warm, dry air passes over water, evaporation will occur, taking heat from the air and thereby causing the temperature to drop. This phenomenon is called *evaporative cooling*. Ancient Egyptians, Greeks, and Romans sometimes used this technique, placing wet mats or porous clay pots in door openings, to cool their buildings. The same concept was used for cooling in ancient India and in the Middle East.

Anasazi solar. South-facing windows and doors, thermal mass walls and roofs, and multiple tiers were hallmark features of Anasazi construction.

Modern Approaches to Temperature

Stable indoor temperatures are probably more important to you and me than they were to our ancestors. The reason for this is simply that we live in an indoor culture. Not only do we tend to have a more sedentary routine at home and work, but our lives don't tend to be in sync with the seasons. In contrast, self-sufficient societies have lives centered more on the growth cycles of plants and animals. Consequently, they spend much more time outdoors and have work schedules that change with the seasons. We're often performing the same tasks in winter as we are in summer. Whether it's hot or cold outside, you still need to sit at the same computer or stand at the same cash register, and therefore want a similar temperature year-round in which to work.

So modern building is understandably focused on the ins and outs of heating, cooling, and insulation. Ironically, however, in many western countries passive solar techniques are little utilized. The reasons for this, I think, are twofold. First, the more people you cram into an area, the harder it is to obtain solar access. In urban centers, where large apartment buildings and skyscrapers are utilized to accommodate the centralized needs of business and living for so many people, the sun is often blocked by architectural obstacles. Second, as I've said before, modern society is general. It spans many climates and consists of the remnants of many cultures tied together by the thread of business. Our buildings are a product of modern business, and as such are mass-produced and

Shady urban jungle. Access to sun can be limited in the urban environment.

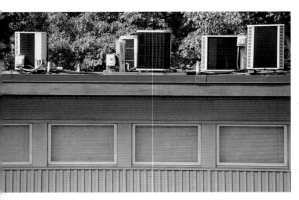

Spaceship with life support. Perhaps the inoperable glass windows on this building were installed to let the "astronauts" housed inside peek at the strange world outside their climate-controlled environment.

Altar to a fake sun. This pile of technology, what I call a "fake sun generation unit," is used to regulate the indoor temperature of a hospital.

Isolation from outside. The only way to gain contact with the outside from inside this building is with a sledgehammer.

nonlocal. If you're planning buildings and building materials in a general fashion without a specific location in mind, the sun is of no use to you and becomes only an obstacle.

Our modern inability to think locally has led to what I call the spaceship approach to temperature regulation. In this approach, the first step is to build a spaceship, a well-insulated building that can be essentially cut off from the outside environment. Since utilizing the sun isn't part of our equation, thermal mass is less important and the focus is on materials with high thermal resistivity, or R-value. Until recently, the modern materials of choice for this job have been fiberglass and rigid foam. These materials placed on or in walls, floors, ceilings, attics, and roofs in combination with insulated glass and air-infiltration barriers can create a fairly airtight interior space resistant to heat loss. The next step is to attach life-support systems to this spaceship. These consist of modern heating, venting, and air-conditioning (HVAC) machinery, which mechanically creates temperature in a central location and pumps it into and through the house.

Theoretically, these habitable machines can maintain the desired temperature regardless of outdoor conditions simply by burning more or less fuel. Ironically, these systems are simply mimicking naturally occurring processes. Air conditioning, for example, uses a refrigerant, a liquid with a low boiling point, to mechanically force evaporative cooling, therefore mimicking the process by which plants can create a lower temperature in the vicinity of a building. In a similar fashion, on a sunny winter day the flames of the gas furnace in a poorly sited house are mimicking the fire of the Sun, which could be accessed directly for warmth.

The advantage of these spaceship houses is that they're independent of their local environment and, therefore, theoretically can be placed anywhere. The disadvantage of this approach is that these buildings create an isolation from the outside that can lead to indoor air quality problems and incredible energy inefficiencies. For example, a few nice big picture windows facing west in a hot climate will put a tremendous strain on the building's cooling apparatus. Consequently, huge amounts of energy are used to produce a temperature that could have been achieved elegantly with correct solar orientation and judicious plantings for shade. The apparent independence of the modern house from its local environment is an advantage for commerce only. It does nothing to help create a truly habitable space, and makes the building forever dependent on a fake sun, sources of heat and cool that must be purchased.

Alternative Approaches to Temperature

Our modern dilemma is how to create the stable temperatures needed for our more sedentary, indoor lifestyles while maintaining a connection to the outside and a consciousness of our energy consumption. As I've said, the sun is both the central issue in the quest for a stable indoor temperature and the most predictable aspect of a given local environment. Since alternative building is an attempt to return to a specific, locally driven approach to housing, it's no surprise that the sun plays a big role in alternative strategies. The most successful alternative approaches combine all the features of locally specific passive solar design: correct solar orientation, use of thermal mass, appropriately placed insulation, and natural ventilation and cooling.

Cold winter solar orientation. This earthship is facing south and is partially bermed into the earth on its north side. South-facing glass is angled to allow deepest penetration of the low winter sun.

SOLAR ORIENTATION

Given the predictability of the Sun's path across the sky at any given spot on the planet for any day and any hour of the year, there's simply no excuse for not orienting a building to make the best possible use of the sun. In very hot climates with mild or nonexistent winters, this might mean avoiding the sun as much as possible by facing your house to the north and creating a shaded atrium on that side of the building, or tucking your house into the side of an east-facing hill. For many climates, it will mean facing your house to the south, or slightly east or west of south, to gain access to the winter sun while allowing the roof and overhangs to shade you in the summer.

PROVIDING THERMAL MASS

Once you've chosen the orientation that will maximize the sun's usefulness, you'll need to place appropriate materials in the sun's path. Some materials will keep the sun out, others will let it in, and still others will collect and store its heat. As we've already learned, such heat collectors are called thermal mass.

In alternative building, the most common place to put a thermal mass is in the floor. Since the sun always enters a building at a downward angle, most of its energy tends to hit the floor. Thermal mass floors are made of a wide variety of materials including concrete, brick, tile, and earth. Earthen floors, sometimes called puddled adobe, are basically a mud mix poured over a prepared base. As with other mud applications (see chapter 2), there are many variations in approaches, mixes, and additives. The end result can be a beautiful, durable thermal mass floor.

"There's simply no excuse for not orienting a building to make the best possible use of the sun."

Earthen floor. This beautiful earthen floor hybrid was made of a mix of sand and clay stabilized with a small amount (about 7 to 10%) of Portland cement. The floor was scored and grouted to give it an abstract tile look, then sealed with a commercial liquid concrete sealer.

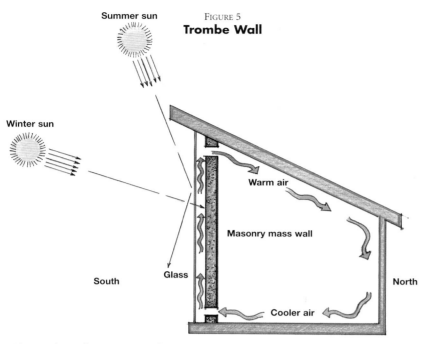

FIGURE 5
Trombe Wall

Summer sun

Winter sun

Warm air

Masonry mass wall

Glass

South

North

Cooler air

The Trombe wall is a conceptually simple method for collecting solar heat and passively moving it to where it's needed. A large overhang prevents overheating in the summer.

There are many other ways to use thermal mass for sun collection. For example, the Trombe wall, credited to the French engineer Felix Trombe, is a simple elegant solar collector consisting of a south-facing glass wall separated from a mass wall by an air space (see figure 5). There are vent openings in the mass wall's top and bottom. As the sun heats this wall, hot air moves through the top vent into the living space. At the same time, cooler air from the room is brought into the collector through the bottom vent, causing the cycle to begin again.

Water has a very high specific heat and can be used to good effect as a solar collector, or thermal mass. For example, 55-gallon drums filled with water can be placed against the interior north wall of a south-facing building, with windows on the south allowing solar exposure, to collect the winter sun. Or the wall can simply be built of a good thermal mass material such as brick.

Exterior south-facing walls also can be used as thermal mass. Walls made of adobe or rammed earth can collect sun striking their outer surface and conduct it through their mass to the building's interior. The problem with this approach is that if the walls are thin enough to conduct heat from

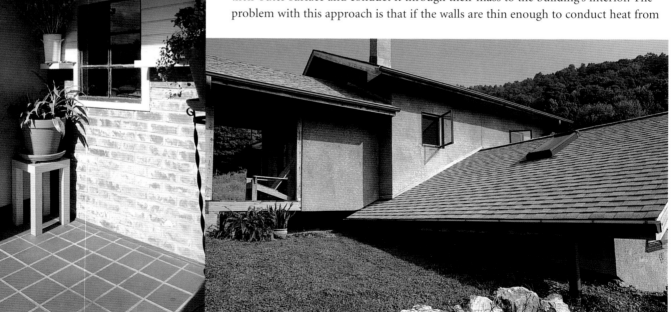

Interior mass wall. This interior brick wall was placed across from a large window to collect and store heat from the winter sun.

Passive solar earth-bermed building. This photo is taken from the northwest side of a south-facing, partially bermed, passive solar house. The south side is open to the sun and has a thermal mass floor to collect solar heat in winter. The smaller roof at left covers a shaded summer porch and winter mudroom/airlock.

the outside to inside during the day, they will probably not be thick enough to prevent indoor warmth from migrating toward the cold outside during the night. Later in this chapter, we'll discuss how materials that combine insulation and thermal mass, such as cob and composite blocks, can compensate for this problem.

The earth itself is a huge thermal mass, a giant heat sink. This mass is so large that it takes a long time for it to heat up or cool down, making it relatively indifferent to the daily fluctuations of air temperatures that make winter cold and summer hot. In most parts of the world, the year-round temperature of the earth four feet below the surface is 55 to 60º F (30.8 to 33.6º C). With walls and floors next to the stable mass of the earth, underground and earth-sheltered buildings access a year-round temperature that's close to the human comfort zone. In a passive solar earth-bermed building, this temperature can be raised indoors by the sun in winter. In contrast, the lack of sun reaching indoors and the fact that the huge mass of the earth maintains a temperature well below that of the outdoors can help keep the building cool in summer.

NATURAL AIR MOVEMENT

Unlike the Sun's methodical march across the sky, air movement is complicated and unpredictable. Nonetheless, natural air movement, as opposed to mechanically induced air movement, is an important part of the heating and cooling equation in passive solar buildings. For example, once you've collected solar heat in your thermal mass, you need to move it around the house. In a two-story building, one approach is to put vents into the upstairs above your thermal mass on the south side of the house. Other vents are placed where cool air is likely to be—for example, against the north wall or under east or west windows. As the thermal mass heats up, warm air will rise off the mass and through the south vents. At the same time cooler air will fall down through the other vents to replace the ascending air, in turn being warmed by the sun and rising. This is called a *convective loop* and, when combined with an open floor plan, can result in the steady circulation of warm air through a passive solar house.

Cooling through natural air movement is more complicated because it requires the services of unpredictable outside air currents. Since wind patterns are determined by so many factors, including the complex variabilities of local terrain, wind is the most site-specific environmental element. If you educate yourself about the prevailing summer winds on your site, you'll be able to place windows optimally for cooling ventilation (see figure 6). Plantings are also an important aide to ventilation and cooling. Obviously, trees planted near the house will shade the building and lower the air temperature there. In addition, though, trees and shrubs can be planted to channel airflow toward the building and slow down or deflect air into the building. Ground covers also can

FIGURE 6
Ventilation and Cooling

Both the orientation and design of windows influence a building's interior air flow and cooling.

Strong air movement   **Strong air movement**   **Weaker air movement**

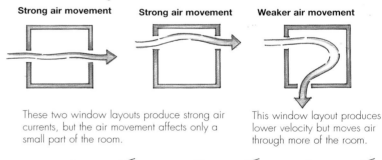

These two window layouts produce strong air currents, but the air movement affects only a small part of the room.

This window layout produces lower velocity but moves air through more of the room.

Choice of window design also has an effect on interior air circulation.

have a significant effect on local air temperature because they dissipate heat through transpiration, another example of naturally occurring evaporative cooling. You've probably noticed this phenomenon when walking from hot asphalt to cool grass. One statistic I've read claims a mature beech tree can evaporate 300 gallons of water per day, thereby dissipating 1 million BTUs (British Thermal Units) of heat, the equivalent of 10 room air conditioners operating 20 hours a day.

Another approach to cooling through air movement is sometimes called "southern air conditioning." In this technique, windows are opened at night to allow cool air in and then closed in the morning to capture that cool air inside as the outside air heats up. This method works best in a well-shaded, well-insulated house, or in a building with thick thermal mass walls.

Unfortunately, natural air movement may not be a workable cooling solution for all people in all situations. In humid climates, encouraging natural ventilation through a building also means inviting large amounts of water vapor inside. This can lead to conditions that encourage the growth of mold and fungus. As we'll discuss later, in chapter 6, this growth can have a significant detrimental effect on indoor air quality. In humid climates where natural ventilation cooling is being used, care should be taken to choose materials that aren't conducive to mold growth.

PROVIDING INSULATION

Through solar orientation, thermal mass, natural air movement, and shading, we are using our local natural environment as a source of heat and cooling for our interior environment. A huge boost to these efforts comes from the appropriate application of insulation.

Let's remember the three ways that heat moves: radiation, convection, and conduction. The materials that make up the bulk of a building are responsible for preventing convective and conductive heat losses. Radiant heat is best dealt with at the outside surface of a building. In a U.S. Department of Energy study, for example, red concrete roofing tiles experienced a temperature increase of 71° F (39.8° C) while white concrete tiles exposed to the same conditions experienced a 21° (11.8° C) increase (see figure 4, page 70). Simply put, if you want to prevent heat gain, use light-colored or reflective roof and wall surfaces. If you want to collect heat, use dark colors such as black, dark green, or deep red.

Don't Believe Everything You Read (Including This)

The saga of the R-value of straw is a good lesson for all of us weekend changers of the world. We're brought up to be wary of politicians and salesmen, but sometimes forget that good-hearted idealists can also be sources of misinformation. In many books and articles you'll find confident claims that straw bales deliver an R-value of between 2.4 and 3 per inch. This translates to claims that straw bale walls can produce R-50 or even R-60. As far as I can tell, these numbers were based on a single 1993 study by a graduate student who measured the heat flow through a single straw bale, not a building or even a wall. Subsequent tests have yielded widely varying results. One test by the Oak Ridge Lab came up with a dismal R-0.94 per inch. The same lab performed a more careful test in 1998 yielding the present "definitive" result of R-1.45 per inch, giving straw bale walls values in the R-27 to R-33 range. These are still good numbers, but they're barely over half of the original, often-repeated, estimates.

In my opinion, there's as much, if not more, misinformation out there inflating the performance of conventional building materials as there is of alternative ones. In any case, not all misinformation is intentional; some is just inaccurate. The point is, don't take everything you read—including this—as absolute fact. You have your own brain and your own powers of analysis that you must use. Learn as much as you can, and make your own decisions.

In modern building, at least, the concept of insulation is fairly recent. The first fiberglass and rigid foam insulations appeared in the U.S. in the 1930s. Though these products are sometimes utilized in alternative buildings, for example rigid foam as perimeter insulation to prevent heat losses through the foundation, other methods of preventing heat flow are much more popular in the alternative world.

Straw Bales

As I pointed out in chapter 2, straw in today's world is basically a byproduct of industrial agriculture, so it can be considered a recycled plant product. Straw bales are excellent insulation against convective and conductive heat loss. Convective losses are prevented because bales are thick and, when covered with stucco, allow only controlled air movement through their width. Conduction is prevented because a bale is made of hollow (air-filled) strands bound together, creating a wide, airy mass. Heat encountering a bale has no direct route through which to move and is therefore slowed down.

This property of bales combined with their width, 17 to 24 inches, gives them an excellent R-value. The exact value is much in debate, but a study conducted at the Oak Ridge National Laboratories, a Department of Energy funded lab, is probably the most definitive to date. In the study, a wall, using 19-inch-thick bales laid flat and plastered on both sides, was constructed under the supervision of nationally known straw bale builders. The measured R-value of the wall was 27.5, or 1.45 per inch. This would extrapolate to R-33 for a 23-inch bale wall (see the sidebar, Don't Believe Everything You Read, left). As we saw in chapter 3, straw can be used as a structural building block with insulative value or as infill insulation in a freestanding structure.

Straw as insulation. Above: These straw bales are being used as infill insulation for a modified post-and-beam wall. Below: These straw bales will serve as both the insulation for and the structure of the wall. Notice the earthbag stem wall lifting the bales off the ground.

Window on waste. Left: Inevitably, framing idiosyncrasies create odd-size spaces that modular fiberglass insulation cannot fit. Off-the-shelf batts will fit in the standard-width cavity between studs, but will require cutting and trimming to fill the others. Right: The result is waste. This fiberglass went through a lot of processing and transportation, using a huge amount of energy, before it ended up as a cut-off in this pile of construction trash headed for the dump.

Recycled Paper

Though sometimes bypassed by alternative building purists, recycled newsprint insulation, commonly called cellulose, is in many ways similar to straw. Both cellulose and straw are organic fibers from plant sources and are the waste products of industry. Made from recycled newspapers, cellulose insulation has a measured R-value of between 3.1 and 3.8 per inch, which is much higher than that of straw. However, cellulose is usually used in conventional wood construction where the wall cavity measures either 3.5 or 5.5 inches, producing an R-13 or R-19 wall respectively. One major strength of cellulose is that it can be used to replace fiberglass in conventional construction. Fiberglass comes in rolls of specific widths to fit between wooden studs. This approach creates waste because it's inflexible, forcing you to frame your building to conform to the precut insulation or to trim that high-embodied-energy, modular insulation to fit your building. The result is extra wood used in framing to accommodate insulation, and lots of strips and pieces of insulation in a pile destined for the dump.

Unlike fiberglass, cellulose, bound together with a small amount of glue and water, can be blown into unfinished new-construction walls in such a way that it fills all gaps, including odd-size spaces such as those around window and door framing and behind electrical boxes. As a result, cellulose can prevent conductive heat losses better than fiberglass. It also means that cellulose creates less waste in installation than fiberglass, which must be cut to fit. Cellulose for wall insulation is most often

Cellulose insulation. Left: A contractor blows insulation material, bound with a little glue and water, into wall cavities. Right: Excess insulation is scraped off and recycled, leaving a level insulation layer that hugs the studs and fills the gap behind the electrical box in this wall.

installed by contractors who blow a damp mixture into wall cavities, then scrape off the excess onto the floor where it's sucked back into the hopper for use on another wall, producing little or no waste.

Cellulose uses much less energy to produce than fiberglass and, unlike fiberglass, keeps its R-value when dampened by condensation. Cellulose also can be blown into attics or pumped into existing walls in a process called dense packing. There's no reason why cellulose can't be used, too, in thicker walls than conventional wood framing provides, therefore delivering R-values to rival and surpass straw bales.

So here we see two materials mass-produced for the same purpose. One, fiberglass, creates waste because it's modular; the other, cellulose, doesn't because it isn't.

Recycled Cotton

Cotton, in the form of postindustrial recycled denim, is being used to produce wall cavity insulation that installs like fiberglass. One brand of natural fiber insulation, for example, is made of 85 to 95 percent recycled denim and five to 15 percent synthetic fiber to add fluff. Like insulation made from newspaper, cotton insulation can take on water while maintaining its R-value. Cotton batts are easier to install than pumped or sprayed cellulose, but don't fill gaps as completely. Cotton's per-inch R-value is reportedly similar to that of newspaper cellulose.

COMBINING THERMAL MASS AND INSULATION

In alternative building, earth materials are often chosen because they're available locally, have a low embodied energy, and make an excellent thermal mass. Mass walls are excellent in preventing convective heat losses. (Just try blowing air through a concrete wall!) But the very reason such materials provide good thermal mass—they absorb, or conduct, heat easily—makes them poor insulators against conductive heat loss. Heat moves easily through them. On the other hand, mass walls tend to be very thick, so a poor R-value per inch can add up to decent insulation in a two-foot-thick wall.

All these factors must be considered carefully in passive solar design. In hot climates with cool nights, walls need to be built thick enough so that the heat of the sun will not reach the inside during the day, giving the wall time to cool off at night. In hot humid climates, however, the nighttime temperature may not fall enough to allow sufficient wall cooling, resulting in overheating during the day. And in cold climates, an uninsulated thermal mass wall that doesn't access the sun's heat in winter—a wall on the north, for instance—would become a cold mass, robbing considerable heat from the house's interior.

Often, combining mass and insulation materials can be a happy marriage. For example, covering the outside of the above-mentioned north-facing mass wall with insulation such as rigid foam or straw bales insulates the mass against the cold winter air while allowing it to function as a mass wall to the interior. The wall could absorb excess interior heat during the day, perhaps from a solar mass floor, and return it to the house at night. Similarly, many modern rammed earth (cement-stabilized soil) walls have insulation built into their width.

Another approach is to build some walls using mass and other walls using insulation. Imagine a house with a well-insulated roof, a south wall built of cob,

Cotton insulation. This cotton insulation is soft to the touch and spongy like a pillow. I wouldn't hesitate to lay down on a big pile of it and take a nap, something I'd never consider on a pile of scratchy fiberglass insulation.

FIGURE 7

Different Wall Systems in the Same House

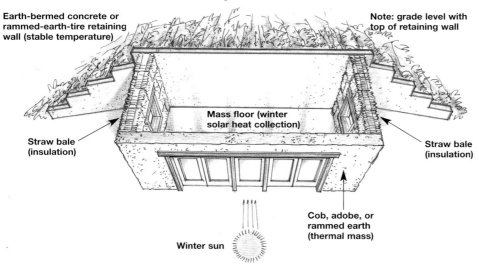

Earth-bermed concrete or rammed-earth-tire retaining wall (stable temperature)

Note: grade level with top of retaining wall

Mass floor (winter solar heat collection)

Straw bale (insulation)

Straw bale (insulation)

Cob, adobe, or rammed earth (thermal mass)

Winter sun

Using a variety of materials to build walls can help to make the most of each material's strengths in thermal performance.

adobe, or rammed earth, east and west walls insulated with cellulose or straw bales, and a poured-concrete or rammed-earth-tire north wall earth-bermed into a south-facing hill (see figure 7). The south wall would collect winter heat, the east and west walls would hold it in, and the north wall would add the thermal stability of the earth's mass. In addition, the amply insulated roof and east and west walls would resist the heat of the summer sun, the lion's share of which they would receive. Such "hybrid" buildings are popping up in the alternative building world, challenging what can sometimes be almost fetishistic loyalty to one material.

Still another approach is to mix mass and conductive insulation together in the same material. The combination of clay/sand (mass) and straw (insulation) in cob, for example, creates a wall that retains some heat while also resisting its movement. Cordwood construction is another example. Wood holds heat well (oak holds more heat by volume than concrete) and also has a decent R-value. Cordwood construction consists of small-diameter logs set in a sandwich of mortar and insulation, creating walls that both hold heat and restrict its flow.

Earthship hybrid. This building uses tires, straw bales, and many other ecologically sensible materials to create a cutting-edge, energy-efficient, passive solar house that blends in with its conventionally constructed neighbors in a sprawling rural subdivision (see also Chapter 7).

Some manufactured alternative materials also effectively combine mass and insulation. Composite blocks made of wood chips bound together with concrete, such as Faswall and Durisol, are an insulative shell filled with thermal mass in the form of poured concrete. They're available in several widths and accept varying thicknesses of insulation inserts, providing R-values from R-8 up to R-28 and the thermal mass benefits of a solid concrete core. The blocks lock together and require no mortar. Hebel blocks, made of aerated concrete, are another version of the concept. Rastra insulative concrete forms are made of recycled polystyrene and also lock together to be laid without mortar.

ADJUSTING THE "SOLAR THERMOSTAT"

At this point, we have our building oriented correctly to the sun and we have our materials placed; we know where we want to plant trees, where to put windows, where the sun will be collected by mass and where insulation will hold that heat in or keep it out. A final step toward creating stable temperature is to install a "solar thermostat." By that I mean we need to adjust the effect of the sun's energy to suit our needs.

Using Glass

Glass windows allow sunlight to enter a building—everybody knows that. But more significantly for our purposes, glass allows the sun's *energy* to enter a building—and then can help keep some of that energy inside the building. By carefully choosing the kinds of glass you use in your building and planning the number, size, and placement of windows, you can regulate, at least partially, the amount of solar energy entering and exiting your home.

For our purposes, we can say that light is energy traveling in the form of waves. The length of a light wave is called its *frequency*. Long or low -frequency waves carry less energy than short or high-frequency ones.

Radiation from the sun is spread over a wide frequency range, but most of the sun's energy that reaches the earth's surface is in three bands: infrared, visible, and ultraviolet. When these high-frequency waves of light are absorbed by physical objects on earth, they are re-emitted as low -frequency, long-wave energy.

Clear glass is basically transparent to infrared and visible frequencies but opaque to low-frequency waves. When sun is allowed to enter a building through glass, its short-wave infrared and visible light heats up surfaces within the space. These objects—furniture or a thermal mass floor, for example—re-radiate that heat as long-wave, low-frequency energy, which is then trapped, or at least temporarily detained, inside the building by the glass. This property of glass makes it invaluable in the collection of solar heat and is a mainstay of passive solar design.

Even so, compared to other building materials a single pane of clear glass is a poor insulator. For this reason, several improvements for window and door glass, also called *glazing*, have been developed. "Insulated" glass, in which two or sometimes three panes of glass are sandwiched together, with a sealed air space between panes, offers greatly increased R-values. Actually, for some reason, the thermal efficiency of glazing is measured by the amount of heat let through rather than resisted. This is called the *U-factor* and it is the reciprocal of R-value ($U = 1/r$). In other words, a low U-factor means a high R-value.

Combining thermal mass and insulation. These blocks made of recycled wood chips bound together with concrete are being poured solid. The insulation value of the wood chips is augmented by rock wool inserts on the inside of the blocks. The poured concrete creates a structurally solid wall with lots of thermal mass.

Double-pane glass. The metal strip in this window separates two panes of glass with an air space. Along with other factors, the width of the space and the gas filling it (air or argon, for example) determine the window's resistance to heat movement.

Thermal mass tile floor. Above: In summer, the tile floor in this south-facing room is shaded from the sun. Below: In winter on a sunny day, the deep red tiles are bathed in sun and collect heat, preventing overheating during the day and slowly radiating heat into the room after sunset.

Other measures that make glazing more insulative include *low-emittance (low-e)* coatings and gas fills. Low-e coatings are microscopically thin reflective layers applied to or between glass panes. These coatings can reflect heat back into the home in winter or back to the outside in summer while still allowing much of the visual spectrum of sunlight to enter the house. While these coatings improve the insulation value of glass, they also reduce its ability to transfer infrared energy, or solar heat. The spaces between panes can also be filled with a gas, such as argon, that insulate better than air. The amount of space between panes can also be adjusted.

As you can see, then, you need to choose glass carefully according to its thermal characteristics. If a window is intended to be used as a solar collector, a source of *solar gain*, then it needs to add more solar heat to the building while the sun is shining than it loses through its poor insulative qualities when the sun isn't shining. In general such windows need to be facing south and are best outfitted with clear double-pane glass. Though the second pane does reduce the amount of solar gain, that loss is more than made up for by the added insulation.

Windows on the east and west sides of buildings generally create net heat losses. The solar gain they provide is not offset by losses created during the long hours when they're shaded. North windows get little or no direct sunlight and therefore are of no use in solar collection. Low-e and *argon-filled* windows are usually only slightly more expensive than clear double-pane glass and offer improved insulative value—but decreased solar gain—making them questionable choices where heat gain is desired, but good choices for windows on north, east, or west walls, where insulation is the prime consideration.

Different commercial window units—even those similar in design and materials—can vary greatly in thermal performance. Luckily, comparing them is made immensely easier by a standardized labeling system, created by the National Fenestration Council (NFC), that provides ratings for a product's U-factor, heat gain, visible-light transmittance, and air leakage. Look for these labels and compare the numbers when choosing glazing for your home.

Finally, remember that, in addition to choosing glass types, you'll also need to match the amount of glass, particularly south-facing glass, to your situation and design. The particulars of where you live, the exact siting of your house, and the amount of thermal mass will greatly affect the amount of glass you should use. Believe me, though, it will be less than you think. Probably the biggest mistake that novice builders make is putting too many windows into a building. Too much south-facing glass can lead to severe overheating during the day and excessive heat loss at night. Study a book on passive solar design and do the appropriate calculations.

Adjusting Thermal Mass

The amount and thickness of your thermal mass is another part of the equation. A thick mass will absorb more heat, but will be slower to react to inside air temperature changes. A thin mass will release its heat quickly, giving fast warming when the Sun goes down, but can also lead to overheating during the day and not enough stored heat to last the night. Again, the correct solution requires calculations for your situation. As a rule of thumb, most sources recommend 4-inch-thick masonry (concrete, brick, stone) floors and interior walls. Remember, this isn't like rearranging furniture. Once you've placed these materials, you can't move them, and the Sun isn't going to change its plans either.

Other Adjustments

Keep in mind that the shape of your building, along with its orientation, will determine the amount of sun that hits its surface. For example, since east and west walls tend to overheat in summer and don't get much sun in winter, a long thin building with one long side facing south limits the east and west wall surfaces while maximizing southern exposure.

The colors of the surfaces of your house also are part of your solar thermostat. As mentioned earlier, light-colored surfaces reflect the sun, while dark colors absorb it. Thermal mass intended as a solar collector, then, should be dark in color. This is why you'll often see the deep red of Saltillo tile covering a thermal mass floor.

Other knobs on your solar thermostat can include movable insulation, whether in the form of curtains or more elaborate constructions, over glass windows and doors to prevent nighttime heat loss. Window and door overhangs planted with deciduous vines will shade glass with their greenery during the summer and lose their leaves in fall to admit winter sun. When placed over south-facing windows and doors, this is called a *solar arbor*.

Solar arbor. When its climbing vines are fully grown this bamboo arbor will provide leafy shade for the glass behind it in hot weather, then shed its leaves in fall to allow sun inside in winter.

SUPPLEMENTING THE SUN

All these measures, and others, can come together to allow flexible use of the sun in cooling and heating your house, often allowing even modern couch potatoes to do without mechanical forms of temperature production. However, even carefully designed houses often need help creating a stable temperature.

A great heat source that complements the open floor plans of most passive solar buildings is a wood-burning masonry stove (see the sidebar, Masonry Stoves and Heating with Wood, at the end of this chapter). Unlike conventional metal wood stoves, masonry heaters use thermal mass to store the heat from a brief, very hot fire and then slowly radiate that heat to the house over many hours. The result is a mild, even heat that doesn't dry the air. Masonry stoves are very efficient, turning most of the available energy in the wood to heat through hot burning and secondary combustion.

Another heat source that utilizes mass to create even warmth is *radiant floor heating*, also called *hydronic* heating. In the most common example of this technique, a liquid (often water) circulates within pipes encased in a poured concrete floor. As it flows through the pipes the liquid, heated by solar or other means, gives off its heat to the concrete's thermal mass. The concrete then radiates the warmth slowly to the room.

Radiant floor heat. Plastic tubing for a radiant floor heating system is placed over insulation and metal mesh reinforcement before the floor's concrete slab is poured.

Hammering It Home

Providing a stable indoor temperature is the most basic function of housing. Because solar energy, or lack of it, is the cause of earthly temperature ranges, a building's relationship to the Sun defines its ability to fulfill this function. Fortunately the Sun's path, which changes through the year from low in the south in winter to high overhead in the summer, is completely predictable for any spot on the planet. This allows us to create buildings that maximize our control over the Sun's effect on indoor temperatures.

Passive solar building is an age-old practice and, in my humble opinion, one of the most elegant examples of the human mind working with nature to improve the human condition. Alternative builders are combining old concepts of passive solar design with traditional and modern materials, such as insulated glass, to create comfortable indoor temperatures for our relatively sedentary times. In the absence of time-tested local wisdom, our modern solar buildings need to be designed with care. Building orientation, thickness of mass, amount of window glass, ventilation patterns, and landscape plantings all need to be planned using our scientific understanding of the thermal performance of materials. In this way, a successful passive solar alternative house will, in most climates, be a true marriage between the traditional and the modern.

Masonry Stoves and Heating with Wood:
A DISCUSSION WITH NORBERT SENF

Q What is a masonry stove?

A masonry stove is a stove that stores heat in a thermal mass. You might burn 50 pounds of wood in a big two-hour fire, and this will heat several thousand pounds of masonry that will still be warm when you have your next fire 24 hours later.

This type of heater has been built in some of the colder regions of Europe and other parts of the world for many years. North American heating traditions come from Britain and France. Neither country has a masonry heater tradition, only open fireplaces, so they were virtually unknown here until about 20 years ago.

In Europe, masonry stoves were traditionally room heaters. When they came to North America, people wanted to heat whole houses with them, and also be able to use them for fire viewing. So heaters have evolved here in North America to fit our needs.

Q There's some debate over whether wood is an environmentally sensible heating fuel. What do you think?

The average North American house consumes about as much fossil fuel as an average North American car. It's a lot easier to get your house off oil than it is your car. So if you're serious about reducing your personal greenhouse gas footprint, your house is a good place to start. The best approach is to reduce the heat load of your house by making it energy-efficient. The next thing to do is replace fossil fuel with renewable fuel for heating. You can take agricultural waste, for example, and turn it into pellet fuel.

The problem with burning wood is the resulting emissions. Wood is potentially a clean fuel, since it contains very little sulfur or ash, and everything else can theoretically be oxidized into CO_2 and water. But this can be tricky. You have to burn the wood fast and hot enough to get a complete burn. Because a masonry heater can store heat, it's relatively easy to burn cordwood cleanly in it, because you can burn it very fast and hot without overheating the house.

Q How do masonry stoves compare to metal wood stoves and brick fireplaces?

With a metal stove, you don't have any significant heat storage. Therefore you have to control the heat output by control-

Future heat. Norbert Senf installing a masonry stove kit.

ling the burn rate of the wood. If you burn cordwood instead of pellets, the only way to control the burn rate is to control the combustion air supply. If you turn the air down enough, the wood begins to smolder. You get smoke, which is unburned tar droplets, the same as cigarette smoke. At this point, the emissions skyrocket. It can be a factor of 100 or more. Not only that, but the proportion of nasty stuff in the smoke goes up as well. There's also increasing evidence that the emissions contribute to global warming.

Metal stoves have come a long way in the last 10 years. The new EPA-certified stoves use advanced combustion technology that allows them to be turned down a lot more before they start to smoke. It's very sophisticated. Therefore, if you use a metal stove, make sure it's EPA-certified. If you have an old metal stove, get rid of it. Sell it to a scrap dealer, not to another user.

Open fireplaces can burn fairly cleanly if you use small, dry wood and have a fast, hot fire. However, they typically smolder a lot because things are kept cool by the tremendous amount of air that moves through them.

Q What's your advice for someone considering putting a masonry stove in their home?
Check out the Masonry Heater Association website at www.mha-net.org. You'll find links to a number of manufacturers, ourselves included, plus a number of masons who care about heaters.

The ideal situation is an energy-efficient house, with a masonry heater located centrally in an open floor plan. This way you get the maximum benefit from the radiant heating aspect which, in my opinion, is the best feature of a masonry heater's performance. It is a very high quality of heat—similar to what you get with a hydronic floor, except that you can cozy right up to it.

Norbert Senf was trained as an engineer and has been a mason for 30 years. He built the first modern contraflow masonry heater in Canada in 1981 and developed the first North American modular masonry heater core. He's a founding member of the Masonry Heater Association and manufactures the Heatkit, a modular masonry stove core kit.

Masonry wood-burning stove. This masonry stove features a large firebox with glass doors, and a bake oven. The fire is burned very hot as heat, gas, and smoke rise to a secondary combustion chamber above the bake oven, where the hot gas is combusted. Heat and smoke are then directed back down the stove through channels on both sides and eventually into the chimney through an opening at its base. This circuitous path, the reason these stoves are called contraflow heaters, takes the heat past the huge mass of the stove, which absorbs much of the warmth and radiates it slowly back into the room over many hours.

CHAPTER 5

SEPARATION

If I WERE MAKING THE UNIVERSE, I'd want to create it once and be done with it. Our world doesn't work like that. Here, everything is a cycle. What we have is a big soup of stuff out of which things constantly take shape, and then fall apart again into the soup. Every plant and animal lives its life nourished by soil, an amazing structure made up mostly of little organic pieces, and then returns to the soil for the whole process to begin again. A rock slowly erodes in the presence of rain, snow, sun, and wind. It breaks down into parts that become available to be formed into something else. Such is our world.

Into this strange setup comes the little human with its desire for shelter. It's a difficult mission from the start. Not only do we want to create a shelter that separates us from the great outdoors, but we want the fruits of our labor, our house, to last as long as possible. To accomplish that, we have to find some way to retard the natural processes of decay that are the rule in our world.

Our main area of concern in this quest is the border between our building and the outside. This border is called a building's *exterior skin*, and includes the outer surface of the roof, walls, windows, and doors. The interior surface of a building is known, logically enough, as its *interior skin*. The job of these exterior and interior skins is to protect the building from the natural forces of decay, be they rain, snow, sun, wind, plants, animals, insects, or even microorganisms.

The Forces of Decay

As we'll see in this chapter, protecting a building from decay, far from being a straightforward problem, cuts to the core of the human paradox of shelter: the elements of nature that we seek out, that we need in order to live, are also the forces that can destroy our buildings. Sun, water, moving air (wind), and abundant life help define a good house site. But they're also ever-present elements of decay, resembling science fiction monsters in their ability to claw and pound their way into the very heart of your house. These forces of nature are simultaneously the enemies of a building and the friends of its inhabitants. There's no hope of creating a lasting building without a healthy respect for this strange relationship.

Let's look at these forces a little more closely.

WATER

When I hear someone talking about "natural" housing, I smile and think of water. No matter what our politics or intentions, there are some things about housing that just aren't natural. Trying to exclude water is one of those things. Water covers much of the planet. Our bodies are mostly water. Water falls from the sky and flows over and through the ground. On this planet, water is almost omnipresent. If there's a way in, water will find it. Our attempt to keep water out of our houses is definitely a David (that's us) versus Goliath situation.

What is it about water? First, it's essentially formless, which means it can take on any shape. Water can fit into the tiniest hole or slightest crack. In addition, water is the only natural substance that exists as a liquid, solid, and gas at normal earth surface temperatures. This means that water may enter a space in one form and then morph to another. So what? Well, water entering a crack or porous substance can freeze and therefore expand, causing more cracking or other problems. Steam can access openings that liquid water can't, then condense into pools that may have no way of escape (see the sidebar, Condensation, on page 91).

Second, water is known as the *universal solvent* because it can dissolve more substances than any other liquid. In other words, it's difficult to find a surface that water won't erode. Third, water

Water damage. Water covers more than two-thirds of our planet and is essential to all life. But it can also act as a destructive agent, as it is in this chemical reaction that's causing steel roofing to rust. The roof is slowly dissolving away.

has the highest surface tension of common liquids. This in essence means that it's sticky and therefore moves easily through *capillary action*. Capillary action is defined as the means by which liquid moves through the porous spaces in a solid. Capillary action is the way in which water moves from the roots of a tree to its leaves and helps to move your blood, mostly water, through your veins. It also allows water to climb up the surfaces of your walls or roof, defying gravity as it sneaks into your house.

Finally, water is a life magnet. Where there's water, there will be things growing and living. Wet wood, for example, decays not because of the water, but because of the insects and microorganisms that the water attracts. Molds and fungi love dark, wet places—such as the insides of your walls if water is allowed in.

SUN

If water is omnipresent, then the Sun is omnipotent on our little planet. The Sun makes all life possible, both as the source of earthly temperatures conducive to life and as the energy behind photosynthesis, the process that powers growth in plants and provides all food, both plant and animal. As we learned in chapter 4, the Sun is also the source of most of our fuels. Coal, petroleum, and wood are essentially just concentrated sunlight stored in plants. Passive solar heat and solar electric power are other uses. The Sun is the origin of all life on Earth, and of most of the energy, both food and otherwise, that we use. Luckily for us, sunlight is abundant, dependable, and accessible.

That's the good news. The bad news is that incessant sun puts a lot of stress on the exterior of your poor little building. The heating and cooling cycles caused by the Sun's daily path can make materials expand and contract. Over time this can cause cracking and peeling. Sunlight, of course, also has an intense drying effect, which can turn materials brittle or make them more porous, allowing them to absorb more water. Also, sunlight's ultraviolet radiation reacts chemically with many materials and breaks them down. You've probably seen, for example, how fabrics or photos fade if left in front of a sunny window.

Sun damage. The Sun is Earth's power supply, its life force. But it also has been a major force in the decay of this wood siding, both by drying the wood and causing it to expand and contract in cycles of hot and cold. Together these actions have opened the grain and warped the wood, allowing water into and behind the siding.

WIND

Air is the ocean in which we swim. Moving air—wind—allows the symbiotic exchange of oxygen and carbon dioxide between plants and animals. We inhale air and extract life-giving oxygen, then exhale to dump carbon dioxide, a poison in our bodies. Plants use this carbon dioxide and produce more oxygen for us to breathe. Circulating air brings us the plants' oxygen and takes them our carbon dioxide. Wind also pollinates flowers and spreads seeds. In these ways and others, wind is integral to our survival.

Wind is the most site-specific aspect of all the forces of nature. The contour of your land, the amount of vegetation, and varying regional wind patterns all combine to create prevalent winds that in many ways will be unique to your site. Wind can cause direct damage, by ripping pieces of skin off your roof, for example. Much more often, however, it enables damage, by driving rain onto a wall or by throwing a branch, or even a whole tree, onto your house.

Wind damage. The same air that we breathe and sometimes feel as a gentle breeze can literally tear the skin off your building.

LIFE

As I've said, life is a cycle. Things are born, grow, live, die, and decay. If we didn't have decay, we'd quickly run out of the raw materials to make more life. Imagine what this planet would look like if the carcasses of everything that had ever lived were still around! Organic materials don't just fall apart. They're eaten and digested. You digest your lunch. Microorganisms, molds, fungi, and bugs will eventually digest any organic matter (wood, straw, etc.) in your house. The only variable we can influence is how long this process will take.

Some things want to eat your house, others just want to live in it. Birds are happy nesting in the eaves of roofs or even in walls. Mice seek out cozy warm spots that are often just a squirm or a few chews away. The list goes on: snakes, raccoons, skunks, opossums, and more. If it's a creature that moves, there's probably someplace in your house that will accommodate it.

"The forces of nature are simultaneously the enemies of a building and the friends of its inhabitants."

Damage from living things. Left: This termite plays an important ecological role as a dead-wood decomposer, but will munch house wood as voraciously as forest debris. Right: This floor joist has been destroyed by carpenter ants, which search out water-damaged wood to hollow out and use as a nest.

Condensation

On earth, air contains water in the form of vapor. The amount of water vapor that air can hold depends on the air's temperature. As air warms it expands, making room for more water vapor. Conversely, cooler air can't hold as much vapor. When air becomes saturated with moisture, the extra water has to go somewhere. It's pushed out of the air and forms on nearby surfaces. This process is called *condensation*. When warm air hits cooler surfaces, its temperature drops, diminishing its capacity to hold moisture, causing condensation. Just where condensation can occur in your house depends on where moist, warm air meets cool surfaces. If there's moist, warm air inside your house and it's cool outside, that moisture will be pulled into your walls from the inside. If the outside air is warmer than inside, moisture will be drawn in from the outside.

This is a concern because where there's condensation, fungi, mold, insects, and associated rot often aren't far behind. It's the perfect example of all our elements of decay coming together to do their thing. Condensation is common in walls, attics, basements, crawlspaces, closets, bathrooms, and kitchens. There's constant debate over how to deal with condensation. Some people say to vent roofs and attics, others say you're crazy to do so. Some people say to use vapor barriers on the side of your walls most often contacting condensation (interior in cold climates and exterior in warm climates). Others say that your walls need to "breathe" and that vapor barriers are wrong, wrong, wrong (see the discussion of breathable walls on page 102 and the sidebar, The Trouble with Modern Products, on page 98). One thing, at least, seems certain: different climates require different solutions. The same air with the same moisture content will behave differently at different temperatures.

Types of Building Skins

Our problem is clear. We have to live where the rain falls, the sun shines, the air moves, and life flourishes. Unfortunately, these wonderful harbingers of life are also powerful forces of decay. The result: your house must be placed smack-dab in the middle of danger. Your house has to keep out the same things that it's designed to let in.

This, of course, is where building skins come in. What options are available? Let's examine the basic kinds of skins first. Then we'll discuss traditional, modern, and alternative approaches.

INTEGRATED SKINS

The structures of some buildings serve as a good portion of their own skins. In order for this to be true, the building must have a monolithic structure (see chapter 3) and be made of materials that resist the elements of decay. Stone is an excellent example. Most stone is resistant to sun, rain, and snow. What's more, stone is heavy by nature, and structural stone walls must be thick. Combined, these properties make wind a minor factor in decay. Perhaps best of all, stone is inedible and difficult to hollow out as a nest.

Concrete and brick share most of the properties of stone, including its resistance to decay. Structural forms made with these materials can also serve as their own skins. Other building techniques such as adobe and cob can, in some climates, withstand their local environment and are sometimes left without further exterior coating.

Does the notion of a self-contained, *integrated* skin sound too good to be true? Well, in some ways it is. Heavy monolithic structures can be built to last a long time, but often perform poorly in other areas such as insulation value (for more on that topic, refer to chapter 4). Also, in most cases only the walls of integrated-skin buildings are integrated. Other surfaces, such as roofs, windows, and doors, require an added, or *applied*, skin. The exceptions to this rule would be an igloo, a concrete bunker, or a monolithic dome made, for example, of brick or fired adobe.

Stone as skin. Some types of stone are resilient to all natural forces of decay. Monolithic walls of stone can serve as their own exterior and interior skins.

Integrated-skin poster child. The exterior of this beautiful mosque at the Taj Mahal is made mostly, if not solely, of integrated-skin materials.

APPLIED SKINS: WALLS

The exterior of any skeletal structure, and of some monolithic types such as load-bearing straw bale walls, requires some kind of applied skin. Such skins are generally tough coatings or membranes, seamless or overlapping (see figure 1). In addition to being durable and resistant to elements of decay, they need to be easy to shape and, to some degree, flexible. They have to be easy to shape because they must be applied with equal success around doors and windows, in tight corners, spanning long distances, and sometimes over complicated shapes. They need to be flexible because all buildings move, shifting slightly over time and expanding or contracting with changes in temperature.

There are many kinds of applied wall skins. Stuccos and plasters are spread on wet and then harden to a durable coating, often rocklike in resistance to decay. Milled lumber is easy to cut and apply and is durable and flexible. Some woods, such as cedar and cypress, contain oils that make them resistant to water and insect damage. Paints and stains are thin final skins, basically sacrificial coatings that water and sun attack first and slowly eat away.

There are also modern versions of these basics, including concrete planks, synthetic stuccos, and the perennial suburban classic, vinyl siding. You can even build a wall to protect your wall, as is the case with stone and brick veneers. You may not realize that many of the brick buildings that you see, especially residential houses, are actually skeletal structures with applied brick skins.

FIGURE 1

Types of Applied Wall Skins

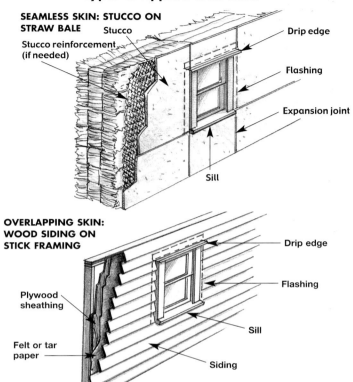

All skeletal structures, and some monolithic types such as those with load-bearing straw bale walls, need an applied skin. Stucco (top) is an example of a seamless skin. Siding (bottom) is an example of an overlapping skin.

Wood siding types. Left: These shingles are made of cedar, a wood containing oils that help resist water and insect damage. Middle: Lap or "German" siding is beveled at the top and grooved at the bottom so each row fits snugly over the previous one, creating a tight seal. Right: This board-and-batten siding was rough-cut and installed green, without kiln drying. As the wide boards dry, they shrink, leaving gaps between them. The thin strips, or battens, are nailed over the joints to cover the spaces.

"A building's roof takes the lion's share of abuse."

APPLIED SKINS: ROOFS

While walls are often partially sheltered by roof overhangs, the roof is usually completely unprotected. Most of the water and sun that fall on a building fall on the roof. In addition, updrafts caused by wind passing over a building can be harsh, tugging severely on a roof's surface. In other words, a building's roof takes the lion's share of abuse. As a result, a roof's skin needs to be absolutely waterproof, able to withstand extended harsh sunlight, and tightly attached to withstand wind.

Most roof skins are formed from materials overlapped to create waterproof seams. For example, *shingles* are thin pieces of wood, tile, slate, concrete, asphalt, or other water- and sun-resistant material laid in overlapping rows and fastened securely with wide-headed nails (see figure 2). *Thatching* is actually a form of shingling. Tight bundles of reeds or straw are laid in overlapping horizontal rows on steep pitched-roof structures. The rows are held in place by steel bars that are fastened to rafters with steel hooks. *Metal* roofs are made of flat sheets formed at the edges to create watertight seams when overlapped. They're attached with strong screws or ring-shanked nails or bolts.

Modern *living* and *green* roofs usually consist of a conventional roof structure covered with a waterproof film of some industrial material, which is usually rubber-, asphalt-, or plastic-based. This in turn is covered with other layers of material, for drainage and insulation for example, and topped off with soil to hold vegetation.

Roof thatching. Left: Thatching is an age-old art, as practiced here by master thatcher Colin McGhee. Right: A thatched roof is both durable and beautiful.

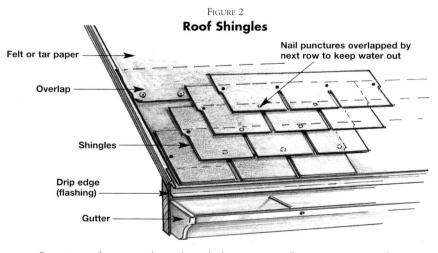

Metal's mettle. A carefully installed metal roof is long-lasting and requires little maintenance.

FIGURE 2
Roof Shingles

Felt or tar paper

Nail punctures overlapped by next row to keep water out

Overlap

Shingles

Drip edge (flashing)

Gutter

Fastening roofing materials can be tricky because it usually means puncturing the roof. When installing shingles, the holes made by nailing one row of material are covered by overlapping the next row, thus keeping water away from the punctures.

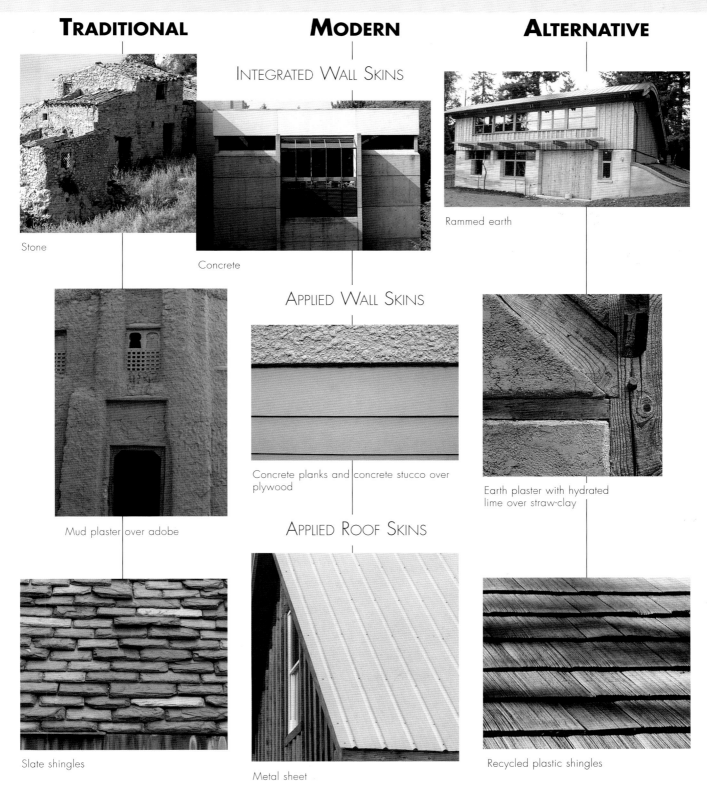

a look at... BUILDING SKINS

TRADITIONAL

MODERN

ALTERNATIVE

INTEGRATED WALL SKINS

Stone

Concrete

Rammed earth

APPLIED WALL SKINS

Mud plaster over adobe

Concrete planks and concrete stucco over plywood

Earth plaster with hydrated lime over straw-clay

APPLIED ROOF SKINS

Slate shingles

Metal sheet

Recycled plastic shingles

Modern vs. Traditional Approaches

The modern approach to providing a barrier from nature's forces is scientific. Scientists in labs work on specific problems: What's the best way to repel water? What characteristics define a material that withstands ultraviolet light? The result has been a constant supply of synthesized products such as plastic membranes, powerful adhesives, and special paints.

One trouble with this approach is that it ignores the dilemma we've discussed here: the enemy of the house is also the friend of the inhabitants. The easiest way to prevent insects from eating is to poison them, but poisoning insects often means poisoning ourselves. If your only concern is protecting something from water, then you may forget that the water itself needs to be protected too, for life to flourish. Modern building products often pollute the environment not only when they're being produced but also through off-gassing and slow leaching of chemical components, both indoors and out, after they're installed. Let's face it, the easiest way to prevent things from decaying is by making them abhorrent to life, an option that would make sense if we weren't alive ourselves. This isn't pie-in-the-sky, touchy-feely stuff. It's simple common sense, a matter of survival. If we make an enemy out of the forces of decay, our environment, then we make an enemy of ourselves.

Making an enemy of the environment is not only dangerous, but often a recipe for failure. Modern building is constantly churning out new products. Housing has been around almost as long as humans, and the problems of decay haven't changed in all that time. Why do we need new products to solve the same old problems? Too often, these products only create their own problems (see the sidebar, The Trouble with Modern Products, on page 98).

Modern materials are overachievers. They're designed to create a sort of "super house" that can withstand any climate. That approach simply puts too much of a demand on our materials, forcing some funky toxic solutions, and doesn't show enough respect for the delicacy of the situation. We become, for example, so focused on repelling water that we forget the nature of water itself. If there's a way in, water will find it. While keeping water out, you have to accommodate what gets in. Rather than repelling water, the more sensible approach is safely redirecting it (see figure 3).

Science can make amazing materials, but those materials can't defeat nature. Sun, wind, water, and life come together in too many varied ways. They bounce off each other, creating an almost endless array of possibilities. The same multiplicity of forces that makes every

Locally specific building. Materials weren't added but taken away to create this amazing building carved out of a solid rock face in Petra, Jordan. Now, that's durable, locally specific building.

Living local lumber yard. Bamboo is an amazingly workable material with considerable structural strength. It also grows like a weed in many parts of the world. Here, a fisherman in Hue, Vietnam, lowers a large, strong, yet light bamboo net structure into the water using only one hand.

Seamless transition. These buildings in Timbuktu seem to grow out of their landscape. That's because they're made mostly from the same soil on which they stand. Over time, sand has accumulated, partially burying the older (middle) building and creating a new street level on which later buildings were constructed.

snowflake unique makes every building site unique. These forces aren't general, and we can't approach them with general solutions.

Fortunately, there's another way. If you focus on the specific local conditions of a building site, you can determine the degree to which rain, sun, wind, life, and other elements will be factors. You can also ask yourself how these different elements will interact and in what specific forms they'll appear.

Climate-specific building can reduce the demands placed on materials. For example, in the desert the skins of buildings will be exposed to extreme heat and UV radiation. They'll also experience the pressures of expansion and contraction due to the heating and cooling cycles of hot days and cold nights. At the same time, they'll rarely be exposed to rain. And when they do get soaked, they'll probably have plenty of time to dry before the next rain. Therefore, you need a material that's happy in the sun and can withstand the occasional soaking. Since you don't need a supermaterial capable of withstanding all extremes of weather, an abundant local resource can often fulfill your needs.

Traditional cultures have had a lot of success finding indigenous materials that are durable in their local environments. People in hot arid climates tend to use a lot of earth mixed with water and perhaps some straw or cow dung to make buildings that stand up to heavy sun and don't need to withstand constant pounding rain. People living in wet forests often use plant materials, such as bamboo, reeds, straw, or palm fronds, for building skins. If they need to repair their bamboo floor or thatched roof, there's no need to call the hardware store and trucking company. These materials grow all around them. To me, the most sublime example of this principle is the igloo. Repelling snow with ice: pure genius! All of these approaches to building skins work great in their locale, but would fail miserably in other climates.

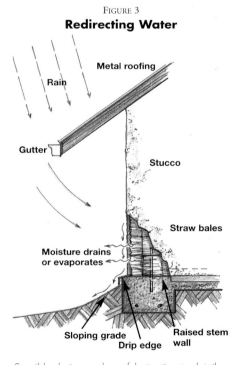

FIGURE 3
Redirecting Water

Rain

Metal roofing

Gutter

Stucco

Straw bales

Moisture drains or evaporates

Sloping grade

Drip edge

Raised stem wall

Sensible design and careful attention to details are the keys to protecting materials by redirecting, rather than trying to repel, water. Large overhangs keep most of the water off this wall. Gutters and sloped grading, along with a raised stem wall, keep water away from the foundation. In the case of this breathable stuccoed straw bale wall, any water that does reach bales through driving rain won't be trapped and can leave the way it came by evaporating over time on hot days. Conversely, conventionally sided wood-frame walls are protected from small amounts of water that get behind siding by an underlayment of asphalt-impregnated felt paper that directs the liquid by gravity to a bottom drip edge.

The Trouble with Modern Products

Bringing a completely new product into the world is a huge leap of faith. No matter how thoroughly you research it, no matter how carefully you manufacture it, you still have no idea how it's actually going to function within our immensely complex real world. As a result, every new product must be considered experimental for many years, until it has been observed in numerous situations over long periods of time.

You might be surprised to learn, for example, that although the following common modern materials and techniques are widely used, they're also still hotly debated in the building world.

HOUSE WRAPS

Most conventionally framed wood buildings built today are enveloped in a cocoon of material generically called house wrap to protect against water damage while sealing the building against air leakage. One manufacturer, Dupont, describes its product this way: "The unique, non-woven-fiber structure of Tyvek® HomeWrap® resists air infiltration and water intrusion, yet is engineered to readily allow moisture vapor to diffuse through the sheet, helping prevent mold and mildew buildup and wood rot. The fibrous structure is engineered with microscopic pores that readily allow moisture vapor to evaporate but are so small that bulk water and air cannot penetrate." This sounds like another wonderful example of better living through science. However, the reality may be more complicated.

House wrap, right or wrong? Is this modern product doing its job or just causing more problems?

One problem that has arisen is that surfactants in cedar, and perhaps other materials, seem to have the ability to compromise the water resistance of some house wraps. If water gets behind the cedar siding, which can happen through driving rain or capillary action, it can cause surfactants to leach out and possibly damage the house wrap, leaving the underlying wood open to water damage. Another problem is that if water does find a way behind the house wrap, it becomes trapped and may eventually cause rot. One way water does this is by exploiting an intentional design feature of the fabric: its permeability to water vapor. Liquid water that finds its way behind siding can eventually turn to vapor, for example through being heated by the sun, pass through the house wrap, and then condense into liquid water on the surface of wood sheathing. This, of course, is the exact situation that the house wrap was engineered to prevent.

ROOF AND FOUNDATION VENTS

It's common practice, usually required by code, to install vents in crawlspaces and roofs. In a roof, the idea is to encourage circulation to lower attic and roof surface temperatures in order to save energy and protect roofing materials. In the crawlspace, the idea is to allow moist air to escape, preventing mold and rot. On the other hand, there are reputable people in the conventional building world who strongly claim that this approach is wrong. They point out that the heat of the sun passes through roofs mostly through radiation, not convection. Radiant heat transfer is little affected by the airflow created by vents. Instead this airflow brings in water from humid outside air, which condenses and is trapped in the attic, often causing mold and rot. Likewise, crawlspace vents can bring in warm air laden with water vapor, which condenses and causes damage.

EIFS (EXTERIOR INSULATION FINISH SYSTEMS)

EIFS is a building skin system consisting of a watertight synthetic stucco, basically a thick plastic paint, applied to foam insulation over some form of wood sheathing. Problems occur if water gets behind the stucco, for example at caulking or flashing imperfections around windows. Once in the wall, the water often has no way out and builds up on the sheathing, causing rot. Thousands of expensive homes have been covered with EIFS, and many have experienced major structural damage in relatively short periods of time. On paper, this system should be waterproof, but in the real world, where human error is a given and water is sneaky, it hasn't always performed as expected.

VAPOR BARRIERS

In many parts of the U.S., the application of vapor barriers is common practice and required by building codes. A vapor barrier, usually plastic sheeting, is a waterproof membrane that prevents humid air from entering wall cavities. Vapor barriers are attached to the "warm side" of the wall (inside in cold climates, outside in hot climates) because this is the area where most condensation should occur (see the sidebar, Condensation, on page 91).

The word "most" should tip you off to potential problems. Vapor barriers are a bold, black-or-white statement in a multicolored world. The idea that there are two kinds of climate, hot and cold, is just plain silly. What about temperate, or hot and dry, or cold and wet climates? More importantly, what about the infinite variety and overlap between these climatic conditions? Vapor barriers are designed to deal with condensation from only one situation, coming in one direction, which just isn't the way the world works. More importantly, we've already pointed out the surreal powers of water to gain access. A vapor barrier is usually attached with staples, causing hundreds of tiny punctures. Then the finish wall, such as drywall or wood, is nailed or screwed on top, adding hundreds if not thousands more punctures in the barrier. If water vapor gets past this imperfect barrier (imagine a steamy kitchen or bathroom) it will be trapped inside the wall cavity, eventually cooling and condensing into liquid. Instead of keeping water vapor out, vapor barriers can actually trap it in. Admittedly, water vapor is a given in air and a potential problem for walls, but this is a pretty lame attempt at a solution. Vapor barriers are a perfect example of how our general modern society can't cope with aspects of nature that are intensely site-specific. For an alternative, see the discussion of breathable walls that starts on page 102.

Are these roof vents effective? The idea here is that hot air will rise in the attic and exit through the ridge vent (bottom photo). This action should pull cooler outside air through soffit vents, shown above, creating air circulation. It sounds good, but does it work?

Alternative Approaches

Alternative builders have to creatively combine traditional and modern approaches to building skins. Let's make this very clear: we live in a time and place where modern materials will be used. Sheet metals for flashing and often roofing; sheet papers such as tar-impregnated felt and (gasp!) synthetic plastics; mass-produced fasteners; energy-efficient double-pane glass; industrially milled lumber; and Portland cement and/or processed lime are just some of the modern products you may find yourself using in the skin of your house.

At the same time, designing with your specific climate in mind often allows you to use abundant local materials instead of industrially conceived, mass-produced stuff. In arid, desert climates, for example, comfortable buildings utilizing thick walls of dirt have been built for thousands of years. Why not take this locally conceived and tested approach and tweak it to your needs, instead of utilizing generic supermaterials with many properties irrelevant to your locale? Often, modern materials can be combined with traditional approaches to expand the types of climate they can withstand. For example, traditional adobe walls can be adapted to wetter climates when used in combination with a metal roof with large overhangs, a water-protective yet breathable stucco such as lime plaster, and raised concrete stem walls. Your challenge is to combine modern and local materials with an understanding of how your local elements of decay manifest themselves. Your goal is to create a skin that withstands your local environment without contaminating it.

The most obvious strategy is to choose a traditional building structure and skin that has its origins in a climate similar to your own. Other than that, simple design features are often as important as materials. Wide roof overhangs help keep rain off walls (see figure 3 on page 97). Lifting organic materials such as straw or wood off the ground on waterproof stem walls of stone or concrete keeps splashing rain and some insects away from walls. Through reflection, light colors can also help protect materials from sun damage. Pigments of any type, in paints or stains, can help protect the materials they cover by acting as a sacrificial layer to the sun's damaging rays. Pigments slowly break down, causing color to fade, but the material underneath is shielded from the sun. Small but crucial details such as *flashing* (see the sidebar, Flashing, right) at all windows, doors, and other skin punctures, as well as waterproof door thresholds and window sills, (see figure 4) are absolutely critical in most climates. Any building, from the most basic hut to a luxurious mansion or well-meaning eco-house, can be devastated by neglecting or poorly installing these simple but crucial details.

Overhangs and stem walls. This little building is lifted off the ground at the corners on stone piers. A porch roof protects the earth-plastered portion of the wall from pounding rain while creating a shady sitting area.

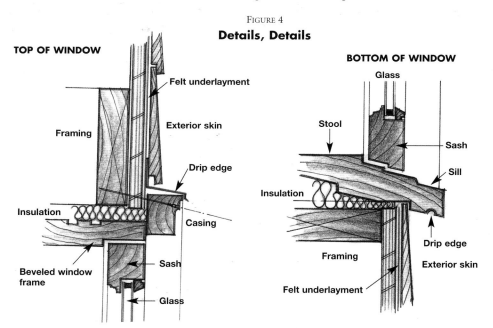

FIGURE 4

Details, Details

TOP OF WINDOW

- Felt underlayment
- Exterior skin
- Framing
- Drip edge
- Insulation
- Casing
- Beveled window frame
- Sash
- Glass

BOTTOM OF WINDOW

- Glass
- Stool
- Sash
- Sill
- Insulation
- Drip edge
- Framing
- Exterior skin
- Felt underlayment

A house consists of many parts that must be installed carefully and with conscious attention to how everything fits together to create a separation from the elements of decay. These drawings show some of the parts that work together at the top and bottom of a window installation in a wood-frame wall.

Flashing

The goal of flashing is simple: to make a seamless, waterproof connection where two materials meet. However, executing flashing can be almost an art. Flashing is installed around all punctures in a building's skin, including doors, windows, and chimneys. It's also necessary at the edges of most materials, such as roof overhangs, and often at the bottom of walls and where walls meet roofs (see figure 5). We don't have the space here for a detailed discussion of this careful wizardry, so this strong advice will have to suffice: Learn about flashing! Don't assume that contractors will do it right. Talk to them about it and check their work. If you're building yourself, learn the basics of flashing and really think about what you're doing during installation. All your wonderful dreams, careful planning, and responsible alternative building techniques can be for naught if you don't keep water out of your structure. Remember, it's not an eco-house if it doesn't last.

Roof flashing. Left: Counterflashing set into the chimney's mortar and step flashing set under the shingles work together to keep rain out. Above: Metal drip edge has a bottom lip that keeps water from dripping onto the siding below.

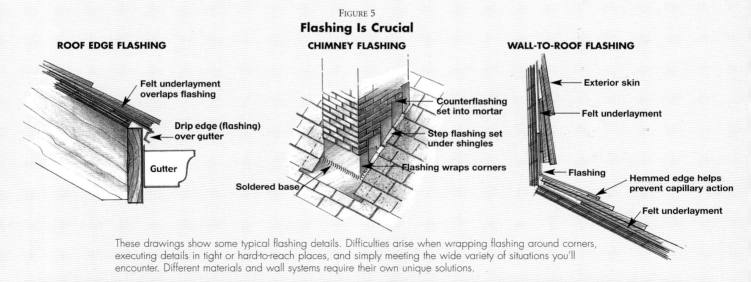

Window flashing. Left: This wooden head flashing reaches behind the siding and is beveled to direct water away from the house. Middle: This window's metal head flashing is set behind the stucco and extends up the wall. Right: When water reaches the notches cut along the bottom of this wood window sill, it will drip to the ground, away from the wood below.

FIGURE 5
Flashing Is Crucial

ROOF EDGE FLASHING

- Felt underlayment overlaps flashing
- Drip edge (flashing) over gutter
- Gutter

CHIMNEY FLASHING

- Counterflashing set into mortar
- Step flashing set under shingles
- Flashing wraps corners
- Soldered base

WALL-TO-ROOF FLASHING

- Exterior skin
- Felt underlayment
- Flashing
- Hemmed edge helps prevent capillary action
- Felt underlayment

These drawings show some typical flashing details. Difficulties arise when wrapping flashing around corners, executing details in tight or hard-to-reach places, and simply meeting the wide variety of situations you'll encounter. Different materials and wall systems require their own unique solutions.

ALTERNATIVE WALL SKINS

Let's look more closely at various alternative approaches to wall skins, and what they may or may not offer for your situation.

"Breathable" Walls

If you spend 10 minutes looking into alternative building, you'll probably run across the term "breathable wall." "Breathable" is a term much like "natural." It sounds good, sounds right . . . give it to me now! In actuality, breathability is another complicated issue that's hard to pin down, and definitely situation-specific. In fact, there's much confusion over what the term actually refers to. Some people claim that thermally efficient walls can be built that allow significant air exchange through the wall envelope, and they dub this concept a breathable wall. Other people use the term to describe a strategy for dealing with water vapor and condensation. For our discussion, the latter meaning of "breathable wall" is what we're talking about.

There are basically two strategies for dealing with condensation in walls (see the sidebar, Condensation, on page 91). One approach is to prevent water vapor from entering the wall cavity, an often ill-fated attempt that utilizes a vapor barrier (see the sidebar, The Trouble with Modern Products, on page 98). The second is to focus on the ability of the wall to take on and expel water vapor; in other words, to breathe.

Some building materials, such as cellulose and earth, have the ability to take on a lot of water vapor and hold it. Therefore, cellulose in the form of straw, recycled newspapers, or recycled cotton, and wall forms made from wood chips, as well as earth in the form of rammed earth, adobe, or cob, can be used to create breathable walls. The idea here is that the wall, when covered with a permeable skin such as lime plaster, will sometimes take on water vapor from humid outside air and then give it back (dry out) when conditions are right—for example, when the outside air is warmer and drier than the wall. This is the same process that's going on continuously in nature. Air is constantly taking on water (evaporation) and giving off water (condensation). Rather than fight this process, breathable walls attempt to become a part of it.

This sounds great and it is. However, it's a general concept, not a specific recipe. I'm always puzzled by people who embrace ideas, such as breathable walls, that are arrived at through scientific analysis, but who don't see the need to carry the science through into the specific application. What will be the range of water vapor loads in your situation? How much water will the straw or cellulose in your wall hold? Will there be enough opportunity for drying? In fact, breathable walls may not be feasible in some climates. In areas where humidity is often high, for example, breathable walls may be forced to take on more water vapor than they'll have a chance to give up. This situation can result in damage to the house through rot and damage to the people through poor indoor air quality caused by molds and fungi. (We'll discuss this problem in more depth in the next chapter.)

This is just another example of why you need to educate yourself and pay close attention to the specifics of your situation. I'm not saying you need to be a physicist to build a wall; I'm just saying that all of these concepts, whether accepted commercial or hip alternative, are only tools to help us in our specific situations. What's important is that it all comes together into a building that works where it's built, and there are no safe conceptual shortcuts that will replace careful attention to the particulars of your building environment.

Stucco/Plaster

Though there are many potentially appropriate wall skins for your building, stucco is perhaps the best example of the synergy possible between traditional and modern worlds. A substance applied to surfaces in a flexible, plastic state that dries to a durable, hard finish is variously called *stucco, plaster,* or *render.* I'll just use the term stucco to apply to this technique in all its varieties.

Stucco has a long, proven history throughout the world. It can be minutely and almost infinitely varied, using different materials in different proportions, allowing it to be applied to a large variety of wall surfaces. In addition, each mix performs differently in relation to various climatic elements, making stucco ideal for adjustment to local environmental conditions.

Stucco is basically a traditional approach that we can tweak, often with the addition of modern processed materials, to adjust it to specific needs. Adobe, for example, is a material that was developed in hot, arid climates. If stuccoed at all, it was traditionally covered with a mud mix similar to the clay mortar used to lay the blocks. Different stucco mixes, incorporating lime for example, can render adobe more resilient to water, therefore expanding its climatic range. If needed, stucco can be made to dry very slowly, a big advantage in sunny climates where quick drying will cause cracking. Conversely, quicker-drying mixes can be used to advantage in wet climates where slow drying stucco can be damaged by rain. Stuccos containing Portland cement are stronger and less water-permeable than mixes based on nonhydraulic lime. The qualities of both of these stuccos can be used to advantage in different situations.

The wonderful variability of this approach is responsible for the fact that most popular alternative building wall systems are usually stuccoed. This is true of both types of straw bale, the exposed sections of Earthships, rammed earth, composite block, and, except in climates where it is deemed unnecessary, cob and adobe.

At the same time, the wide variety of properties attainable with stucco also make it a popular center of controversy in the alternative building world. Should it be breathable? What is the correct mix? What kind of substrate is needed? These and other questions have no correct answers. They will be determined by the specifics of your situation. If you go with stucco, just remember that not all stuccos are created

 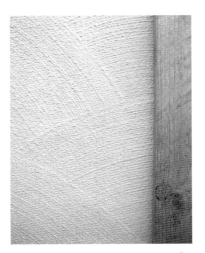 

The beauty of stucco. Left to right: Traditional, modern, and alternative applications of stucco.

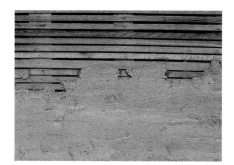

Earth on wood. This earth plaster is being applied over recycled, scrap-lumber lath.

equal. Stuccos can look almost identical, but due to different mixes can perform very differently in relation to water and sun. The beauty of stucco for the alternative builder is its adjustability for local conditions, so you'll have to do your homework to find the mix that's right for your situation. Mainly, this will entail understanding how water and sun work together in your climate. A stucco master familiar with your local climate should be courted with expensive gifts and constant, baseless flattery.

STUCCO MIXES

As we've said, the advantage of stucco/plaster is that it's variable to meet your climatic needs. My advice is to find a master in your area and stick to that person like glue (or stucco!). Don't look to general texts (including this one) when it comes to determining stucco mixes for your location. Still, here's some general information on various types of mixes to get you started:

EARTH PLASTERS Earth mixed with water and organic fibers such as grass, straw, or animal hair are probably the original stuccos. These mixes are easy to apply, breathable, and, of course, very beautiful. They can, however, be susceptible to water damage. In dry climates, that's no problem, but in wet climates they're usually used in combination with large roof overhangs and other measures to keep them dry. Reportedly, you want to start with a soil that is less than 30 percent clay. Various additives, including anything from animal dung and blood to asphalt emulsion, can be added to affect stabilization and resistance to water. For more on this subject, see the sidebar, An Introduction to Earthen Plasters, on page 106.

Lovely lime. This building in Pisa, Italy, is covered with a durable lime-based plaster. Lime plasters have been used for centuries in Europe and other parts of the world.

LIME PLASTERS Lime is produced, to put it simply, by burning limestone. Though lime has been used in building for thousands of years, today it's produced in large kilns and is basically an industrial product. Nonhydraulic lime is mixed with sand and water to form a very slow-drying plaster that is breathable, inhibits mold, and is unattractive to some insects. Hydraulic lime is the result of adding fired clay to the lime production process. Hydraulic lime plasters set much faster than nonhydraulic mixes and can be more durable. Portland cement is often added to lime plasters to speed up the set and help prevent cracking, but this practice is (surprise!) controversial. Lime-based plasters repel liquid water but are permeable to water vapor, which makes them useful in the creation of breathable walls.

CEMENT STUCCO Cement stucco is relatively new on the world scene. It consists of Portland cement, lime, sand, and water in various relative proportions. Portland cement is made predominately of limestone with a bit of clay and silica and fired in a kiln, which, as far as I can tell, makes its manufacture similar to hydrated lime. Cement stuccos set quickly and are very durable. Though they do take on and expel water, they're not as breathable as lime or earthen plasters. Stucco mixes containing Portland cement have become a whipping boy in many alternative building circles. They are accused of trapping water in walls and of having a sinfully high embodied energy. I find this criticism often misleading. It's true that

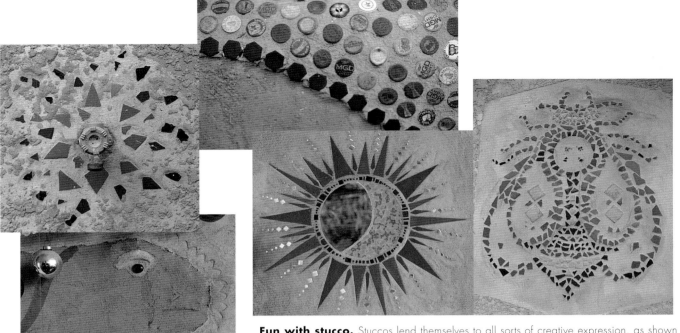

Fun with stucco. Stuccos lend themselves to all sorts of creative expression, as shown here. Clockwise from top: bottle caps in earth plaster, tile mosaic in cement stucco, tile and mirrors in earth/lime plaster, design in earth plaster, fun around a faucet.

conventional cement stucco is a bad match with cob and other wall systems that depend on a high degree of water permeability. However, Portland cement can be mixed with vermiculite or other porous aggregates to create a stucco with increased permeability. As for embodied energy, Portland and hydrated lime are both energy intensive to produce. As we've said before, it's how a material is used and how it performs over its lifetime that determines its overall energy performance. The fact is that Portland cement is just another material contributing to the continuum of possible stucco mixes. Like all materials used to make stuccos, its properties are useful in some situations and problematic in others.

Other Alternative Wall Skins

There are, of course, other appropriate wall skin options. In many areas, wood siding still makes sense. I've worked on a house where the framing and siding were milled from trees cleared from the site, a great example of locally specific building. Wood is durable, flexible, easy to shape, and often lends itself to creative applications. Partially bermed and underground houses use the earth as their effective skins. However, in these situations, some form of industrially produced waterproof membrane is almost always used between the dirt and wall structure. The chart on page 108 summarizes some other alternative wall skins and their various properties.

Leftover-log siding. The siding on this little building is made from the scrap rounded edges of logs left over from milling lumber.

An Introduction to Earthen Plasters
by Mollie Curry

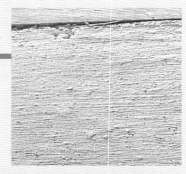

Earthen plasters complement and contribute to the sensuous, organic, alive feel of a well-built natural home. Smearing and smoothing them on with hands or a trowel is my favorite part of the building experience—and it means you're close to finishing! You can select from a huge range of possibilities for shape, texture, and color, making rooms that feel good to be in, and buildings that seem to rise up organically from their surroundings. The play of light on the slightly (or greatly!) undulating, hand-sculpted, soft-looking surface of an earthen plaster imbues your home with a playful, soothing magic.

Though cement stuccos are harder than earthen ones and resist erosion due to rain better, they are less breathable and have the potential to trap moisture behind them, which can cause structural damage. Earth plasters are also more earth-friendly than ones with Portland cement or lime, due to the high energy input that goes into making those limestone-based materials.

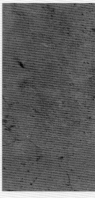
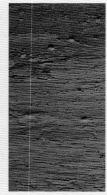

People in all climates make natural plasters out of what they have and what works for their purposes and cultures. As a result, there are hundreds, if not thousands, of different recipes. Some use fermented animal manure—and nothing more. Others mix manure and clay about half and half and use that. (The smell dissipates when the plaster dries.) I've even heard of one plaster that was made entirely of recycled paper.

Much more common in North America is a combination of clay, sand, and some form of fiber, usually straw. Cob and adobe are made of these same basic ingredients, but plaster has finer sand grains and chopped straw, so it's smoother. People also usually mix it wetter than cob, so it'll smear on the wall easily. An even thinner mix, with some additional ingredients, can make a beautiful paint. Adding shiny mica creates a magnificent sparkle!

Even in North America, cow and horse manure are common added ingredients because they contain microfibers and perhaps some enzymes that help make the plaster stickier when wet and more durable once dried. People may also add any number of other seemingly bizarre ingredients, from blood to sodium silicate, to make the plaster stronger, more water-resistant, easier to apply, or a beautiful color.

As in cob, the clay component in earth plasters usually comes from local subsoil, often collected by digging a site for the very house whose walls it will grace. Subsoils vary greatly from place to place. In fact, they may be vastly different even within yards of each other. They may contain sand and mineral silt as well as clay in any number of percentages. Sand and clay are great for natural plasters. Sand lends strength and mass, and clay contributes a strong, binding stickiness. In analogy with cement stuccos, the clay in an earthen plaster acts like the Portland cement, the sand is the same in both, and the straw is like the strands of fiberglass used in a "surface-bonding cement."

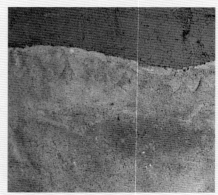

Earth plaster gallery. The spectrum of possible earth plaster colors and textures is limitless. Here are four different Earthaven earth plasters, each uniquely beautiful.

In terms of particle size, silt is between clay and sand, and offers the beneficial properties of neither. Silt is undesirable because it weakens the plaster, but some amount is tolerable, especially if you add other strengthening agents. Of course, your soil could be the perfect "ready-mix," or it could need sand or clay or something else to make it into good plaster.

Where I live, we have a subsoil with a high mineral silt content. As a result, we've experimented with adding hydrated lime to many of our earthen plasters in an attempt to make them harder. Lime also seems to help the plaster dry out quickly when it gets wet. Contrary to our experience, other people have reported that lime makes their earth plasters crumbly, so experiment.

In addition to their high embodied-energy drawbacks, both lime and Portland cement are alkaline and thus somewhat caustic. This makes them more hazardous to your skin and eyes, and less fun to apply. Instead of lime, I prefer using noncaustic strengtheners such as wheat paste, milk, paper pulp made from newspapers and junk mail, and/or manure. Other possible alternatives include white household glue, prickly pear cactus juice, and even blood and eggs. You can also separate the silt and clay. Just mix your soil with water in a big container and let it sit; then pour off the water and remove the clay, which settles last, from the top. However, this has never seemed worth the effort to us. Another option if you don't have enough clay in your subsoil, or if you have a lot of silt, is to add some potter's clay to the mix.

Earth plasters work well in a variety of climates on both the exterior and interior of buildings. In a rainy climate, appropriately large roof overhangs and adequately high foundations are important elements of a house with either earthen or cementitious plasters. This doesn't mean that earthen plasters can never get wet. It takes repeated driving rains to damage a good earth plaster. And the clay in earthen plaster actually draws moisture out of earthen, straw, and even wooden walls because of its hydrophilic nature.

If your interest in earth plastering is piqued, I hope you'll learn more by taking a workshop and/or reading some good books on the subject to help you do the necessary soil assessments and test batches. Books with good information include *Earth Plasters for Straw Bale Homes* by Keely Meagan, *The Cob Builders Handbook* by Becky Bee, and *The Beauty of Straw Bale Homes* by Athena and Bill Steen.

Mollie Curry lives at Earthaven Ecovillage in the mountains of western North Carolina, where she has helped construct a variety of natural buildings

Earth plaster step by step. Top to bottom: Gather your materials... mix 'em up... have fun plastering...ahh, an attractive, durable, plaster wall.

ALTERNATIVE WALL SKINS FOR SOME ALTERNATIVE WALL SYSTEMS

System	Skin Type	Options	Resistant to	Comments
Adobe	Integrated or applied	Nothing or earth plaster in dry climates; lime or possible concrete stuccos in wetter climates	Sun, wind, life	Historically a dry-climate material; susceptible to water damage; can be adapted to different climates by adjusting exterior skin and using proper detailing such as large overhangs and raising adobe off grade.
Cob	Integrated or applied	Nothing in dry climates; earth or lime plaster	Sun, wind, life	Similar to adobe, though historically found in wetter climates; use methods for adapting to wet climates much like those for adobe.
Cordwood	Integrated or applied	Nothing or wood sealant added to exposed end grain to protect against moisture	Sun (partial), wind	More susceptible to water than other wood construction because open wood grain is exposed to the weather; natural curing of wood can cause shrinkage and produce gaps between wood and mortar; proper curing of wood before installation is important.
Superadobe	Applied	Earth stucco	Sun, wind, life	Stuccoed roof surface is a weak defense against water; possibly limits this construction to dry climate.
Composite Block	Integrated or applied	Nothing; earth, Portland or lime stucco; any plank siding	Water, sun, wind, life	"Modern" low-maintenance answer to traditional breathing wall systems; wood chips create spaces to take on water, concrete surrounds wood chips to protect against water damage; alkalinity in concrete unattractive to mold; concrete core structurally strong; termite-proof.
Earth-sheltered/ Earthship	Applied	Water-proof membrane w/ earth; stucco on exposed areas	Water, sun, wind, life	If using tires, difficult to waterproof well because of irregular surface; can be a problem in wet climates and areas with groundwater.
Stone	Integrated	N/A	Water, sun, wind, life	The ultimate material from the point of view of durability. Poor thermal properties and labor-intensive construction are the setbacks.
Straw Bale (load-bearing)	Applied	Earth, Portland or lime stuccos	Sun, wind, life (partial)	Proper detailing to prevent liquid water in bales is very important (as with all organic building materials). Not attractive as food for insects, but can be a good nest; seal appropriately against entry. Water vapor is main concern; breathable wall created with a semipermeable stucco is common practice, but may cause problems in humid climates.
Straw Bale (infill)	Applied	Earth, Portland or lime stuccos	Sun, wind, life (partial)	Same as load-bearing straw (above).

ALTERNATIVE ROOF SKINS

Roofs are a tough issue. We find ourselves in a time and place where modern materials are almost a must in the construction of a long-lasting, watertight roof.

One possible exception is thatch. Thatching is an age-old technique consisting of attaching bundles of straw or grass to a roof structure in overlapping horizontal rows up to 12 inches thick. Thatched roofs, especially when Norfolk reed is used, can reportedly last 60 years or even longer and are incredibly beautiful. But perhaps paradoxically, this traditional technique requires a lot of experience, skill, and time and is therefore relatively expensive, at least if professionally installed. However, thatch's beauty, sustainability, and durability make it an excellent roofing choice.

Reed-newable resource. Left: This reed bed in New Jersey will be harvested to produce thatching. Right: A fine, finished thatch roof.

Other traditional roofs, such as slate and tile, are also on the pricey side for the mere mortal, but can be incredibly durable. Living or green roofs are a wonderful idea and well worth checking out. Again paradoxically, these natural roofs require some modern materials, real thought, and careful execution (see the sidebar, Green Roofs: A Discussion with Charlie Miller, at the end of this chapter). One modern material you'll definitely need is a strong waterproof membrane such as Bituthene®, a composite sheet of rubberized asphalt and cross-laminated plastic film. The thought and careful execution comes in the delicate process of installing the membrane and covering it with organic material without puncturing it. Finding and fixing a leak under a bunch of dirt and plants would not be a job for which I'd volunteer. If you go for a living roof, don't let your political correctness get in the way. Buy the best membrane you can find and have it professionally installed if you're unsure of your skills.

Conventional roofing is still the most common choice on most alternative buildings. Metal roofs are long-lasting and relatively easy to install on simple roof designs. Flashing details for metal roofs can be tricky and sometimes expensive, as is the case with skylight flashing kits. If you have neighbors, give them a break and consider painted or nonreflective metal. Regular old galvanized roofing shines like a supernova. Another option is roofing products now becoming available that are made from recycled materials.

In my never-ending search to be uncool, I'll state publicly that asphalt shingles also are a viable option. Organic mat shingles (as opposed to those made with fiberglass) consist of a felt mat impregnated with asphalt and covered with small stones. High-quality asphalt shingles are much cheaper than metal, easy for one person to install, accommodate roof punctures such as chimneys and skylights with relative ease, and can last 30 to 40 years or more. Thatching might have been the peasant's roof in the past, but today it's asphalt shingles. On the downside, old asphalt shingles often end up in landfills. However, used asphalt shingles are presently being recycled as material for road aggregate base, pavement, and pothole repair, as well as in new shingles and even for fuel oil. In any case, poor quality asphalt shingles, the thin ones you see on most houses these days, don't last very long and are the Styrofoam® cup of the building industry: something that's quick and easy to use and then throw away. If you end up using asphalt shingles, go with quality.

Living roof. A living, or green, roof can be an attractive alternative in many situations. This living roof is on Dan Chiras' Earthship hybrid home, featured in chapter 7.

Recyclables come home to roof. This shingle looks like a cedar shake but is actually manufactured from postindustrial recycled materials such as plastics, cellulose fibers including hemp, and rubber elastomers from used tires. The finished product is itself completely recyclable.

Hammering It Home

This chapter's goal has been to open up the amazing world that is the border between a building and the outside. This zone is like the surface of a planet, with its own air circulation, temperature variations, water profile, and little ecosystem of life. The skin of every building is, in a very real sense, a world unto itself. It's a human-made world and its purpose is to protect the building structure that lies beneath. It has to do this by repelling nature's most abundant and powerful forces, the elements that we actually seek out when placing a building. These elements are great when they're your friend and horrible as your enemy. They take different forms and combine to create a myriad of possibilities. They are everywhere and simply cannot be defeated.

Protecting a building from decay is a riddle, a true mystery of life. What is it that creates life while destroying it? The answer: Water, sun, air, and life itself. How do we keep these things out while letting them in? To answer this riddle, the alternative builder needs to get to know the nature of these elements as they pertain to his or her exact situation. Your climate will guide you to the best approach to protecting your building. This may sound like a daunting task, but what could be more fun than learning about the place where you live? Is there a traditional building style that was developed in your area? If so, have people adapted it to meet modern lifestyles? How do conventional builders in your area approach the elements of decay? What types of alternative buildings seem to be popular where you live? How do the people building them approach the elements of decay? Start looking at buildings. Start talking to people about buildings. You will not create a good building from a book.

Dynamic beauty. The skin of every building is a world unto itself, interacting with its environment. As you can see from these examples, a building suited to its climate acts together with the elements to become an amazing, slowly evolving work of art. This page: (top) multistory "apartment buildings," each housing several families, carved from soft sandstone at Cappadocia, Turkey; (left) a Mayan ruin on the Yucatan Peninsula; (above) a carved wood building in Bhak Tapor, Nepal. Next page: (top) an abandoned castle in Erice, Sicily; (middle) the Taj Mahal near Agra, India; (bottom left) a village in Tuscany; (bottom right) an ornate carved sandstone building in Jai Sal Mer, India.

If you learn anything from this chapter, let it be this: Looks can be deceiving. Two buildings standing side by side can look identical. Hidden elements, such as the wrong stucco mix, a vapor barrier on the wrong side, or poorly installed flashing, can cause one building to have serious problems relatively quickly while the other may last hundreds of years. In other words, a modern alternative house is an intellectual concept. It has to be conceived and thought through intellectually, based on its local environment and how the forces of decay manifest themselves there. Just as important, this conception has to be carried through carefully in the details of construction. You can't judge your building from how it looks; you have to understand it from the inside out. You have to give the natural elements of decay the respect they deserve. Making something that can withstand the pressures of the world while encouraging life to flourish within it is truly an amazing feat. Perhaps this is why well-preserved old buildings are some of the most beautiful artifacts of human existence.

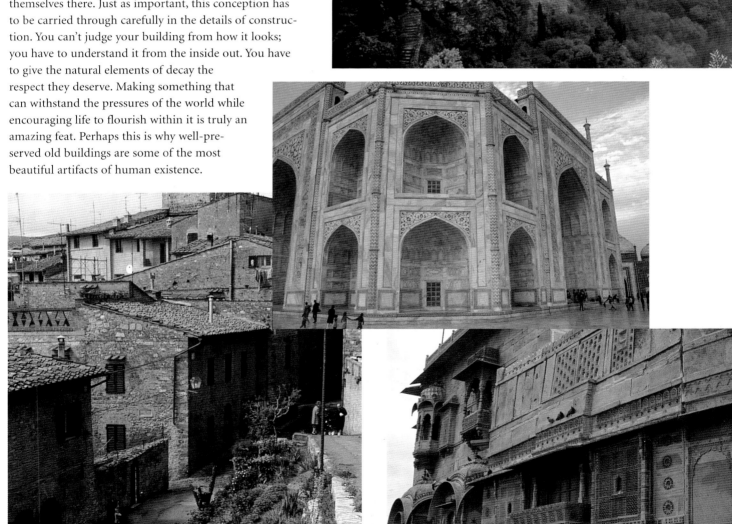

Green Roofs:
A DISCUSSION WITH CHARLIE MILLER

Q What is a green roof and what are its basic components?

A: A green roof consists of a thin veneer of materials that support a dense plant cover, drainage layers that allow the free flow of water, and some form of waterproof membrane.

With few exceptions, the layers in green roof systems are arranged so that the particle size increases with depth. This mimics many natural systems, where surface layers of topsoil, rich in loam and organic matter, overlie sandy subsoil and eventually a foundation of fractured rock or shale. As in nature, we want the plants to send their roots into the deepest zone where moisture and temperature conditions are most stable. Irrigation, when required, is introduced in the deepest layer.

Using green roofs, it's generally possible to support larger plants using shallower depths of planting media than would otherwise be possible. This is because plant roots can extend horizontally over large areas, which increases access to moisture and nutrients. Also, containerized plants often suffer from temperature shock, whether hot or cold, due to the container's large surface area compared to the volume of soil. Green roofs have a lower surface area. Moisture conditions change more gradually, too, due to the free flow of water.

Q Surprisingly, green roofs seem more popular in urban settings and large-scale commercial applications than on single-family homes. Why is this? What are the issues that make green roofs so attractive in the city?

The benefits of green roofs are most apparent when they're applied either to large structures or to clusters of smaller buildings in a single district. These benefits include cooling of the surrounding air (i.e., reduction of the so-called urban heat island effect), reduction in the volume and rate of runoff, improvements in water and air quality, and restoration of habitat for birds. Isolated single-family residences also realize some of these benefits. But individually their area is too small to affect the local environment. For this reason, urban municipalities are more likely to promote the use of green roofs than are suburban communities. In Germany, for example, municipal promotion through tax credits and other incentives make green roofs very attractive to urban building owners. In Munich alone, subsidies have led to the "greening" of approximately 4.2 million square feet of roofs in the last 15 years.

The transformation created by green roofs is more dramatic in urban areas where open space is often presumed to be an inevitable casualty of development. Green roofs can restore the experience of open space in even the most highly urbanized communities. They soften the appearance of the urban landscape, provide open space for public recreation, and create intimate private areas. In fact, the experience of being on a green roof is exhilarating because it combines the intimacy of private space with an openness to the elements and nature.

Q What are some of the advantages of putting a green roof on a residence?

One obvious advantage is that green roofs vastly prolong the service life of the roof structures they cover and protect. This is because the main destructive processes that plague conventional roofs, freeze-thaw cycles and the sun's ultraviolet radiation, are severely curtailed with a green roof. On a conventional roof, the waterproof membranes, shingles or metal, take a terrible beating. With a green roof, the membrane is protected beneath layers of plants, growing medium, drainage, and often insulation. It's protected from the sun's ultraviolet radiation and from daily temperature swings, thus prolonging its life tremendously.

Another big benefit of green roofs is that they improve a building's thermal performance in several ways. For one, they prevent radiant heat transfer by providing a shading effect. Green roof foliage absorbs radiant energy and prevents it from reaching the surface of the growth media, thus preventing heat transfer to the building's interior. At the same time, a green roof provides evaporative cooling. When it's hot outside, moisture trapped in the roots and leaves of

Green in more ways than one. A green roof can provide not only a pleasant outdoor living area, but also energy savings and protection for the structure below.

plants in the vegetation layer evaporates, taking heat from the air above the roof.

Also, green roofs prevent heat loss through advection. The vegetation creates a layer of dormant air immediately above the roof surface. Without a green roof, wind blows across the roof surface to either heat or chill it. This concept is familiar to us as 'wind chill.' Buildings experience wind chill, too. The higher the air velocity the greater the thermal transfer. Thick green roof material isolates the roof's surface from air movement and consequent heat loss. A dry green roof can prevent convective heat loss, too, much like a simple layer of insulation. But the insulating value is reduced when the green roof is moist, which is most of the time in temperate climates.

Thermal mass is the most important property of green roofs. Especially when moist, green roofs can absorb and store large amounts of heat. The effect is to create a 'buffer' against daily temperature fluctuations. Even a three-inch green roof drastically reduces temperature variations in the roof surface. Temperature extremes are eliminated. The result is that heating or cooling equipment doesn't have to respond to those extremes; also, overall heat transfer through the roof is reduced. Conventional insulation, while optimized for insulation value, has virtually no heat-storing capacity and cannot function as a heat sink. This is an instance in which a green roof can work in combination with conventional insulation to provide a benefit greater than either used separately.

Q What advice do you have for someone thinking about installing a green roof on their new house?

First, don't approach your project with preconceptions of what a green roof should be. Techniques exist to create a stunning range in roof appearance and performance. Be open to using materials and plants you may not be familiar with. Make sure that the system is adapted to your climate and conditions. Also, I strongly recommend that systems be installed by green roof professionals. All installations should come with good warranty protections for durability of the waterproofing and other elements.

Charlie Miller is the founder and president of Roofscapes, Inc., which designs and installs green roofs throughout the United States.

CHAPTER 6

CONNECTION

LET'S REVIEW. In chapter 1 we decided that the human body is a really good house that in certain situations needs help doing its job. That job is to maintain and protect human life, and consists of creating a separation from and constant exchange with nature. We also concluded that the body accomplishes this feat by providing four essential functions: a self-supporting structure, a stable temperature, separation from the outside, and connection to the outside. Housing was created to help the human body do its thing. Housing augments the body by mimicking it and providing the same four basics.

So far, we've explored this amazing parallel between the body and housing as it relates to the first three functions. Now we'll consider the fourth: connection. The human body is rendered quickly useless—in other words, dies—when deprived of a connection to the outside. We need an almost constant influx of air, food, water, and sunlight in order to survive. Simultaneously, we need to expel carbon dioxide, feces, and urine. If left in our bodies, these substances are toxic to us. This steady bringing in and taking out is the constant exchange that makes our lives possible. It is the final function the body provides to maintain human life. Housing must create the same exchange with the outside as the body's. A house must allow in air, food, water, and sunlight while removing toxins. If a house doesn't do this, it too is useless and dead.

Traditional Approach to Exchange

For much of human history, people spent most of their time outdoors. This simplified the demands on housing because most of the exchange with the outside was done outside. Getting food and making a living, either by growing, raising, hunting, or gathering, kept people outdoors many hours a day. This is still true in many parts of the world. Cooking and eating often took place outdoors, as did the excretion of bodily wastes. Sources of water and fuel, wood for example, were outside. House sites were chosen based on their nearness to food, water, and fuel. If you

Working outside. Children weeding a field in Nepal's Kathmandu Valley.

Location, location, location. Above: A young girl in Mali carries the day's firewood. If you use firewood for fuel, you don't want to live far from its source. Right: Using a large mortar and pestle, a woman in Mali grinds millet. Open space and a shady spot to work make this a good place to build.

used any of these things inside, they were carried in. A single simple opening, the door, would accommodate you for this purpose.

The sun coming through doors and windows provided light. People tended to go to bed when it got dark. Air exchange, giving us access to oxygen and allowing the expulsion of carbon dioxide, was amply available through windows, often without glass, and doors. In many types of construction, air also moved through walls and around gaps in window and doorframes. Smoke from fires was sometimes accommodated by a simple hole in the roof or, more efficiently, through a chimney.

Modern Approach to Exchange

The modern world is an urban world. According to the Population Reference Bureau, 75 percent of the population in "more developed" countries resides in urban centers. For example, while eight percent of people in Burundi and 16 percent of those in Cambodia live in cities, 75 percent of the population of the U.S. and 97 percent of those in Belgium live in urban centers. Urbanization translates to a loss of self-sufficiency and an indoor lifestyle. Most of us don't grow our own food, fetch our own water, cut our own firewood, or build our own houses any more. Most of us work, eat, sleep, and recreate indoors.

This cultural change has triggered a corresponding change in housing. Buildings are no longer sited based on their access to food, water, fuel, and sun. Cities function by bringing many people close together, with needed goods and services produced elsewhere and shipped in to the population *en masse*. Houses, then, become receptacles for these shipped products. True, some things still come in the old way, through the front door. Food, for example, is centrally produced and shipped, but then it's brought home from the supermarket and walked right into the house just like Grandma used to do. However, just about everything else is piped in.

Water is brought in through pipes from large reservoirs or other sources, sometimes from quite a distance. We urinate and defecate in this same water and send it out through other pipes to be treated at a central sewage plant. Fuels, in the form of natural gas or propane, for furnaces, cookstoves, water heaters, etc., can travel hundreds or thousands of miles through pipelines before they eventually make their way to the individual pipes of a house. Heated and cooled air is moved throughout the house in large pipes, or ducts. Even sunlight has been "upgraded" into a pipeable product: Electricity is moved through pipes filled with wires, called conduit, to

Semi-open door. This door to a church in Mali allows plenty of air exchange in the hot African climate

Arbitrary siting. There's plenty of room in this suburban neighborhood for all the houses to be sited to take advantage of the sun. Instead, the buildings have been plopped down haphazardly without regard to solar orientation. There's also a conspicuous absence of vegetable gardens.

bring fake sunlight into homes any time of day or night. Piped electricity is also used to heat water, food, and air.

This is the spaceship approach to building, the box with attached life-support systems, that we discussed earlier in this book. On the plus side, this tactic solves the problem of creating housing for large numbers of people. In a crowded urban environment, ample drinking water, sanitation, room to grow food, and fuel for heating can be hard to come by. Bringing these things in from outside the local area is sometimes the only option. On the downside from the point of view of exchange, this approach cuts us off from direct access to the outside world. In these buildings, almost everything we take into our bodies is altered by some synthetic additive. In the process, it creates a sort of chain reaction of strange side effects.

Let's look at water, for example. Centralized water is a hygienics nightmare. How do you collect enough water for thousands or millions of people and pipe it to them while keeping it clean? Our solution has been to treat it with chlorine. According to whom you believe, this is either the stupidest or smartest thing we've ever done. Both sides of the debate agree that chlorine is poisonous and was used as a weapon in World War I. That's why all those old WWI photos show guys wearing gas masks. If you aren't familiar with the topic of chlorine and the ongoing debate over its safety, I strongly suggest doing a little research. It makes great late-night scary reading.

At any rate, after we drink or otherwise use this questionable mix, it goes down the drain to be combined with everything else that anyone with a drain decides to get rid of. This includes water from toilets, runoff from streets, and everything hosed off the floor at any gas station or factory. All of this water is collected, the solids are removed, more chlorine is dumped in—and then the liquid is set free again to start the process over.

It's a similar story with indoor air quality. Again, there's a scientific debate. Yet, everybody knows that sniffing glue or paint for recreation will rot your brain. I've been in apartments that had been repainted and carpeted two years before and I could still smell the clearly noxious off-gassing fumes. What's the difference between sniffing glue in a bag, and inhaling it from the carpet while watching television? Enclosing those kinds of materials within a living space without adequate natural ventilation is asking for trouble.

Electricity addict. Without electricity, this skyscraper is a useless monolith, inhospitable to human habitation.

While we're focusing on the negative, I might as well mention that these spaceship houses are also the final nail in the self-sufficiency coffin. A good analogy is someone in a hospital on life support; an iron lung, catheter . . . the whole business. The modern spaceship house is much like that. It's just a box hooked up to life support. If you turn off the electricity, it no longer functions. It will quickly get too hot or too cold; the air will become stale and more noxious than usual; the food in the fridge will spoil; and if you have a well, the pump won't work. If you're in a office building and want to get out of this unpleasant, nonfunctioning box, you'd better hope there aren't electric locks on the stairwell doors, because that elevator won't be going anywhere.

Alternative Approaches to Exchange

"We need to choose building sites based on their access to food, water, sun, and air."

Well, that sure was a harangue, and to be fair I probably should cut modern building some slack. Let's face it, the real problem with modern building is that it's saddled with the task of creating safe, comfortable housing for six billion people. I wouldn't want that job. Still, our quest is for a good house for you and your little tribe, so we simply have to improve on some of this modern stuff. And again in the case of connecting to the outside, the alternative building approach is to lean toward a traditional mindset while accommodating the realities of modern existence.

Our first lesson from the traditional approach is: *choose your outside.* You can't create an exchange with something if it isn't there. We need to choose building sites based on their access to the things we need: food, water, sun, and air (see figure 1). For this reason, it's no accident that an interest in alternative building is often coupled with a desire to leave the city. It's difficult to control your water and food supply while living in an urban environment (though not impossible; see the interview at the end of this chapter). Often, even clean air and access to the sun can be hard to come by.

However, the concept of exchange with the outdoors is not about finding paradise. It's about maximizing your access to the things you need, not as a consumer, but as a life form. Any building site can and should be viewed from the perspective of creating the best connection to and exchange with the outside.

FIGURE 1
The Perfect House Site

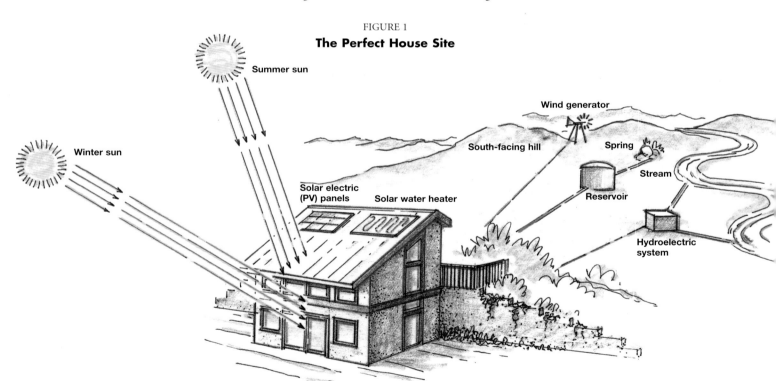

Where I live, and in most temperate climates, everyone is looking for this house site. Watch people's eyes roll when you say, "We just want a private little south-facing location with a strong spring and a good stream"—as if it's a simple request that nobody else has thought of. We can't all have the perfect spot. Alternative building is about maximizing what you have access to.

SUN

As we discussed in chapter 4, sun is by far the most predictable natural feature on the planet. Though it may be behind clouds, you can determine exactly where the Sun will be in the sky on any hour of any day at your building site. In unpredictable nature, we don't get many chances like this, and we simply have to take advantage of it. Chapter 4 is all about harnessing the sun for temperature control. Let's think about it now in terms of light.

The Sun, along with its reflection on the Moon, is the only consistent naturally occurring light source for Earth. Of course, you've got your fireflies and the occasional forest fire, but let's not get picky. Artificial lighting is relatively new on the scene and, I have to say it, just isn't "natural." Flying insects, for instance, find artificial light confusing. They mistake bright light for their usual navigational guide, the Moon. Flying in a straight line relative to the distant moon translates into flying circles around a nearby light bulb. The result: a slow, confused death.

Now, admittedly we have a better handle on the light bulb issue than insects. But there's also evidence that a life based on artificial light may not be the best thing for humans. Science has revealed the existence of daily cycles governing many body functions such as temperature regulation, blood pressure, hormone levels, and heart rate. These cycles, or *circadian rhythms*, are controlled by molecular processes in the brain we call *biological clocks*. These clocks are reset by sunlight. They can also be reset by artificial light, potentially disrupting our natural biological processes. Modern medicine is investigating and treating possible links between biological-clock malfunction and illnesses ranging from jet lag, insomnia, and depression to high blood pressure, mental illness, and even neurological disorders such as multiple sclerosis.

Sunlight also plays an important role in the production of vitamin D. Calciferol, or vitamin D, is most important in its role of maintaining normal blood levels of calcium and phosphorus. Though added to some processed foods, such as milk, vitamin D occurs naturally in only a few foods, such as fish and fish oils. Luckily, our bodies synthesize their own vitamin D when our skin comes in contact with the sun's ultraviolet (UV) rays.

These scientific studies simply underscore what seems to me like common sense. The human body has a much longer history, as in hundreds of thousands of years, in the sun than it does out of it. Isolating ourselves from sunlight is a new experiment that may not be a good idea. My point is simple: Encourage natural sunlight to enter your house.

The city never sleeps. Can a body truly sleep in a city that never does?

Glass and Sunlight

Unless you live on an open houseboat or an island paradise, much of the year sunlight will travel through glass to enter your house. In chapter 4, we talked extensively about the thermal properties of different glass types. Now let's talk about glass from the point of view of natural light.

Any glass will alter natural sunlight by filtering some of its wavelengths. Coatings and gas fill will further filter light. Some coatings, for example, are designed to limit

Daylighting. Careful design and consideration of factors such as reflective and nonreflective surfaces, diffusion, and contrast can create spaces with pleasant, natural indoor lighting.

UV radiation partially, because it fades carpeting and upholstery. Then again, you'll remember that UV radiation is what triggers vitamin D production in the body. Whether light passing through such coatings limits vitamin synthesis more than clear glass, which already stops much of the UV spectrum, I don't know. My point is that glass changes sunlight, and some glass changes it more than others. In this context, choosing glass is a tradeoff between improvements in insulation and the further filtering of natural light.

Even if you don't go for the idea that sunlight is healthier than artificial light, you have to admit that it's cheaper. Why burn coal to make electricity to light a dark room that could be illuminated by the sun? The use of sunlight instead of artificial light for indoor illumination is called *daylighting* in architectural circles. A lot of thought goes into the proper daylighting of a building. You can move a lamp, but you can't move the sun, so issues like brightness, contrast, and glare need to be considered in the design phase. For example, sunlight that is diffused or reflected from nonshiny surfaces is often more suitable than direct light. Skylights and windows that reach high onto walls admit the most sunlight for their size. The intricacies of daylighting are outside the scope of this book. In any case, they will be affected by many other aspects of your design. For example, different activities call for different quantities and qualities of light. My goal for now is to convince you not to place glass based solely on a good view or even for solar gain. Your house is like a big permanent light fixture. How well it illuminates things is up to you.

Homestead siting. This cabin was built in the shadow of a dark, north-facing slope, which makes it a cold spot in winter. However, there's plenty of nearby water in the form of a strong spring and small creek.

WATER

Where I live, in the hills of western North Carolina, it's easy to find an old homestead where the house is placed in a dark hollow away from the sun. The sunniest land was often reserved for raising food and livestock. However, I've never seen such a homestead very far from a good water source. In self-sufficient societies, no one would've considered building a house that didn't have a close, clean, secure water source. A combination of urbanization and technological ingenuity has changed all of that. Even many ancient cultures, including those in Persia, India, and Egypt, piped water into urban centers. The ancient Romans built 230 miles of aqueduct, 30 miles of which were above ground and the rest in underground conduits, to supply their capital.

Today, large urban centers such as Los Angeles and New York City pipe water many miles to supply their massive demands. We build some large cities, such as Las Vegas, in the middle of deserts. Houses there have the same suburban prerequisites, a green lawn and swimming pool, as in water-rich areas. As we've noted, large-scale "mass production" of water delivery demands drastic hygienic measures, including the use of the poison chlorine, and produces a strange toxic product, centralized sewage. It also requires drastic changes to the ecosystem. Dams, for example, flood huge tracts of land that have never been under water, and divert water from land where it has flowed for millennia. In short, the whole thing isn't very well thought out. It's all a big, risky experiment.

Sources of Water

Seventy percent of the earth's surface is covered in water. There's also water held in the air and stored in the ground. Since the earth doesn't gain or lose water, this is the same old H_2O we've always had. All this water is continually moving around in what is called the *hydrologic cycle* (see figure 2). Surface water in rivers, lakes, and oceans is evaporated by the sun and condenses in the sky to form clouds, eventually falling back to earth as precipitation. This rain, snow, sleet, and hail either becomes runoff, recharging rivers, lakes, and oceans, or it enters the ground. From there it's either used by plants, which return some to the air as vapor through *transpiration*, or it percolates down through soil and rock to become *ground water*.

The area of soil, sand, and rock that collects ground water is called an *aquifer*. The highest level of water in an aquifer is called the *water table*. All ground water, rivers,

Essential water. Ready access to water is a critical site requirement in most parts of the world. Here, a Turkish shepherd draws water from a well.

FIGURE 2
The Hydrologic Cycle

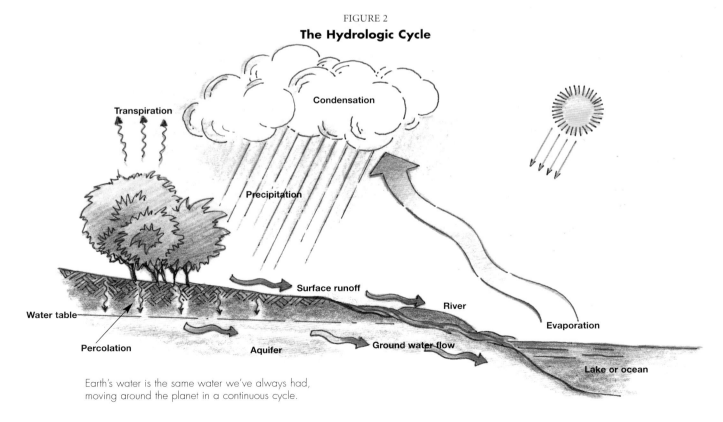

Earth's water is the same water we've always had, moving around the planet in a continuous cycle.

"A reliable source of clean water is essential."

~

and freshwater lakes combined make up only 0.3 percent of the planet's water. It is this small percentage of terrestrial water that all land-loving organisms must share.

Water is naturally purified in its journey through the hydrologic cycle. When water evaporates from the surface of oceans, lakes, rivers, and plant leaves, most contaminants are left behind. This process is called *distillation*. When water falls back to earth as precipitation, it may pick up biological contaminants. Microorganisms in topsoil can break these organisms down into nutrients that are then taken up by plant roots before the water percolates farther into the aquifer. This process is called *biological land treatment*. Once water is in the ground, the cool temperatures and the absence of light prevent the growth of algae and plant life. Rock and sand act as a filter to further purify water as it moves deeper into the aquifer. Many substances that humans introduce into the air and onto the land can disrupt this natural purification cycle. For example, sulfur dioxide and nitrogen oxides from industry and auto emissions can combine with water in the air to produce an acidic soup, commonly called *acid rain*. Industry has a long history of dumping chemical wastes directly into surface water. In addition, anything that we dump onto the land has a good chance of making contact with the water that covers 70 percent of this planet.

In order to achieve the goal of a healthy exchange with the outdoors, it's essential to have a reliable source of clean water. Therefore, taking control over the supply of your own water, and responsibility for its purity, are mainstays of alternative building. If you want to access water yourself, there are three possible sources available: springs, wells, and rainwater.

SPRINGS

A spring is a place where ground water emerges naturally. For example, water percolating down through porous rock can hit an impervious rock shelf and be forced to move horizontally. If this shelf ends up at the surface, a spring is the result. The ground area through which the percolated water feeding the spring moves is called the *recharge zone*. Depending on the spring, this area can be large or small. The rate and regularity of flow from a spring depends on many factors, including the size of its recharge zone. Observing a spring over a long period of time, especially through periods of drought, will give you a good indication of its regularity. Springs are often marked on plat maps or mentioned in deeds, so old documents may give you some indication of the history of water sources on your land. Neighborhood old-timers may know about the performance of your spring, so ask around. I know of a spring in my area, for example, that ran so strong through a bad drought many years ago that people came with horses from miles around to collect its water.

Spring water's drinkability is determined by various factors. As we've said, distillation, biological land treatment, and aquifer filtering do a good job of purifying ground water. However, some springs are heavily augmented by surface water, which can add biological and human-made contaminants. If your spring's flow increases greatly or becomes cloudy after it rains, surface water is probably accessing your spring. In any case, activity at an elevation above your spring, such as grazing cattle or any kind of industry, can be a source of contamination. For this reason, it's best to have control over the land from your spring to the top of the nearest ridge. In any case, it's a good idea to test spring water for contamination. If things are in there that you don't want, filters can usually be purchased that will take them out. These filters range widely in price, often based on the fineness of the material they're designed to

Springhead. This is the head of our spring. I used a thick, flexible piece of plastic to dam the area, and sealed the bottom of the dam with clay, to catch the water. I attached a PVC water pipe to a gasketed fitting in this dam, filled in around the dam with gravel, and covered the whole thing with plastic and then soil and leaves. I've since buried the pipe to keep it from freezing in winter. The vertical PVC is an overflow/vent pipe.

remove, and can be installed at the house's water main or at individual fixtures.

The area where a spring emerges is called the *springhead*. At this point, water can be dammed, or *headed up*, and piped to a reservoir, usually made of concrete, molded plastic, or fiberglass. In my area, concrete was the standard for years, but now plastic reservoirs, which are inexpensive and lightweight and therefore easy to install, are widely used. If the reservoir is elevated above the house site, pressure for household water use can be supplied by gravity. The elevation difference from the reservoir to its destination is called the *head*. Water pressure is measured in pounds per square inch, or psi, and is defined by the equation $P = H/2.3$, where P is water pressure and H is the head in feet. This means that every 2.3 feet of elevation will give you one psi of pressure. If your pipe is very long, friction will begin to affect this measurement. Some appliances, such as tankless hot-water heaters, require a minimum water pressure, so it's a good idea to figure the amount of head you have to work with before designing your plumbing system. Bury high-quality pipe—PVC is usually used—below the frost line to prevent freezing. A gravity-fed spring-water system uses no external power once it's installed and can give years of trouble-free service.

Reservoirs old and new. Left: This concrete reservoir, most of which is buried, is starting to blend in with its woodland surroundings. Above: This 500-gallon plastic reservoir is light enough for one person to install. It sits high above the house (visible at top of photo) to create plenty of water pressure.

WELLS

A well is a human-made channel that accesses ground water. Wells can be dug by hand and lined with stone or brick, a prerequisite piece of scenery in any Western movie. The more common modern approach (see figure 3) is to drill a relatively small-diameter hole down below the water table. Usually this hole is then lined with a *casing*, a plastic or metal pipe, to prevent collapse. A screen, or strainer, is attached to the bottom of the casing to filter out sand and other debris. Pea gravel can be poured around the casing as another layer of filtering and to serve as a passageway for water above the bottom of the casing to reach the screen. Most wells require a pump, and therefore some form of power, to get the water to the surface. Some wells, called *artesian wells*, don't require a pump because of natural pressures that push the water up to daylight. From there, water is either pumped directly to the house, by way of a pressure tank, or to a reservoir for a gravity feed to the building.

The depth of wells varies widely and depends on the distance the water table lies from the surface. This is difficult to predict, and because most

FIGURE 3

A Drilled Well

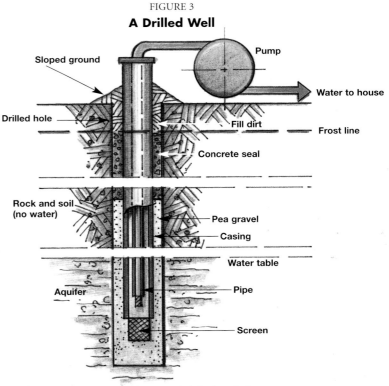

This is a cross section of a typical drilled well; there are several variations, but most have similar components. Wells are often drilled using truck-mounted machinery.

well drillers charge by the foot, having a well dug can be a nerve-racking affair. Picture the budding homesteader, nervously clutching a checkbook, waiting helplessly as the big drill rig goes down yet another waterless foot. Nearby wells are sometimes of similar depths, so it's a good idea to ask neighbors about their wells. On the other hand, wells close to each other can be of vastly different depths. It's really a crapshoot. As with springs, water quality is very site-specific, too. Testing your well water is a good idea. Again, filters can be purchased to deal with most undesirable elements.

RAINWATER

Springs and wells are ways of accessing ground water. Another approach is to bypass the ground and intercept this water as it falls to earth. Precipitation can be collected and stored as a source of domestic water. The concept is simple: some form of sloped surface—the bigger the surface area the better—collects falling water and directs it to large storage tanks called *cisterns*. From here water is either gravity-fed or pumped to the desired location: a field for irrigation, or household plumbing for domestic use. Let's see, let's see . . . where can we find a large, sloped surface for collection? Duh, how about the roof! Rainwater collection, or *catchment*, systems are elegant because they turn the negative of having to shunt water away from your building into the positive of collecting that same water for your use. They're also often the only way for urban dwellers to gain some control over their domestic water supply.

A truly functional rainwater catchment system is more complicated than my conceptual example. First, you'll need an appropriate roof surface. Aluminum and steel are probably the most common, though slate or tile are also suitable. Basically, any surface that won't leach undesirable materials into the water will work. For this reason, shingles made of asphalt or preservative-treated wood are a bad idea. Water from the roof is collected, usually in gutters, and flows by gravity through pipes or directly into a cistern or series of cisterns. Unless you're collecting water off the roof of one building to supply another, the cistern will not be at an elevation sufficiently

Rain catcher. Rainwater that falls on this roof is collected in the gutter and piped to this homemade ferrocement cistern to be stored for domestic water needs.

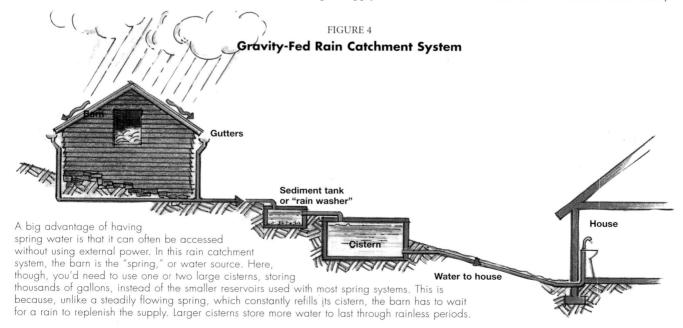

FIGURE 4
Gravity-Fed Rain Catchment System

Barn

Gutters

Sediment tank or "rain washer"

Cistern

House

Water to house

A big advantage of having spring water is that it can often be accessed without using external power. In this rain catchment system, the barn is the "spring," or water source. Here, though, you'd need to use one or two large cisterns, storing thousands of gallons, instead of the smaller reservoirs used with most spring systems. This is because, unlike a steadily flowing spring, which constantly refills its cistern, the barn has to wait for a rain to replenish the supply. Larger cisterns store more water to last through rainless periods.

above the house to allow gravity-fed pressure. Therefore, pumps and pressure tanks are usually used in conjunction to help move the water. The storage tanks, made of a variety of materials, including concrete, fiberglass, molded plastic, and steel, can be placed or buried near the house or even inside—in a basement, for example. Water is heavy and these tanks are large—5,000 gallons or more of storage is not uncommon—so they need to be carefully and securely placed. From here water is either gravity-fed or pumped to a pressure tank, which then supplies water to household fixtures. A completely gravity-fed system could be accomplished by collecting water from an outbuilding, such as a barn, and storing it in a large cistern far enough above the house to provide the desired water pressure (see figure 4).

Roof to roots. Harvested rainwater doesn't always have to be collected in a cistern for domestic use. This sculptured roof directs runoff into a courtyard planter at Casa Esperanza School in Tijuana, Mexico.

Often water from the roof is first passed through some sort of crude filter to remove dirt and large contaminants before entering the cistern. This filter can simply be a small tank in which dirt and small rocks are allowed to settle. Such a tank can also be partially filled with gravel in an attempt to catch more impurities. Also, the cistern or cisterns into which water from the small tank flows can provide further opportunities for unwanted materials to settle out (see figure 5).

The final component of the system is a commercial filter or series of filters placed in the main water line or at individual fixtures. In certain situations, well and spring water that tests negative for contaminants can be somewhat safely assumed to stay that way. With catchment water, you never know for sure what you're getting

FIGURE 5
Filtering Sediment from Rainwater

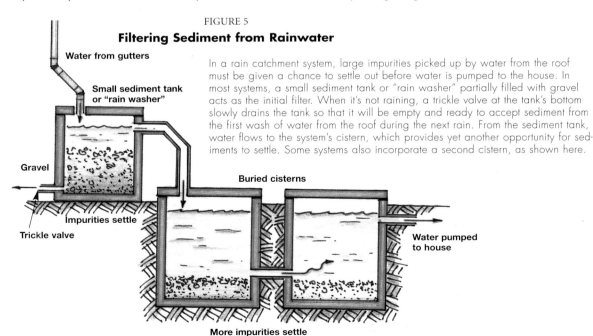

Water from gutters

Small sediment tank or "rain washer"

Gravel

Trickle valve

Impurities settle

Buried cisterns

Water pumped to house

More impurities settle

In a rain catchment system, large impurities picked up by water from the roof must be given a chance to settle out before water is pumped to the house. In most systems, a small sediment tank or "rain washer" partially filled with gravel acts as the initial filter. When it's not raining, a trickle valve at the tank's bottom slowly drains the tank so that it will be empty and ready to accept sediment from the first wash of water from the roof during the next rain. From the sediment tank, water flows to the system's cistern, which provides yet another opportunity for sediments to settle. Some systems also incorporate a second cistern, as shown here.

FIGURE 6

Greywater System

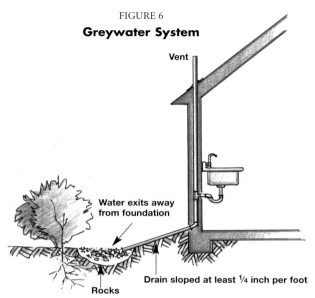

Basic greywater systems take the water from each drain separately to an appropriate place for the water to be utilized. This conceptual illustration is simplified; greywater systems need to be planned carefully. Indiscriminately dumping greywater is irresponsible and can create health hazards.

because you aren't receiving the benefit of any ground filtering and treatment. Bird droppings on the roof or contaminants from industry and auto emissions can vary your water's content from one rain to the next, so filtering is probably a good idea. Filtering systems range widely in cost and effectiveness, so research a system carefully before buying. Be especially conscious of the cost of replacement filters, because once you have a system, you're locked into its maintenance costs. On the other hand, rainwater can be cleaner than many ground water sources. If environmental conditions become so bad that we can't collect water from the sky and make it drinkable with a reasonable amount of filtering, we'll have more urgent problems to deal with—like the end of life as we know it.

Water Out: "Waste" Water

The whole concept of "wastewater" is downright strange. As I've already pointed out, our planet's water isn't produced or destroyed; it's constantly circulating in a never-ending cycle. You can't throw water away; it just keeps coming back, sometimes to haunt you. I don't know who first came up with the idea of putting human feces and urine in drinking water, but I'd liked to have been around simply to hear the strange logic that got the whole ball rolling. Of course, now it's just the way we do it. To be fair, I realize that sanitation is a big concern in human civilization and that piped sewage is an attempt to create a safe, healthy environment. Still, can't we use our big brains to come up with a better way than soiling this precious essential, water?

In the case of domestic wastewater, the big bad bogeyman is human feces. Once you put feces in water, it's unfit to drink and isn't safe to leave just lying around. On the other hand, if you leave out the feces and replace toxic cleansers with biodegradable soaps and cleaners, you're left with a basically benign mix consisting mostly of water, dirt, and food particles. This mixture, called *greywater*, is no longer waste, but a good source of nutrients and water for plants around your house (see figure 6). In a typical household, greywater constitutes a majority of water use; some estimates put it at 80 percent. Toilet flush, and water used to wash diapers, is called *blackwater*. Water containing large amounts of meat grease or other food oils is also sometimes lumped into this category.

By separating grey and blackwater, we can reclaim a majority of our domestic water

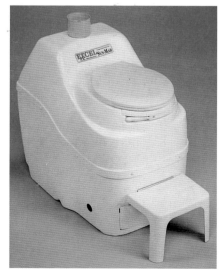

Composting toilet. Commercial models such as this one offer a compact and effective alternative to the ubiquitous flush toilet.

Sawdust toilet. This is the sawdust toilet in our house. The metal trash can holds sawdust.

for reuse. And we can eliminate the concept of "wastewater" almost completely by totally disassociating urine and feces from our domestic water supply.

First, though, we'd have to get over our fear of the stuff. In his entertaining and informative book, *The Humanure Handbook,* Joseph C. Jenkins calls our society's discomfort with urine and feces "fecophobia." Let's face it, we're all full of it, so how bad can it be? In fact, our "waste" is actually a mineral-rich resource of organic matter that should be returned to enrich the soil from which it came. This can be accomplished through proper *composting,* which is simply the process of turning organic matter into *humus,* the organic component of soil. Compost is created through a progression of decay involving myriad organisms, including bacteria, fungi, worms, and insects.

There are many commercial *composting toilets* on the market, created specifically to destroy pathogens in human waste. Some, such as those by Clivus Multrum, have a large storage tank that must be installed below the toilet—in a basement, for example. Others, such as those by Sun-Mar, are small units that occupy little more space than a conventional toilet. Some models use electricity to generate pathogen-killing heat. Commercial composting toilet systems are expensive, but are time-tested and work well. If you're in a situation where you can use composting toilets to avoid needing a septic tank (in some areas, sanitation codes require you to have a septic tank whether you use it or not), they could end up saving you a lot of money.

Another option, advocated by Joseph C. Jenkins, is the sawdust toilet/compost bin combination. In this basic setup, which I've adopted in my house, the toilet is simply a five-gallon bucket with a toilet seat. After each use, urine and feces are covered with a healthy layer of sawdust to add carbon and prevent flies and odor. When the bucket is full it's emptied, along with kitchen scraps, into a compost bin and covered with straw, weeds, or yard clippings. This system is very inexpensive and easy to maintain. According to Jenkins, its main advantage is that it encourages *thermophilic composting,* a process of decay that generates sufficient heat to kill all pathogens that can survive in the human body. Nitrogen-rich human feces combined with sawdust, kitchen scraps, straw, and yard weeds, all high in carbon, create a healthy carbon-nitrogen ratio, the hallmark of good compost. The result, claims Jenkins, is thick, rich humus that's safe for use on vegetable crops. Of course, I'm not necessarily saying that sawdust toilets are for everyone. In fact, in many jurisdictions and applications they can be illegal. Just do some research and decide for yourself.

There are other elegant methods for reclaiming human waste and the water that carries it. *Constructed wetlands* mimic the biological land treatment of natural wetlands to purify blackwater with the help of microorganisms and water-loving plants. And "Living Machines," commercial systems developed by ecological designer Dr. John Todd, are compact, indoor versions of constructed wetlands consisting of a series of water-filled tanks that serve as homes for the requisite plants and microorganisms. With the help of sunlight and a managed environment, a diversity of organisms, including bacteria, plants, snails, and fish, break down and digest organic pollutants. Finished water from a Living Machine is clean enough for reuse

Humanure compost. The Jenkins family has grown their own food using humanure-enriched compost for the past 25 years.

applications such as irrigation, toilet flush, and automobile wash. Most current Living Machine systems are designed for municipal, corporate, or educational applications, but single-family systems are on the horizon.

Of course, it's important to be concerned about sanitation, and for that reason the entire subject of composting toilets and other nonstandard approaches to dealing with greywater and blackwater may seem scary to you. To get some perspective, let's look at the more common methods: septic and sewage systems.

In rural areas, septic systems are the usual code-approved approach. Septic systems consist of a two-chambered tank and some sort of *leach field*: a series of trenches that are filled with gravel, foam peanuts, or other material that creates space for liquid. All domestic water, both grey and black, is dumped into the tank, where some solids are allowed to settle out, giving bacteria that thrive in this airless environment, called *anaerobic bacteria*, time to digest them. Everything that doesn't settle out or get digested leaves through a pipe at the tank's far end. This liquid, called *effluent*, slowly fills the trenches of the leach field, where it can be further purified through biological land treatment.

As with composting techniques, septic systems break down wastes through bacterial digestion. However, septic systems use anaerobic decomposition and don't achieve temperatures that guarantee the deaths of all possible human pathogens. In addition, no useable compost is produced. Furthermore, septic systems can be short-circuited by too much water. An excess of water from the house to the tank can cause a backup into the house, or force effluent too quickly into the leach field, therefore preventing adequate bacterial digestion. In addition, too much precipitation can saturate leach fields and bring raw effluent to the surface, creating a stinky swamp and possibly contaminating surface and ground water. The results

Septic system components. Left: No, this isn't a concrete coffin . . . well, actually it is: a septic tank, the final resting place for a household's solid waste. Right: This leach field setup consists of perforated plastic pipe surrounded by foam peanuts that in turn are wrapped in plastic netting. After the trench has been covered with dirt, effluent from the septic tank will flow into the leach field. The foam peanuts make room for the sewage to spread away from the plastic pipe. Gravel was once used instead of peanuts, and sometimes still is.

Modern sewage plant. In many urban areas, everything that's flushed down a toilet, poured down a sink, hosed into a gas station drain, or washed into a storm sewer is collected in the same system of pipes and brought together as a grimy soup to be treated at a modern sewage plant.

of all of these problems can be dangerous to human health and the environment. A 1986 United States Environmental Protection Agency (EPA) study found that 46 states in the U.S. reported septic tanks as a source of ground water pollution. Nine of these states found septic systems to be their *largest* source of ground water pollution.

The municipal approach, centralized sewage collection, is pretty much a giant version of the septic system. According to Art Ludwig, author of *Create an Oasis with Greywater*, 20 percent of all U.S. communities still are dumping sewage directly into surface waters such as rivers with only basic removal of solids for treatment. Other, more sophisticated systems take the sewage through a number of steps, including filtration, sedimentation (settling), aeration, and biological digestion. The final step is disinfection, which usually relies heavily on chlorine (see page 117). As with septic systems, municipal sewage treatment can falter when faced with too much water, contaminating surface and ground water. This says nothing of the effects of dumping untold tons of chlorine into the environment.

Human waste can be a health problem. Alternative systems reduce this risk better than conventional measures because they isolate, manage, and transform human waste on a small scale. Conventional septic and sewage systems struggle against the same basic flaw: they see water as a medium for waste. Human waste (and this goes double for industrial toxins!) has no place in the water cycle. If we take responsibility for our waste products instead of flushing them "away," we can often find uses for them. Such is the case with our urine and feces, which really should be returned to replenish the soil from which they came.

AIR

The earth is surrounded by a blanket of air, called the *atmosphere*, that extends about 350 miles above the surface of the planet. Scientists separate the atmosphere into zones, or layers. The closest zone to the surface, extending to about 9 miles above the earth, is the *troposphere*. This is the layer where all weather takes place and is the air we breathe. It's comprised mostly of gaseous nitrogen (78 percent), oxygen (21 percent), and argon (one percent). Water vapor is a variable component, amounting to anywhere from almost nothing up to seven percent of the air we breathe. The balance of the troposphere is made up of small amounts of various gases, including ozone and carbon dioxide, and suspended particles called *aerosols*.

Chalk up another miracle to creation. Air is a clear, homogenous mix of gases that maintains a consistent composition, even though components are constantly being added and removed (see figure 7). For example, animals use up oxygen and add carbon dioxide to the air. Plants use carbon dioxide and add oxygen. Water vapor is constantly coming and going. Yet air remains evenly mixed, allowing life forms to take in and get rid of the elements they need in order to survive. This feat is accomplished by the constant movement and mixing of air molecules, the phenomenon we call air circulation or wind.

FIGURE 7

Air: The More It Changes, the More It Stays the Same

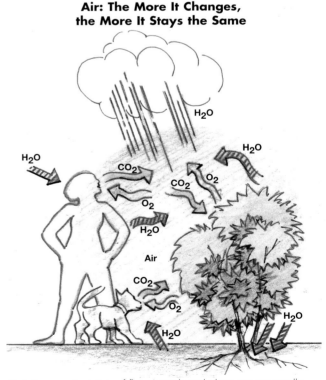

Air is in a constant state of flux. Animals and plants are continually taking from and adding to the composition of air, yet it remains remarkably predictable.

Outdoor Air Quality

Unfortunately, humans have actually started to affect the overall composition of the planet's air. For example, an increase in atmospheric carbon dioxide, mostly from industry and automobile exhaust, is the culprit behind the much-publicized phenomenon of global warming. Ozone depletion, an equally dubious accomplishment, is the result of releasing substances such as chlorofluorocarbons from various sources, including refrigerants and aerosol cans. Ozone filters out frequencies of ultraviolet light that are damaging to life on the planet, human and otherwise, so its reduction is a serious concern. These are just two examples of the many ways in which we're altering the air we breathe.

The first challenge, then, in maintaining a healthy exchange with outdoor air is to access some healthy outdoor air. Obviously, this is another reason why alternative building is sometimes linked to rural living. However, air, like water, just keeps coming back. There's no escaping air pollution. The only sane approach is for us all to work together to find a solution.

Indoor Air Quality

In a study conducted by the EPA to compare the quality of outdoor and indoor air, 335 individuals wore small pumps that sampled air near their faces. At the same time, similar pumps were placed in these people's back or side yards to sample outdoor air. At the end of every day, each participant's breath was tested. Subjects lived in three U.S. cities: heavily industrialized Jersey City, New Jersey, somewhat industrialized Greensboro, North Carolina, and nonindustrialized Devil's Lake, North Dakota. In the study, 20 toxic chemicals were looked for, and 11 of these were found in all situations. The study found that in Jersey City, people breathed in two to five times more toxins per day indoors at work and at home than they would've sitting in their back yards for the same time period. This was true even with people who lived less than one mile from an industrial pollution source. The results were even worse at the two less industrialized test sites, where hazardous-chemical levels were five to 10 times higher indoors than out.

I describe this study in such detail because it makes a shocking point. We tend to think of pollution as outside. We know that cars and industry are fouling the air. We also know that this pollution must have an effect on our indoor air. So it comes as a surprise to realize that our buildings and the activities performed within them can produce levels of pollution that far exceed the world outside.

Another surprise is that it's not just human-made substances that create this phenomenon. Radon is a colorless, odorless, radioactive gas that occurs naturally all over the world as the result of the decay of uranium 238, found in soil and

Pure isolation. The air inside this building is isolated from the outside air.

"Our buildings must be wholehearted participants in the cycle of air circulation on our planet. "

rock. In the ambient outdoor air, radon levels are typically very low. However, according to many experts, if a house is built over radon-active soil, concentrations of this gas can accumulate that are dangerous to humans. Radon's main health effect is lung cancer. An estimated 7,000 to 30,000 lung cancer deaths each year in the U.S. are attributable to radon. The U.S. Office of the Surgeon General lists radon as the second leading cause of lung cancer. The EPA considers indoor radon to be the most serious environmental carcinogen to which the general public is exposed. In one study over a seven-state area, radon levels above the EPA safe minimum were found in a third of the houses tested.

Perhaps we never should've moved inside. In the case of radon, if the experts are right, creating a separation from the outside can be deadly, even without the help of human-made toxins. The good news is, testing for radon is inexpensive and easy to do. If radon is found in elevated levels, relatively inexpensive measures can be taken that are designed to reduce accumulated radon. If you're building a new house, there's no reliable way to predict possible indoor radon levels. But for a few hundred dollars you can follow simple radon-prevention construction techniques. To get more information on radon, see the sources listed in chapter 9.

In any case, we see that indoor air quality can be adversely affected by a number of factors. There are two lessons to be learned here. First, we have to be careful about the materials we use to construct our buildings and the substances we store and use inside them. Second, we absolutely don't want to isolate our indoor air from the outdoor air. As bad as the air at large may be, it's most likely no worse and perhaps much better than what we can maintain indoors. Our buildings must be wholehearted participants in the cycle of air circulation on our planet.

When it comes to air, then, we want to create as much of a transparency between the inside and outside as possible. At the same time, a central purpose of housing is to create an indoor air temperature and humidity level that's different than the one outside. To do this, we need to create a separate indoor temperature without really separating indoor and outdoor air (see figure 8). When you think about it, this is a strange goal. During warm periods of the year in many climates, this is accomplished relatively easily by encouraging ample natural ventilation through windows and doors. As we saw in chapter 4, if built into the design of a house, natural ventilation—along with shading, evaporative cooling, and ample thermal mass—can be an effective strategy for cooling while allowing a healthy amount of air exchange. However, as we pointed out in chapter 5, this strategy may bring too much moist air into the building in a humid climate, possibly fostering the growth of mold and a consequent decline in indoor air quality. And in winter

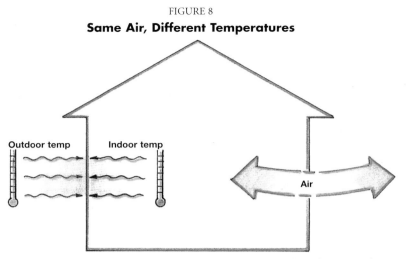

FIGURE 8

Same Air, Different Temperatures

Outdoor temp   Indoor temp

Air

Housing presents an interesting dilemma. In order to maintain healthy indoor air quality, we want our indoor air to be the same as fresh outdoor air. However, in most climates we also need to create different air temperatures indoors than exist outdoors. To do this, we have to isolate indoor air to some extent. As with most human endeavors, the answer is to find a balance between the two conflicting goals.

Fresh air welcome. This window to a monk's chambers in Lhasa, Tibet, has a beautiful awning to shade it. Plants and a lace curtain provide privacy but also allow for the free flow of fresh air.

Mechanical air exchanger. This unit brings in fresh outdoor air and expels stale indoor air. To learn more about it, see the section on Cindy Meehan-Patton's home in the next chapter.

in most climates, windows and doors are closed, and air exchange with the outdoors is considerably curtailed. These conditions complicate the problem of maintaining a healthy air exchange and may require other solutions.

Various sources claim that thermally efficient walls can be constructed that will allow significant amounts of air to move slowly through them. This would be a wonderful trait in a thick wall with thermal mass, because air exchange could be accomplished without drastic temperature change. Such a wall is often referred to as "breathable," though others (including me; see the previous chapter's section on the subject) define a breathable wall as one that can absorb and release water vapor. Walls realizing either definition of "breathable" would lead to improved indoor air quality. For example, a wall that's able to take on and release water vapor should create an environment less conducive to mold than a wall that traps water vapor. A wall that allows air to move through it without causing significant interior temperature change would improve air quality by being a constant source of outside air. This, of course, is exactly what we're trying to accomplish. There's debate over how to build such walls, or even if they're a practical strategy for air exchange. You'll have to do your own research and make your own decisions on the topic (see also chapters 5 and 7, and the sidebar, Bau-biologie and Breathing Walls, on the next page).

Air exchange is another debated and confusing topic for which I can give you no definitive answers. Unless through your own research you become confident in the existence of thermally efficient walls that allow appreciable air movement, a balance must be struck between good thermal performance and air exchange. Again, creating a building that fits your local environment and your lifestyle will help you to solve this problem. For example, if you're a smoker who absolutely has to smoke indoors, you'd want to focus on all-season air exchange and allow some winter heat loss to increase ventilation. If you live in a cold climate, spend some time looking into the breathable-wall issue and attempt to find the best approach that allows maximum air exchange while maintaining temperatures efficiently. A clean-burning source of heat is a big help (see the discussion of masonry stoves on page 86).

One of the best things that you can do is visit a variety of buildings in your area at different times of the year, being conscious of your perception of air quality. Variables such as stuffiness and odor are indications of the degree of air exchange. What are the differences you see in the design and construction and furnishings of a stuffy building as compared to one with fresh, healthful air?

Using nontoxic materials and a sensible design go a long way toward creating sufficient air exchange. If there's a problem after that, it may be more with lifestyle than with the building. We put a lot of pressure on our poor little houses by making them such a huge part of our daily lives. Lifestyle changes, such as smoking outdoors or quitting altogether, and engaging in more outside activities—especially in winter—will greatly increase your access to fresh air. Indoor air-quality concerns play a big role in the designs of several of the houses we'll be looking at in the next chapter, so we'll learn more about the topic there.

Masonry wood-burning stove. This is the masonry stove in our house. The core was built by stove mason Tom Trout. We faced it ourselves with brick, scrap granite, slate, and various artifacts.

POWER

This chapter is largely about maintaining an exchange with the outdoors. We've been discussing how to sustain a flow of sun, water, and air in and out to mimic the healthy balance these things offer us outside. But today's home life involves more than using natural outdoor elements at comfortable indoor temperatures. For most of us, modern life also entails coexisting with any number of machines and gadgets that we need in order to function in our society. For example, I'm able to live and work outside of an urban area because I have a computer and Internet connection that allows me to plug into my society. If you aren't fortunate enough to have a gravity-fed water system, you'll need a pump to access water. These and all the other little humming boxes that nestle in our homes have one thing in common: a hunger for electrical energy.

The topic of electricity—what, exactly, flows through those wires and ends up at your wall outlet—is a real mind-bender, one that we don't have the space to go into in detail here. The image of an orderly line of little dots, or electrons, flowing single file from the power source to your toaster is definitely not the way it works. For our purposes, we can simply identify electricity as a refined form of energy. It can be moved to exact places in exact amounts, which makes it ideal for delicate equipment that requires consistent and precise infusions of power.

Bau-biologie and Breathing Walls
by Helmut Ziehe

Translated from the German, the term Bau-biologie (a trademark in the U.S.) means "building biology," and is the study of the relationship between the building environment and human health.

In addition to creating shelter, the goal in building a house is to provide a comfortable indoor living climate. Such an environment is not only a function of the right temperature, but also depends on good indoor air quality. There are four parameters that play a role in creating that quality: temperature, air exchange, humidity, and electroclimate. Furthermore, we have to consider the exterior climate, the building materials used, the number of occupants, and the kinds of activities that will take place in the space. Add to all these variables seasonal and daily climatic changes, and it's obvious that creating a comfortable indoor living climate is not an easy task. But if indoor air quality isn't carefully considered, the result may well be structural problems for the building, and health problems for the people living or working in it.

In Bau-biologie, we say that a person has three skins: the first is your actual skin, the second is your clothes, and the third is the exterior walls of your dwelling. This "third skin" has many functions beyond being the dividing line between interior and exterior. The Bau-biologie approach to providing a comfortable indoor climate is to create a breathable third skin, a "breathable wall." We aren't talking about a wall with holes that permit large amounts of air flow. Instead, we're talking about a water and gas exchange on a molecular level as the result of vapor pressure differences. In other words, we're talking about diffusion, which is a naturally occurring phenomenon that happens to one degree or another depending on the type of material used.

When there's air on both sides of a barrier and the air pressure is higher on one side than the other, air will tend to move, or diffuse, from the high-pressure zone toward the low until a balance is created. The type of material in the barrier determines how quickly, if at all, this diffusion occurs. Airy materials, such as cellulose of any kind (straw, wood, recycled newspapers), obviously will allow more diffusion through them than dense materials, such as concrete.

However, if very dense material, such as glass or plastic, is placed in front of the airy material, a "vapor barrier" results that prevents diffusion. This is precisely what is happening in a conventional home that utilizes, for example, fiberglass insulation and a film of plastic, or vapor barrier, to create an "airtight wall." The result can be a building with a comfortable indoor temperature, but bad indoor air quality—a combination that doesn't add up to a truly comfortable or healthy living environment.

Helmut Ziehe is an architect and president and chairman of the board of the Institute for Bau-biologie and Ecology.

The power grid. Positive: power at the flip of a switch. Negative: massive air pollution from generating plants, and inefficiency caused by transmission losses through miles of wires and electronics.

Most electricity is produced at large, central power plants and transported to its destination through a connected system of high-voltage transmission lines, substations, transformers, and distribution cables. This system is collectively called the *power grid*.

In the U.S., about 55 percent of electricity is produced by burning coal. The balance of electric energy is produced by nuclear power (22 percent), natural gas (10 percent), oil (2 percent), and large-scale hydropower (10 percent). There are several problems with this approach. First, most of these methods produce air pollution, as well as create other environmental problems. Coal-fired power plants, for example, are responsible for a significant percentage of the emissions that are causing acid rain. In addition, according to the group Environmental Defense, 80 percent of global CO_2 emissions, the main gas that contributes to global warming, are produced by electrical power plants. Nuclear power, on the other hand, produces dangerous pollutants, radioactive wastes, with a huge potential for environmental devastation.

Inefficiency is the second problem with these centralized production methods. When you make electricity in one place and then ship it, sometimes more than a thousand miles, to its destination, large amounts of energy are wasted. This happens because the wires through which electricity travels resist the flow and cause friction, which uses up energy as heat. The amount of loss depends on many factors but it can be considerable, especially over long distances. In addition, many electrical devices are poorly designed from an energy-efficiency standpoint. For example, the incandescent light bulbs that you probably have in your house convert about 90 percent of the electricity that they receive into heat instead of light. Only 10 percent of the electricity that reaches your bulb, a good percentage of which was already lost in transmission, actually produces illumination. Finally, as we mentioned above, centralized power is another nail in the self-sufficiency coffin. When you're plugged into the power grid, you're often at the mercy of weather, which can knock out your lines, and the sometimes-questionable antics of governments and corporations.

Light bulbs or heat bulbs? Both of these bulbs produce about the same amount of illumination. The bulb at left is a compact fluorescent that uses 13 watts of power. The bulb on the right is a standard incandescent that uses 60 watts of power. Why the difference? Incandescent light bulbs lose about 90% of the energy fed into them as heat—as you know if you've ever touched a lit bulb.

If all of this is true, why do we use centralized power? Because it's relatively inexpensive and easily available. However, there are hidden costs that don't show up in your power bill, but that we all end up paying nonetheless. According to the National Academy of Sciences, for example, acid rain causes enormous financial losses in damage every year to buildings, crops, forests, and lakes. The economic impact of health care costs resulting from fossil-fuel-based electricity production is similarly massive. We pay these and other energy production costs, including military expenses to protect foreign energy sources, in many ways, including taxes, health insurance, and food prices.

Interestingly, alternatives to centralized electricity production come from the same outdoor elements that we've been discussing: sun, water, and air. The advantage of all these systems is that they produce a modern necessity, electricity, on-site, using natural elements that we've already sought out while placing our building. The energy of the sun shining, wind blowing, and water falling is simply utilized, without being significantly altered, as it goes about its business. Though the materials used to create these systems are usually mass-produced and are therefore a part of the pollution problem caused by modern production, once installed these systems are clean-running and noninvasive.

Solar Electricity

Some materials exhibit a property, known as the *photoelectric effect*, that causes them to release electrons when they absorb photons of light. These electrons can be captured as an electric current. This process, called *photovoltaics*, is the direct conversion of light into electricity. Photovoltaic systems generate electricity from sunlight. A photovoltaic cell, also called a *solar cell*, is a thin wafer, usually made of silicon, across which an electric current is produced when the cell is exposed to sunlight (see figure 9). A group of these solar cells con-

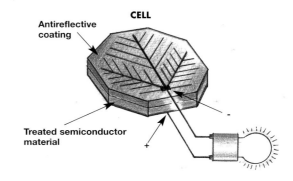

FIGURE 9
Solar Cells

CELL

Antireflective coating

Treated semiconductor material

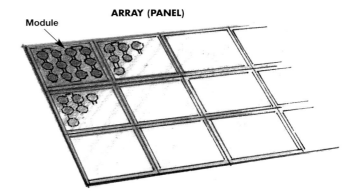

Module

ARRAY (PANEL)

A solar cell is made of specially treated semiconductor material that creates an electrical field, positive on one side and negative on the other. An antireflective coating reduces reflection of sunlight to less than five percent. When light energy is absorbed by the semiconductor, electrons are freed and are able to flow across the field. Wires or contacts on each side (top and bottom) capture and direct the current. Solar cells are wired together in a framed group, or module, to produce a certain voltage—usually 12 volts. Modules, in turn, are often connected together in an array to produce more power.

How Long Do PV Modules Last?

I wanted to know the current estimate for PV-module life expectancy, so I asked the tech support people at Real Goods Trading Company, a well-known retailer of alternative energy products and many other items geared to sustainable living. Here's their answer.

PV modules last a long, long time. How long, we honestly don't know yet, as the oldest terrestrial modules are barely 30 years old and are still going strong. In decades-long tests, single-crystal and polycrystal modules have been shown to degrade at fairly steady rates of 0.5 percent to 1 percent per year. First-generation amorphous modules degraded faster, but there are so many new wrinkles and improvements in amorphous production that we can't draw any blanket generalizations for this module type. The best amorphous products now seem to closely match the degradation of single-crystal products, but there are no long-term data. All full-size modules carry 10- to 20-year warranties, reflecting their manufacturers' faith in the durability of these products.

PV technology is closely related to transistor technology. Based on our experience with transistors, which just fade away after 20 years of constant use, most manufacturers have been confidently predicting 20-year or longer lifespans. However, keep in mind that PV modules are only seeing six to eight hours of active use per day, so we may find that lifespans of 60 to 80 years are normal. Cells that were put into the truly nasty environment of space in the late 1960s are still functioning well.

On-site PV power. PV modules like this one can produce power anywhere there's sun.

nected together in a frame create the basic unit of modern solar power systems, the *photovoltaic (PV) module*. Several modules connected together to produce even more power is called an *array*.

Using this technology, we can generate electricity from sunlight. However, when the sun isn't shining, the flow of electricity stops. Therefore, we need some form of storage capacity. We can, for example, use solar power to pump water to a reservoir as the sun shines (see figure 10). This energy is then stored for later use, as the water will flow by gravity whether the sun is shining or not. Similarly, to store electricity directly, we need some form of battery. Electricity generated by solar modules can be stored in batteries for later use.

Solar technology is elegant and, compared to giant coal-fired power plants, has relatively few components (see the sidebar, PV vs. Grid Power). It's also highly evolved

FIGURE 10
Storing Solar Power

Both of these systems use photovoltaics to store the sun's energy for later use, night or day, sunny or cloudy.

WATER STORAGE

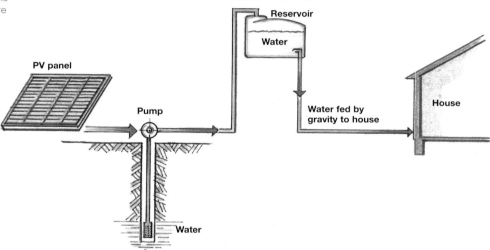

Here the PV panel produces electricity to run a pump when the sun shines. The pump pushes water to a reservoir, storing the solar energy as potential energy until someone in the house below turns a faucet—and the water flows by gravity.

BATTERY STORAGE

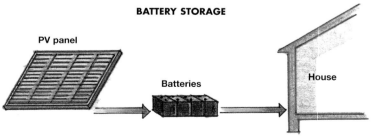

Here the PV panel charges a bank of batteries with sun-generated electricity that can be used when needed.

and well-tested, due in part to its widespread use in space exploration. Satellites and spacecraft have long utilized photovoltaic systems for power. Today there are many manufacturers of high-quality solar components that can be used for domestic, on-site electricity production. The equipment is relatively straightforward, widely available, and dependable. PV modules, for instance, typically carry 10- to 20-year manufacturer warranties (see the sidebar, How Long Do PV Modules Last?, on page 135).

You can choose either a *standalone* photovoltaics system in which batteries, and often a backup gas-powered generator, provide stored electricity, or a *grid intertie* system (see figure 11). In the latter setup, you connect your PV system to the utility company's electricity supply. When you're producing an excess of current, your surplus feeds the grid and the utility pays you for the electricity. When the sun isn't shining and you need more electricity than your system can provide, you use it directly from the grid and pay the utility company, just like regular customers. Another version of the intertie system simply substitutes grid power for the gas generator to charge batteries when solar power is insufficient.

The specific components required to set up a photovoltaic system vary, of course, depending on the system. One essential element in most setups is a device called an inverter. It changes direct current (DC), such as that created by PV panels as well as by wind and water turbines, into the alternating current (AC) that can be used by common appliances and lights.

FIGURE 11
PV Systems: Standalone or Grid Intertie

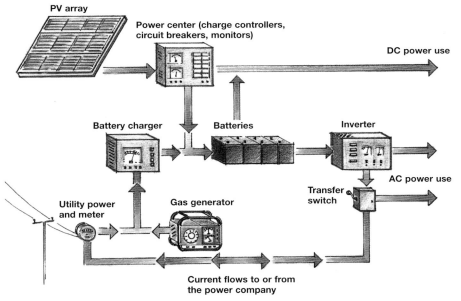

This is a simplified schematic showing PV system setup possibilities. A standalone system would use the gas generator to charge the batteries when solar was insufficient. A grid intertie system would replace the gas generator with a connection to the utility power grid. In such a system, the batteries could also be left out. When more solar electricity was produced than used in the house, the excess would flow to the grid and be purchased by the power company. When there wasn't enough solar energy to produce needed electricity, the power would flow from the grid and be purchased by the user.

PV vs. Grid Power

Cost: Solar electricity usually requires a considerably higher initial investment than hooking up to the grid. The exception is a rural building site that doesn't have easy access to grid power. In this situation, the cost of a PV system can be less than paying the power company to run long lines to a house. PV technology is constantly changing, so mentioning specific prices or estimated payback times here would be of little value. Go ahead and price a system. What do you have to lose?

Maintenance: Once installed, PV systems require only periodic maintenance. Modules require no regular upkeep. If storage batteries are a part of your system, they will need to be cared for. Check the water level on lead-acid regularly—once a month is recommended. As for grid power, maintenance is required, but you don't have to do it—you just have to pay for it as part of your monthly bill.

Reliability: PV systems and grid power are both reliable. Many PV modules carry a 20-year warranty and may realistically be expected to last even longer (see the sidebar, How Long Do PV Modules Last?, on page 135) In most PV systems, there are no motors or moving parts, except for backup equipment such as a generator. Inverters, devices that change DC current coming from panels into AC current for conventional appliances and lights, are perhaps the most delicate component in the system. PV systems are modular, so problems are usually easily isolated and solved by replacing the component. PV power's reliability advantage comes during bad weather. In a storm, a tree falling on a power line miles away, or some other problem far from your house, can cause you to lose grid power. With a PV system, as long as you have enough solar energy coming in or stored in batteries, you won't lose power, regardless of storms or emergencies.

Solar Water Heating

The sun's energy also can be used to replace, rather than produce, electricity for certain applications. As we've said, electricity is a highly refined power form, sort of the vintage wine of energy. Electricity is necessary to run delicate devices that need exact and consistent amounts of energy. However, we use it in some situations that don't fit this description. Heating water is one example. The heating of water is a simple process: you add energy in the form of heat to a body of water, and the water's thermal mass stores the heat. Insulation can be added to the storage tank to increase efficiency.

Electric water heaters are a perfect example of complicating something simple. To use such a heater, coal, for instance, must be mined and transported to a power plant, where it's burned to produce electricity, which is then sent through miles of wires and electronic equipment to reach the heating elements in your tank, which heat the water.

The same effect can be achieved by simply setting that tank of water in the sun.

Solar water heating is another application of passive solar heating as discussed in chapter 4. This time, though, we're storing heat to create hot water, not hot air.

There are many types of solar hot-water heaters. The simplest are called *breadbox* or *batch heaters*. These units combine water heating and storage by simply placing a tank of water in an insulated, glass-covered box and placing it in the sun. You can construct one of these heaters yourself or buy it. Another approach is to run pipes of water through an insulated, glass-covered box. The smaller amount of water heats more quickly and is either pumped to a storage tank or moved through a *convective loop* (see figure 12). In a convective loop, water rises in a pipe when heated and enters the top of a storage tank. This action pushes cold water out the bottom of the tank and into the solar collector, creating a continuous loop as long as the sun is applying heat. This is an example of *thermosiphoning*. The hot-water outlet is at the top of the tank to access the hottest water; another line returns cooled water to the tank to be heated again.

Another variation is to use a series of high-tech vacuum bottles, sort of like giant coffee thermoses, to collect heat and store water. The small-diameter bottles heat up quickly and are insulated, so they hold the heat well. Some of these systems use antifreeze liquids, pumps, and heat exchangers to supply hot water, allowing their use in cold climates where other solar heaters may be vulnerable to freezing. All of these systems are placed facing south, and are often angled to maximize solar gain. They're frequently mounted on roofs.

Evacuated tube water heater. These evacuated tubes mounted in a manifold are part of a hot water system. The manufacturer (Thermomax) claims that their systems will produce hot water even on cold, cloudy winter days.

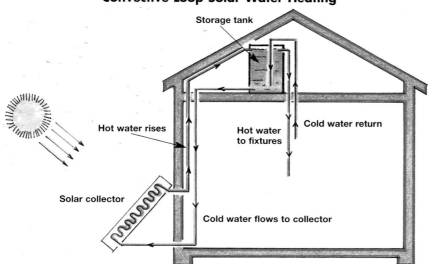

FIGURE 12

Convective Loop Solar Water Heating

Storage tank

Hot water rises

Hot water to fixtures

Cold water return

Solar collector

Cold water flows to collector

In this simple example of a convective loop water-heating system, water passes through pipes in a solar collector, where it's heated by the sun. The hot water rises through convection to the storage tank, pushing cold water out the bottom of the tank and into the collector. The water circulates continuously as long as the sun applies heat. In cold climates where water in the collector might freeze, antifreeze or some other liquid with a low freezing point is circulated instead of water to a heat exchanger, which in turn transfers the heat to water in the storage tank.

A passive solar heater can be part of a larger system that will guarantee a constant supply of hot water. For example, the solar heater can be plumbed as a preheater for a *tankless hot-water heater*. These units, also called *instantaneous* or *on-demand heaters*, are standard in Europe and steadily catching on in the U.S. They don't store hot water but use natural or propane gas to heat it as it passes through a coil of pipes. As a result, these heaters don't waste energy storing water 23 hours a day for the one hour you may need it. They also never run out of hot water, because they create it on demand. Tankless heaters are a larger initial investment than tanked heaters, but most, such as the Aquastar, have replaceable parts and are designed to last a long time.

A system that combines both a passive solar heater and a tankless heater provides the luxury of energy efficiency and inexhaustible hot water. With the turning of a couple of valves, you can access only solar hot water when the sun is shining and then switch back to a combination when the sun isn't enough. For more details on this type of setup, see the sidebar below.

Our Combination Water Heater

Our homemade system provides unlimited hot water. It consists of a tank from an electric hot-water heater painted black and set in an insulated box under a skylight in our bathroom roof. When the sun is shining, water in the tank is heated. Using a series of valves, we have this tank plumbed to move water directly to faucets, or we can send it through our instantaneous water heater for an additional boost if the sun is insufficient that day.

Tank seen from roof. The electric water heater tank is painted black and suspended below a skylight. Flashing and silver paint help make the interior surfaces more reflective.

The view from indoors. Inside this insulated box is the tank from the previous photo. The side comes off for tank inspection and removal. You can see the water pipes going in and out as well as a drain pipe, which I installed in a sealed plywood drain box in case the tank ever starts leaking. At bottom right, you can see our "in-laws" toilet. Though we use a composting sawdust toilet, we had to install a conventional toilet for code reasons.

Tankless heater. Here you can see our tankless heater and the pipes coming down from the loft to bring water to and away from the heater. The valves to direct water to the solar heater, tankless heater, or both are in the loft. We use the narrow, metal-runged ladder on the left when we need to switch the valves. It takes about three seconds. The two white pipes are from the tankless heater overflow valve and the drain box for the solar heater. They're plumbed to a floor drain in the bathroom slab.

FIGURE 13

Small-Scale Hydroelectric System

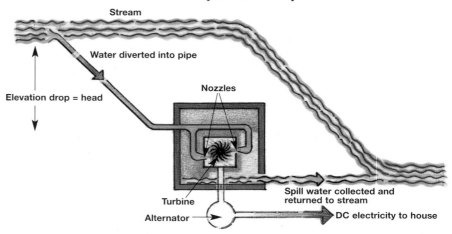

A steady flow of water with a good head (the vertical distance from the water source to the turbine) can be utilized in a simple system with few parts that produces plenty of current for domestic use.

Water and Wind Power

A *turbine* is basically a wheel that is made to spin by a fluid, which by definition includes both water and wind. Either can be used to turn a turbine to produce electricity. The picturesque windmills you see in old movies or on farms are turbines being used to pump water or grind grain. Windmill technology has been vastly improved in recent years, allowing smaller and more efficient units to produce electricity.

A wind turbine is simply a set of blades that spin in the wind. These blades turn a shaft that drives a generator, which produces electricity. Like PV systems, wind turbines produce DC current, so wind power can be hooked into the same system as your PV modules. Wind makes a good partner for solar power, because the weather is often windy when the sun isn't out. As we've said, wind is the most site-specific environmental element. In order to really establish whether your site can efficiently produce wind power, you need to determine its average wind velocity. The best method for doing this is to use a device, such as an *anemometer*, to measure wind speed at your site. An anemometer is mounted on a pole at the approximate height of your proposed wind turbine, where it measures average daily wind speed. It's best to get a full year's worth of data before making conclusions.

Falling water also can be used to turn a turbine to generate electricity. The process is called *hydroelectricity*. Large and small dams all over the world have been built to harness

Wind power. Wind turbines, such as these manufactured by Southwest Power, can be installed singly or in multiples.

water for this purpose. If you have a steady source of falling water, a stream for example, a small-scale hydroelectric system is an exciting possibility.

In a typical setup, water is diverted from the stream through a pipe to one or more nozzles that direct a spray of water onto a turbine, causing it to spin (see figure 13). This turbine is connected to a generator, often simply a DC car alternator, which produces electricity. The amount of electricity produced depends on the rate of water flow and the distance, in elevation, that the water falls. Therefore, a small amount of water falling from a great height can produce the same amount of electricity as a lot of water falling only a short distance. Once generated, the electricity can be used directly or stored in batteries, making it compatible with solar and wind systems. A good source of water can produce electricity 24 hours a day and in some situations generates enough current to bypass the need for battery storage. If you're blessed with a strong water source on a good site, hydroelectric power can be relatively inexpensive, costing considerably less than either PV or wind.

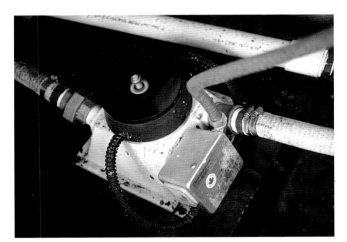

Small-scale water turbines. Turbines designed to generate hydroelectricity are available in a range of types and power outputs. Top left: A Stream Machine 800-watt turbine. Top right: This 200-watt turbine, installed over a small waterfall in Vietnam, has an integrated water dam. Bottom left: This Power Pal turbine, manufactured by Asian Phoenix Resources, is made in 200-, 500-, and 1,000-watt models. Bottom right: A 20,000-watt Pelton wheel turbine and generator from Canyon Industries.

Hammering It Home

*"He or she who is
without sin, throw
the first PV module."*

As I've said, my goal in writing this book is simply to help you start thinking about things that will lead you toward a good house. One aspect of that road is creating a healthy exchange with the outdoors. It's difficult to discuss that topic without bringing up pollution and the many woes that our modern existence seems to be bringing to our planet. There are many things we can do to encourage the healthy exchange with the outdoors that we need to survive. Often, a happy side effect is the reduction of our impact on our local environment. However, the real goal of alternative builders is often much grander: a sustainable way of life.

Sustainable practices are simply ways of doing things that can be continued indefinitely. I don't know if it's possible to combine a modern lifestyle and housing for six billion people sustainably. I do know that, from an objective point of view of sustainability, building a house, and even having children, is a selfish act. I'm reminded of a bumper sticker I once saw: "Save the world, kill yourself." That absurd sentiment sums up our modern predicament. With our growing population and resource-gobbling lifestyles, adding to the population or even participating in modern life can be a source of guilt. In my opinion, all you can do is be aware of how your actions on Earth affect the planet, and do your best: build the best house you can, one that will satisfy your needs and make you happy while also being as environmentally responsible as possible. The options I outline in this chapter are fun to learn about and, in my experience, interesting and satisfying to put into practice. Do what you can, and don't let anyone point a finger at you for not doing "enough" or for doing something the "wrong way." We're all in this together. He or she who is without sin, throw the first PV module.

In the final analysis, the success of our indoor and outdoor exchange, as well as our environmental impact, probably depends more on lifestyle choices than anything. Trading in your conventional downtown apartment and constructing a state-of-the-art eco-house in the country may sound good for you and the planet. However, that "Think Green" bumper sticker won't change the fact that you're probably wasting more energy and creating additional air pollution on the two-hour daily commute than you'll ever save living the rest of your life in your spiffy new house. By the same token, installing a huge PV system to run untold numbers of gadgets is, in my opinion, much less praiseworthy than conserving utility-grid energy through simplifying your needs. As far as ecological impact goes, I'll put my money on the little mobile home with a big vegetable garden and clothes drying on the line over the huge alternative house with all the modern comforts.

To achieve a real exchange with the outdoors, we have to spend more time out scratching in the dirt, growing food, and returning compost to the soil. We need to prefer putting on a sweater over tweaking a thermostat. This is the way that most people on earth have always lived. It's more fun, it's rewarding, it's healthful, and, who knows, it just might make a difference.

The sin of size. We don't need to discuss the materials choices, energy systems, or siting of this modern house before criticizing it for being irresponsible. It's simply too big. Three large stories (including the full-size daylight basement) for a single family is a resource extravagance that, in my opinion, the planet won't be able to sustain indefinitely.

Experiments in Urban Sustainability:

A DISCUSSION WITH OLE ERSSON

Maitri and Ole Ersson are getting the best of two worlds: the independence and self-sufficiency of country life, plus the social stimulation, diversity, and economic opportunities of city life. Here's a conversation with Ole about their endeavors.

Q How did you get interested in sustainability?

My interest goes back to childhood, when I had my first organic garden. I've gardened organically on and off ever since, and it's an important element of many of the projects I've undertaken. Organic gardening differs from other gardening in that one of its main and characterizing principles is its sustainability. Besides producing much of one's own top-quality food in a way that's psychologically and spiritually rewarding, its techniques enrich and actually create new soil by recycling nutrients that some people consider "yard waste." In a sense, organic gardening has served as a source of inspiration and a model for how to create a healthy ecosystem.

Q People often combine an interest in issues of sustainable living with a desire to leave the city. Your website is entitled "Experiments in Sustainable Urban Living." Are you experimenting in the urban environment by choice, or is that just where you find yourself right now?

It's a choice. I certainly understand the feeling that many people have, the desire to escape the city and create a little paradise in the country. My wife and I undertook such a voyage with our young family many years ago. We purchased an old church at a county auction and spent two years remodeling it as a residence. The nearest village was two miles away. The county seat, population 25,000, was 20 miles away. Our neighborhood consisted of about half a dozen families, few of whom shared our interests in ecology and sustainability. The economic base was rather limited and nearby job opportunities were few. I would've had to drive almost an hour to work as a computer programmer. Instead, I worked full time (or more) on our project and, after two years, and clocking thousands of miles and hundreds of hours in the car, we finally finished it—and couldn't wait to move back to our community of friends in the city! I don't mean to demean country living, but we found that it wasn't for us. Deep down, we enjoy having a variety of friends, and let's face it—people are the one thing in rural areas that can be in short supply!

We've rediscovered a lot of the fun we had "homesteading" back then—and much more—right here in the city. Both my wife and I are able to have rich professional lives, which would've been more difficult, and for some people would be impossible, in the country. We have a community of friends who share our passions. We have ample spiritual, psychological, mental, and financial support. Now, as a family physician, I'm able to bike less than 15 minutes to work in the heart of downtown. I rarely use a motorized vehicle,

Straw bale hot water heater. Coiled flexible water pipe is buried beneath a layer of composting wood chips and household waste in this straw bale greenhouse. Cold water from the house flows into the coil, where it's warmed by heat produced by the compost to 90° to 130° F, then returned to the house for domestic use.

Urban rainwater catchment. This 1,500-gallon cistern collects rainwater from the Ersson's roof and supplies them with most of their household water needs.

and really need it only for hauling cargo or family outings. Our lives are as full as we like of the social stimulation that was lacking in the country. And we don't even have to own a car if we so choose.

Q **Most urban dwellers depend on big institutions, such as municipal governments and large grocery store chains, to provide them with the basics of life. You've found some creative ways to directly access some of the "necessities" of modern life in your urban setting. Could you describe a few of your projects?**

Yes, one of our focuses has been to see how many of the necessities of modern living we could tackle ourselves in more sustainable ways than the norm usually found in American cities. Shelter, food, and utilities and sevices such as water, energy, and sewer are needs that everyone shares. By applying simple ecological principles and old-fashioned values like simplicity and thrift, we've found rewarding ways of dealing with these issues.

For instance, we've raised a good portion of our food organically on a small city lot, and utilized our rooftop—a rarely exploited but plentiful resource in any city—for container gardening. We've almost eliminated our "garbage" and sewer bills by embracing recycling and simple organic composting-toilet technology. We harvest rainwater that provides almost all our household water needs for most of the year, and extract waste heat from compost to produce all the hot water we require.

Currently, we're planning a super-energy-efficient straw bale home in another part of the heart of the city that will better integrate the many things we now do in our existing home.

Rooftop garden. Pumpkins in plastic buckets are set into, and tied onto, a wood framework to create a simple roof garden.

Q **What has been the reaction of neighbors and local government authorities concerning your experiments in sustainable living? Do you have any advice for other urban dwellers with similar interests?**

Our neighbors have been very supportive of our projects. We've hosted tours and made presentations to many hundreds of individuals, including school children, college students, and various groups and organizations. As you can see if you've visited our web page, we've garnered favorable publicity for our projects in the local press. Several city officials, including Portland's senior plumbing inspector and the city counselor who overseas wastewater issues, have visited our home. In fact, the interest we generated prodded the city to develop its own rainwater harvesting guidelines.

Q **What advice do you have for others who are interested in developing more sustainable ways of living?**

My suggestion to others with similar interests is to get together with like-minded individuals for mutual support and inspiration. Plunge in and get your hands dirty! I always finish a project thinking "why didn't I try this a long time ago?" Don't hesitate to work with the local bureaucrats to help expand their—and your own—thinking. In the end, everyone benefits from this kind of work.

Articles with more details about Ole and Maitri's many sustainable living projects and plans are on their website, listed on page 226.

CHAPTER 7

APPLICATIONS

So far, this book has been an introduction to housing through the lens of alternative building. We've been learning about materials, concepts, and approaches that will help you on your journey toward a good house. Now it's time to look at some actual buildings, some specific real-world examples of how specific real-world people approached the interesting goal of building a good house.

My goal for this chapter is to show you a wide variety of approaches to "alternative building." To that end, I asked the owners of six different alternative homes the same set of questions about their houses. I based the questions on the information we've covered, including the four fundamental functions of housing: structure, temperature, separation, and connection. Since we've taken the time to begin at the beginning and learn about housing conceptually from the ground up, we'll be much better able to understand the homeowners' answers, and, therefore, their houses. I can't thank these people enough for taking the time and energy to reflect on their buildings. I learned a lot from what they had to say, and I think you will, too.

That's not to say that I think these are perfect buildings. I don't agree with all the choices that these folks made, nor do I share all the beliefs and assumptions that they express. In fact, if you read these interviews closely you'll find statements here or there that are contradicted elsewhere in the book. You'll also find contradictory approaches to achieving the same goals. Who's right? Who cares! In fact, these contrasts are exactly why I chose these particular buildings. The important thing is that these houses are interesting examples of modern people creating buildings that are specific to their local environment and to their needs and beliefs. As I've said throughout this book, that's my definition of a good house. The point here is not to compare these buildings or to decide which one you like better, but to listen and learn from people who've been through the process of creating a house.

Four of the six buildings featured in this chapter are located in my general climatic region. I chose them for two reasons: First, I live in a very wet area that has fairly hot summers and fairly cold winters, so buildings around here are exposed to a large range of environmental trials. This makes them good starting points for our real-world practical education on how buildings interact with their environment. Second, my intent here isn't to do a survey of all possible options available to you. Instead, I'm trying to get you to start asking the right questions. Looking at how different people dealt with a similar climate is a good way to accomplish that goal. To round out our survey, I chose two buildings from entirely different climates: hot and humid (Texas), and cold and dry (Colorado mountains).

This chapter is a chance both to check out some houses and to practice for a process you should continue on your own. I've written the questions here, but eventually you should be asking similar questions, and many more, about any building that interests you, whether it's because you like it or you hate it. In your search for a good house, every building with which you come in contact is an education far more detailed and enlightening than anything I can hope to give you in a book. The human world is a living laboratory of buildings, buildings, buildings as far as the eye can see. Once you learn what to look for, how the functions of housing express themselves in your specific situation, you'll find yourself surrounded by answers.

DAN CHIRAS'S EARTHSHIP HYBRID

"GO THE DISTANCE. DO EVERYTHING YOU CAN TO CREATE A HOME THAT'S EASY ON THE ENVIRONMENT, SAFE AND HEALTHY, AND AFFORDABLE."

Dan Chiras describes himself as "a writer, public speaker, green building consultant, and practitioner of sustainability." He's the author of numerous articles and 15 books, including the best-selling college textbook, Environmental Science: Creating a Sustainable Future, and The Natural House, a guide to building sustainable homes.

Dan is passionate about issues of sustainability and our environment. He has taught classes and written books on the subject for many years. However, he had little actual building experience when he decided to become the general contractor on the construction of his own Earthship hybrid house. His clear understanding of the alternative concepts he was trying to implement, his ability to research, and his passion to "do it right" helped him succeed. Dan's house seems almost a textbook example of the modern "alternative" house.

Q **Describe your land and building site, and outline what led you to choose it. What did you do to analyze your site?**

My home site is in a sprawling subdivision in the mountains outside of Denver, Colorado. Homes are on two-acre lots. I chose my lot primarily because it offered me an opportunity to tap into the sun's generous supply of energy, which I planned to use for three purposes: producing my own electricity through PVs, or photovoltaics; heating my home; and growing some of my own food.

Because I'd lived nearby, just a few miles away, for 10 years, I knew the path of the Sun at different times of the year. So one

Chiras house.
Dan Chiras' house is part Earthship, part straw bale, part conventional framing. Its careful design emphasizes energy efficiency and the use of recycled or renewable materials and resources.

Long and thin. For maximum solar gain, Dan's house faces south and is one room deep along its west-east axis.

A roof living over your head. The roof over the house's earth-sheltered portion is planted in grasses and wildflowers.

visit to the site told me that it would provide plenty of sunlight to meet my energy needs. I looked at other factors as well; drainage, for example. Because the land was gently sloped and thick with grasses, I could tell there would be no major drainage or erosion problems. I knew that the forest to the west would shield me from the harsh summer sun without blocking too much solar gain in the winter. I also felt that these trees would help shield me from the harsh winter winds, but that they would also diminish my capacity to generate electricity with a wind turbine. As it turns out, though, the winter winds in this valley blow north and south, so I've been able to install a small wind generator to supplement my photovoltaic panels.

The one thing that concerned me was that the land sloped to the east. Solar homes work best if built on south-facing slopes. That arrangement makes it easier to earth shelter a home, and also ensures that the building will be in its own little microclimate because south-facing slopes are always a bit warmer. I figured with a little excavation, however, I could still nestle this home into the hillside to stay warmer in the winter and cooler in the summer.

Q What led you to choose your overall building approach? Briefly describe your building and its major characteristics.

My house consists of four semicircular, bermed tire walls and a modified post-and-beam, straw bale living room all built together in a thin line facing south. The south wall of the house is conventionally framed with 2X6s.

I chose to build a home out of tires because I'm a strong advocate of using recycled and salvaged materials. It seems a shame to me that we build about 1.2 million new homes in this country each year primarily out of wood cut from forests while we throw away about 250 million auto tires. Moreover, building with tires offered me an opportunity to build thermal mass into my home, and to create curved walls. I'm not enamored of those boxlike rooms in a stick-frame home.

I chose an Earthship hybrid because I wanted to build a structure that fit in visually with the rest of the neighborhood. Although the bermed walls are made of tires, the rest of the house is conventionally framed. A standard Earthship would've stood out like a sore thumb. I didn't want to live like my neighbors, but I didn't want to be obtrusive, either. My home is one room deep throughout its length, with south-facing glass, so the sun warms each room independently. There's no need to move warm air around with fans or ducts.

The house is earth-sheltered. The office and bedrooms are built into the hillside, and the roof over these rooms is covered with dirt and replanted with grasses and wildflowers. The north wall of the kitchen is earth-bermed and covered by a superinsulated metal roof. The living room is made from straw bales and is not earth-sheltered.

Q What makes up the load-bearing structure of the foundation, walls, and roof of your house?

In most tire homes out West, the walls don't require a foundation. We had to excavate pretty deeply to earth shelter this home, and the subsoil was quite compact. Thus, the soil required no compaction whatsoever in preparation for tire wall construction. The foundation in front is a standard poured concrete stem wall.

By the way, we packed the tires using a pneumatic tamping device run by a large compressor, which greatly reduced labor. Connecting the walls made from different materials was a challenge. Tire walls that abutted straw bale and frame walls were buttressed by concrete that we formed and poured on the foundation adjacent to the tire wall.

The main roof is framed with 12-inch wooden I-beams, which we attached via a wooden 2X10 top plate bolted to a concrete bond beam formed and poured on top of the tire wall. The bond beam was poured so that it would provide a level plane on which the roof could rest.

Forms for concrete. Here you can see the forms for a conventional concrete footer and stem wall, used on the south side of the house, and for the bond beam atop the tire walls.

Bond beam connection. The concrete bond beam served as a surface on which to connect the tire walls and wood roof framing.

Wall-in-one foundation. Tire walls are wide and stable enough to serve as their own foundation.

Wood here, tire there, straw there. Dan used engineered lumbers and chipboard products to save wood on the framing for the south wall and roof. The tire wall to the east, as yet without framing, will define the kitchen. The straw bale living room will abut the kitchen to the east.

Q What creates and maintains the stable temperature within the building?

My home stays a remarkably constant temperature year-round, although it's a little cooler than I anticipated. Thermal constancy results from a number of factors: the living roof, berming, superinsulation in the walls and ceilings, over 20 tons of thermal mass, and passive solar heating.

The tire walls are bermed into the ground, so they access the huge mass and stable temperature of the earth. In addition, they're insulated with 2-inch rigid foam to reduce heat loss to the cooler-than-room-temperature earth. This home was insulated to the hilt. The ceiling contains 12 inches of recycled cellulose insulation (about R-38). I then applied rigid foam insulation on the inner and outer surfaces of the roof framing, bringing the ceiling insulation to R-65 in most places. In the ceilings under our living roof, the insulation is as high as R-70. The wood frame walls contain 6 inches of the same rigid insulation. The living room walls are insulated with straw bales.

We poured a concrete slab with radiant floor heat as an auxiliary heat supply to the passive solar design. We insulated the stem wall and slab-on-grade foundation for the straw bale portion of the home, but we didn't insulate under the main slab. That was a huge mistake. I've found that my backup heating system has a heck of a time keeping this place warm when the sun's not shining. There's too much heat leaking into the ground. I've tried to remedy the situation by installing crushed rock and horizontal or wing insulation along the perimeter of much of the house. The rocks keep the area dry. The wing insulation, about R-12, extends 2 feet out from the house and reduces heat loss from the foundation to the surrounding earth. We don't yet know if it will make a noticeable difference.

My overhangs are designed for this latitude to regulate solar gain during the fall. We could use a shorter overhang in the spring, when it's still cold up here, and a

Rigid retrofit. Stone and rigid insulation were installed around the building to attempt to remedy heat loss through the uninsulated slab.

longer overhang in the fall, when it's still hot. Overhangs always tend to be a compromise. In retrospect, I'd go with shorter overhangs to get more early-spring solar heating, and draw window shades in the fall.

Q How does the building deal with destructive forces—sun, water, wind, animals, molds, insects, etc.?

I designed the exterior to reduce maintenance. The exterior skin is synthetic stucco over cement stucco base coats. The cement stucco has cracked a fair amount, requiring repair. I consider this a bad choice of material. If I were to do it over again, I'd probably try a lime-sand plaster. The roof's nonliving portion is covered with metal roofing. We used metal-clad wood frame windows with argon-filled, low-e double-pane glass. Without my knowing it, the builders used redwood trim. That would've been acceptable had they used sustainably harvested redwood.

My tire walls are insulated and draped in two layers of 6 mil plastic. We installed a French drain along the periphery to reduce water contact with the wall. Vapor barriers are installed on all framed walls and ceilings, and under the slab.

Q How does the building maintain a nurturing exchange with the outside?

This home is daylighted through south-facing windows and clerestories. Skylights in the hallway leading to my office and the bedrooms provide ample light year-round for plants. Skylights lose a lot of heat, so we've installed homemade insulated slider panels consisting of 1-inch rigid insulation covered with fabric.

Moveable insulation. Skylights help provide daylighting, while insulated sliding panels cover the windows to cut heat loss on cold winter nights and snowy days.

Windows connect us visually to the outside. When the sun shines in, the house comes alive. It's so inviting. Because I've protected most rooms from direct sunlight, the house is quite functional, too. Over the years, I've toured a lot of passive solar homes. One of the biggest problems with many is that they're designed to let sunlight stream into living areas; they're sun-drenched. They perform well heatwise, but the rooms are often so heavily bathed in sunlight that they're unusable during much of the day. Excess direct sunlight can produce overheating, cause damage to interior fabrics and finishes, and create glare that triggers headaches and eyestrain.

There are some simple design tricks to control sunlight and eliminate glare. In my house, the front airlock shields the living room from direct sun and greatly reduces glare. My office is sheltered by a bathroom located adjacent to the office along the south wall. Trombe walls are extremely effective in this regard, too. Clerestory windows can be helpful by delivering sunlight to back walls.

I've also brought the outside into my home by introducing numerous plants. They're all over the place. There's a 40-foot-long planter on one side and two smaller, 15-foot planters on the other side of the hallway leading to the bedrooms and office. Potted plants are in each room. It's a jungle in here. One of the advantages of this is that my home is quite moist. It's great on the sinuses in this otherwise fairly dry climate. The downside of this moisture is that the house is cooler than I'd like. The moisture has caused some mold buildup, too. Unfortunately, an infestation of whiteflies has made it impossible to grow any food in our planters. I've tried everything to get rid of them, but to no avail. The cat views the planters as a gigantic litter box! The interior growing space intended for food production has been turned over completely to hardier plants, such as tropicals, cacti, and succulents.

Q Can you tell me anything else about your home's materials or detailing?

In designing and building this house, I tried to abide by the biological principles of sustainability: conservation, which in this context means efficiently using only what you need; recycling; restoration; and the use of renewable resources. So my home reflects this approach in a great many ways, starting, of course, with its overall design and construction. Also, the appliances, lighting, and other electronics are energy-efficient, and the showers, toilets, and garden irrigation are designed to conserve water. We used many recycled materials, including carpeting, carpet pad, and tile, and asphalt for the driveway; the doors and wood for the cabinets were salvaged; and we used reclaimed paint, too. We also recycled all aluminum, glass, wood, cardboard, and other waste from the construction site.

Q Looking back, what would you do differently?

First, I'd arrange things so that we didn't build over the winter. Second, I'd never build cathedral ceilings. They create too much volume to heat, which is partly why my house is cooler than anticipated. Third, I'd spend more time and money to protect my tire walls from ground moisture. Fourth, I'd use an earthen plaster for all interior wall finishes, rather than a cement stucco. We're now in the process of replastering many of the walls with earthen plaster. Fifth, I'd watch over the subcontractors a bit more carefully. Never have subs working while you're away. For example, I had my driveway installed while I was gone on vacation. The guy not only performed shoddy work that required expensive repairs, but he sold some of my topsoil! Also, always seek the advice of professionals. In retrospect, for example, I should have hired a professional to train my crew on stucco application.

Q What advice do you have for aspiring builders?

Well, although I'd read a lot, and had done odd jobs, I was still a construction greenhorn when I started my house project. Nonetheless, I made sure that I was my own general contractor. This let me choose the builders and subcontractors who were going to do the work. It also gave me control over materials purchasing, which allowed me to chase down sometimes-elusive alternative materials. I had to show up every day or so, too, to discuss details with the builders or to coordinate subcontractors, which kept me involved with the project. I also did some of the work when I could, such as tire packing, stuccoing, and interior finishing such as tiling and painting.

So my advice is to learn everything you can about building before you start. Read books on building homes and on natural building. Be your own contractor if you can, and search for really good subcontractors who are interested in natural building. In my experience, a lot of subs like to do things the way they've always done them. They'll often dismiss proven alternatives to conventional construction because they have no idea what you're talking about and don't want to spend the time finding out. Fire them and search for others.

Also, be realistic. Building is difficult, trying work. It requires interpersonal skills as well as skill in construction. It also demands enormous patience and perseverance. Schedules slip and completion dates are rarely realized. Costs typically escalate by 10 to 50 percent over what was projected, especially if you start changing things.

Perhaps most importantly, I say to go the distance. We can't cross the chasm between our currently unsustainable way of building homes and truly sustainable shelter by taking small leaps. Do everything you can to create a home that's easy on the environment, safe and healthy, and affordable. Remember, there isn't a building material that goes into your home that doesn't have a green substitute. Spend a little extra if you must to buy healthy, resource-responsible building materials.

Inner growth. Numerous plants, including these growing in long hallway planters, bring the outside in and help humidify the air.

GEORGE SWANSON'S "BREATHABLE" HOT-CLIMATE HOME

"ASK QUESTIONS, AND CHALLENGE THE ASSUMPTIONS OF THE BUILDING CULTURE."

George Swanson offers natural home consulting, design, and construction services throughout the United States. In recent years he has completed more than 40 low-toxic, fully "breathing" buildings in 11 different states, using a variety of wall systems, including straw bale, rammed earth, wood-chip block, and aerated-concrete block.

I grew up around Austin, Texas, so I know how brutal the combination of heat and humidity can be there. This Austin-area house, designed by Swanson, uses mass-produced materials in an attempt to efficiently emulate the thermal and air quality performance of time-tested but labor-intensive traditional building methods, such as straw-clay and cob construction. George has combined this approach with design elements that creatively deal with the region's intense climate.

Q **Describe your land and building site, and outline what led you to choose it. What did you do to analyze your site?**

I designed this house for a chemically sensitive client who owns acreage near Austin, Texas. Both my client and I shared a long-time interest and study of Vedic architecture. Many of the Vedic concepts are the forerunners and basis of the ubiquitous, currently popular Feng Shui principles—with emphasis on the importance of orientation to the compass points, especially to the east. In choosing the lot, we applied the classic Vedic criteria of north- and east-sloping land and open areas.

Swanson house.
This home by George Swanson combines ancient principles of Vedic architecture, modern alternative materials, breathable walls, radiant cooling, and other features designed to create a comfortable, healthful living environment in a challenging climate.

Cool and light. Belying the notion that "cool" has to mean dark and shadowy, the house's airy open design, with windows carefully placed for effective daylighting, creates a pleasant, well-lit interior.

Q **What led you to choose your overall building approach? Briefly describe your building and its major characteristics.**

We adhered to the traditional Vedic principles of an eastern entry, a southwest kitchen, a central atrium, and few or no doors or windows to the west and south. Other requirements that tempered the Vedic approach included a Feng Shui interior flow, natural nontoxic materials, natural lighting, natural air exchange and humidity control, and traditional Texas Hill Country aesthetics.

Our main concern was creating an energy-efficient building that maintained a healthy indoor environment. This meant devising strategies that create stable temperatures, don't encourage mold growth, and do allow good air exchange. Put simply, we tried to create a building that breathes by combining organic cellulose and thermal mass. Our cellulose came in the form of recycled wood chips under the slab, in the poured floor, and in the walls; straw in the walls and between floors; and recycled cotton fiber in the attic. Our mass was concrete and rammed earth used in the foundation, slab, and walls.

Q **What makes up the load-bearing structure of the foundation, walls, and roof of your house?**

Our site had solid limestone rock at a depth 8 inches below grade. We poured a continuous, steel-reinforced concrete footer that was tied into the limestone every 24 inches by rebar placed in holes drilled into the rock. We also placed rebar in the concrete that extended out of the footer every 16 inches into the hollow cavities of our block walls, thus tying them to the foundation.

The walls are constructed of 12-inch-wide, clay-treated, concrete-stabilized wood-chip block, specifically Faswall block. Though they look much like a standard concrete block, these blocks are only one-third the weight. Each 16-inch-long block has two hollow cavities, each approximately 8 by 5 inches. We placed 4-inch straw panel inserts in the cavities toward the outside of each block, and filled the remaining cavity space with either concrete and rebar or rammed earth, depending on the structural requirements. About every fourth cavity was concrete and rebar.

The roof is conventionally framed with prefabricated, engineered roof trusses placed 24 inches on center and sheathed with ⅝-inch plywood.

Q **What creates and maintains the stable temperature within the building?**

The building holds temperature very well. The walls are a combination of thermal mass and insulation wrapped in a jacket of breathing material. The thermal mass is concrete and rammed earth, the insulation is the 4-inch straw panel inserts I just mentioned, and the breathable jacket is made up of the hollow-core, clay-impregnated wood-chip blocks. The thermal mass is actually "outsulated" by the straw panel inserts set into the outer portion of the blocks' hollow cores. This isolates the concrete and rammed earth thermal mass that fills the inside portion of the hollow block forms, so that this mass won't be exposed directly to outside temperature fluctuations. In addition, the block itself has insulation value because it's predominantly cellulose in the form of wood.

The house's poured floor, unlike a conventional concrete poured floor, also has intrinsic insulation value because it's comprised of a mixture of 70 percent clay-treated wood chips and 30 percent concrete over a 2-inch bed of dry clay-impregnated wood chips. The dry bed of chips also prevents the migration of moisture, eliminating the need for a plastic vapor barrier. In addition, the chips add a bit more spring to the composite floor, making it more comfortable to walk on.

Insulation in the attic is comprised of 18 inches of blown-in cotton, with insulation dams at the fascia edge to create an air space through the boxed eaves to the ridge for roof ventilation. Fourteen-inch floor trusses between the top and bottom floors are filled with shredded straw treated with borax and a clay soup. Natural cooling ventilation is created through the central open atrium, which has a cupola "cool tower" and a closable attic fan at the top.

Of course, in addition to evaluating how a house holds temperature, it's important to scrutinize how it creates the temperature in the first place. There are two basic approaches: radiant and convective. Radiant heating and cooling is long-wave energy that cuts through the air temperature to heat or cool your dense bone mass. Convective heating and cooling, such as that produced by a conventional HVAC system, is air movement that affects only your skin temperature. Your bones can retain cool or heat for approximately three and one-half hours, and your skin for only 10 minutes. This 10-minute cycle of constant skin temperature change created by convective air movement is unhealthy. Therefore, radiant heating and cooling is vastly preferable.

Creating radiant heat is relatively easy. Sunlight, fire, and hot water are all sources of radiant heat. Since this house is well-insulated, with a lot of mass to help keep its temperature stable, radiant heat for its 2,400 square feet can be supplied by one hot-water radiant unit that's heated from the household water heater. In order to get bank financing for the house, we were required to install small baseboard electric heaters in each bedroom; they've never been used.

Radiant cool, on the other hand, is available through cold water only. Therefore, accessing radiant cool is more difficult because it forces the building envelope to deal

Ventilation, naturally. The home has no ductwork. All venting is driven by natural convection created by a cooling tower and strategically placed wall vents and door transoms. The tower extends above an open atrium (left) and is capped with a roof cupola (right). On hot days, the attic fan mounted in the cupola pulls air from wall vents and door transoms up through the cooling tower and out the cupola.

with changing levels of air moisture. Fortunately, the wood chips, straw, concrete, and rammed earth in the walls of our building are able to take on and let off water vapor as the humidity changes. Radiant cooling for the building is provided by a closed-loop, cool-water swamp pump. A swamp pump is an evaporative cooler. It brings cool water moving through pipes into contact with warm indoor air, causing evaporation, which takes heat from the air. The result is radiant cooling. Our swamp pump accesses cool water from 1,800 linear feet of pipe at the bottom of a 28,000-gallon cistern buried 9 feet deep. In addition, dense trees to the south of the building are fitted with water misters that drip onto the concrete tile roof to slow down attic heat buildup in summer. This water is collected and recycled into the cistern. Also, the western side of the building has a continuous, deep porch and narrow slit windows to protect the interior from the hot western sun. The house is performing so well that we haven't even needed to use the swamp cooler over the last two summers.

Q How does the building deal with destructive forces—sun, water, wind, animals, molds, insects, etc.?

We were careful to place durable materials in the path of natural forces. For example, the crystallized wood chips used in the Faswall blocks, as well as in and under the slab, are processed with a fine clay treatment that acts like diatomaceous earth, killing insects by scratching their exoskeletons and causing them to dehydrate. The crystallization process of treating the wood chips also extracts all the sugar, acid, and oils from the wood, thus removing possible food sources and discouraging mold and fungi. In addition, the clay/cellulose wall system promotes the rapid diffusion of water and air molecules from the dense concrete and rammed earth mass. The end result is a wall surface environment that isn't conducive to mold growth and is very unattractive to insects and rodents. We used a one-coat, low-cost, site-mixed, durable, breathable stucco to cover and complement our breathable wall system.

Roofs in Texas take an incredible beating from the sun, so we installed a light-colored concrete tile roof: concrete to handle the UV and freeze-thaw cycles, and a light color to reduce temperature buildup. We used 4-foot, 6-inch overhangs on all sides of the roof to protect the exterior walls from direct sun, wind, and rain.

Radiant cool, and heat too. This view is from the main entry into the foyer, or "Brahmastan." The small, rock-covered garden to the right is open to the earth below and has a recirculating water mister that accesses cold water from the bottom of the house's underground cistern, providing evaporative cooling. The upper grill past the fountain houses a closed loop of cold cistern water flowing over a car radiator, another source of radiant cooling. The water is pumped by roof-mounted photovoltaic panels. The lower grill houses another car radiator, this one plumbed to the home's main hot water tank. During cold weather, hot water is pumped through the system to produce radiant heat.

No mold. The window in this bathroom is set into stuccoed wood-chip block above the protective tile. Although the area has been soaked with water daily for more than five years, the unprotected section shows no signs of mold or moisture damage.

Q How does the building maintain a nurturing exchange with the outside?

As I've said, this building utilizes a "breathing wall" system. With a breathing wall, the entire wall mass is a passive air exchanger. Though air doesn't pass through the wall freely, differences in air pressures between the inside and outside cause some air to diffuse slowly through the wall. Any air that travels through literally miles of clay-impregnated wood chips is usually 70 to 90 percent of the indoor temperature by the time it reaches the inside. This is in marked contrast to the cold or hot air traveling through leaking doors and windows. That's why we chose quality windows. The combination of a breathable wall and quality doors and windows means slow conditioned air exchange through the entire wall mass, not air leakage through doors and windows. This creates some air exchange without creating temperature fluctuations.

Another good way for humans to access clean air is, of course, to go outside! So it's important to create comfortable transitions between the inside and outside environments. The house's 8-foot-deep porch covers the western side of the building, which invites people outside even in the uncompromising heat of a Texas summer.

Cool kitchen. The louvered box above the cabinets houses yet another car radiator that's plumbed to the cistern to produce cooling. Says Swanson, "Don't try this on a sheetrocked, nonbreathing conventional building; every sheetrock screw would show rust in two weeks from the moisture created by the evaporative cooling." In contrast, the wood-chip block walls in this kitchen are rust- and mold-free.

As for systems, the home has a "gravel marsh" wetland septic system that processes all black and greywater from the home through two fully sealed, 7 x 25-foot, 20-inch-deep gravel beds. These beds feature miniature bulrush and cattail plants, which produce mineral-rich, potable water that we pump to raised organic garden beds. This is the full septic system for the four-bedroom, three-bath home.

Water is provided by a rain catchment system featuring a 28,000-gallon cistern. Three-quarters of the cistern is buried, and the quarter above grade is terraced with rock, and is the home of plants that provide additional shading for the vulnerable southwest corner of the home. The tank is the sole source for all water needs for the property and provides enough storage to supply water through a six-month period without rainfall. The concrete tile roof is self-skinning, which means it's designed for freeze-thaw climates. This feature ensures that the tile's top surface remains non-porous to keep the drinking water clean.

About one-third of all the electrical needs for this all-electric home is provided by a 20-panel southern array of 120-volt rooftop solar panels. All the lights and fans and a few selected outlets are direct 12-volt solar, eliminating the need for an inverter. The system has eight 12-volt golf cart batteries and can operate up to five days without sun. If the batteries run low, the system recharges itself automatically from the grid.

Gravel marsh septic system. Two 25-foot-long gravel beds, one planted in cattails and bulrush and the other with hyacinths and lotus, make up the home's septic system. Blackwater flows through the beds 20 inches below grade, so there's no odor. The system discharges nutrient-rich potable water that irrigates nearby garden beds.

Q Can you tell me anything else about the home's materials or detailing?

By carefully choosing modern materials and applying some intelligent design, we were able to emulate the great physics and feel of a hand-packed straw-clay or cob building without the excessive building cost. In order for a building to breathe, materials need to be able to adjust to humidity changes by taking on and letting off water freely. Most organic fibers, such as the wood chips, cotton, and straw we used, do this quite well. Secondly, air exchange has to be encouraged. Air pressure differences between the inside and the outside environments will naturally allow exchange through a wall if no impenetrable barriers are put in the way. A thick wall that combines thermal mass with organic insulation without employing vapor barriers is the best way to accomplish this. Third, we have to encourage what I call "electromagnetic breathing": the balance of paramagnetic (positive) and diamagnetic (negative) charges of materials.

An example of this natural "breathing" occurs between human bone (+) and tissue (-), which creates a push-pull pulsation that is largely responsible for maintaining, replacing, and flushing cells from the human body. It has been proven that if your heart was strictly a pump it would need to be roughly the size of a small house to pump blood through the 60,000-plus miles of major blood vessels in an average adult. Placing these delicate mechanisms, our hearts, out of the context of the natural balances of earth and vegetation has been a dangerous development. I believe that it's no minor

Landscape cistern. A 28,000-gallon rain-catchment cistern provides all water to the home and its surrounding gardens. When full, the cistern holds a six-month supply. The cistern is kidney-shaped, with 9 feet of its volume buried underground. The 3 feet above ground are terraced with rock, creating raised beds for plants. Notice the 8-foot-wide porch overhang, which covers the west side of the house and protects it from the harsh afternoon sun.

coincidence that modern urban people have many times the number of heart failures of their agrarian ancestors. In my opinion, it's important to our health to build walls out of biocompatible materials that create a natural electromagnetic balance.

Most of the civilized world has been, and still is, constructed with biocompatible materials and building techniques. Historically, biocompatible construction has meant the bringing together of naturally occurring thermal mass materials—such as wood, earth, stone, cement, and plaster—with insulation such as wood chips, straw, assorted other forms of cellulose, and air gaps in ways that allow these materials to "breathe" properly. The result has been some of the most comfortable dwellings on earth.

PV system. A roof-mounted photovoltaic system provides one third of the electricity for the all-electric home. If the sun doesn't shine for an extended period, the system automatically recharges its batteries from the municipal power grid.

But traditional approaches were developed in a specific context that often doesn't fit the modern paradigm. Among the traditional methods of combining insulation, thermal mass, and breathability are straw-clay, cob, straw bale, and cordwood construction. All these systems work great, except that they evolved under the assumption of low-cost labor, 10 kids in the family, and unlimited time—10 years with all 10 kids helping. Straw-clay construction, for example, requires building two full frames, an inner and outer, usually separated by about 18 inches. Temporary forms must then be built on the outside of both frames and stuffed by hand with clay-soaked straw, layer by layer, until the wall is completed. The results are beautiful, but it's an unbearably time-consuming process. Having personally built cob, straw-clay, and straw bale buildings, I can attest to the somewhat labor-intensive and torturously slow methods involved in these traditional systems.

The modern solution to labor- and time-intensity is mass production. A few examples of modern mass-production-based attempts at blending thermal mass, insulation, and breathability are AAC block (aerated autoclave concrete), clay-treated wood-chip block, compacted strawboard panels, pumicecrete, concrete-bonded foam-chip block, and ultralightweight fiber-reinforced concrete tilt-up walls. Of these materials, only the wood-chip blocks have also proven to be electromagnetically balanced and therefore 100 percent biocompatible.

But all the modern alternative systems I've mentioned, much like their historical predecessors, typically consume between 40 to 70 percent less energy, and typically have a longevity several times greater than conventionally built structures. They're usually sounder structurally, and are many times quieter acoustically than their modern counterparts. In addition, they're more resistant to mold, mildew, fire, and earthquakes. And, unlike their ancestors, these modern alternatives to conventional building are cost- and time-competitive.

Q What advice do you have for aspiring builders?

My advice for would-be builders is to ask questions and challenge the assumptions of the building culture in which you find yourself. With even the most cursory review of the most common building systems currently available in North America, it quickly becomes apparent that the protection of your health and well-being has taken a secondary role to short-term profits for reaching short-term goals. That being the case, it's up to you to educate yourself about the possibilities and options. Ultimately, only you will determine if the space you live in will be a healthy environment. Your lungs, heart, and nervous system deserve the best.

CHUCK MARSH'S LITTLE BUILDING IN AN INTENTIONAL COMMUNITY

"WE NEED TO BE DESIGNING BUILDINGS THAT CONNECT US TO THE NATURAL WORLD RATHER THAN DISCONNECT US FROM IT."

Chuck Marsh describes himself as "an amateur natural builder, a pretty fair earth plasterer, and a small-time cultural evolutionary who just can't seem to stay in the house when the outdoor life calls." He's also a permaculture/ecological design teacher and consultant, a landscape horticulturist, and a founding member of the Earthaven community, a growing "permaculture-based ecovillage" in western North Carolina.

One of Earthaven's many happy obsessions is experimentation with and development of sustainable building techniques appropriate to their situation. Through building and working together on community homes and structures, Earthaven is slowly developing experience relevant to their exact environmental and social situation. In other words, Earthaven is engaged in alternative building, as we've defined it in this book, on a village scale. It's in this context that Chuck Marsh has constructed a small building that will eventually serve as his office, but that's presently his temporary abode while he plans and constructs his permanent house.

Marsh house. Chuck Marsh will use the experience and insight he gained while creating this small, post-and-beam frame, passive solar structure—his future office—to build his house. For now, though, the comfortable earth-plastered building is home.

Q Describe your land and building site, and outline what led you to choose it. What did you do to analyze your site?

I've been involved in the Earthaven ecovillage project since its inception in 1992. We spent two years searching for a place before buying our land, about 320 acres of forest, in 1994. We spent several more years getting to know the land, and planning and developing the community infrastructure, before opening up permanent site-holding leases for selection.

Choosing my site was a combination intuitive, social, and practical process that took several years. I'd chase solstice sunsets and sunrises around the land and watch solar shadows move across the hills. I'd use my body as an observation tool, feeling temperature, wind, and humidity changes. I'd observe surface water flows during downpours. I did this all over the Earthaven landscape, often alone and sometimes with fellow members. This was a process of discovery that ultimately led to our community land-use documents and settlement locations, our neighborhoods.

Not the first. Chuck wasn't the first person to decide that this particular spot would make a good place for a home. He found these ancient artifacts on his house site.

In the end, I chose my site-holding and neighborhood for its relative proximity to the village center area, easy physical access, workable slope, solar access, and excellent microclimatic qualities. As it turns out I'm not the first person who's considered it a pleasant location. I've found numerous Stone Age artifacts on the site, indicating long-term settlement in the distant past.

Once I settled on a site, a quarter-acre "lot," if you will, I pitched a tent nearby. With the help of some friends, I mapped the site, including creating a contour drawing with contour intervals every foot. We then engaged in permaculture-based landscape planning, exploring all sorts of placement options and defining my needs for home and landscape and life. This took a lot of time, but I think it's wise to spend time planning in an effort to avoid costly errors down the line. Through this process, we sited the small hut/office/sleeping loft/shop that I've built, as well as my future home, other possible structures, and earthworks for small ponds and gardens.

Q What led you to choose your overall building approach? Briefly describe your building and its major characteristics.

The hut's design was somewhat serendipitous. I needed a first structure on my site to serve as a temporary dwelling and permanent office while I built a house. We had some peeled poles from clearing the site, so we decided to use them as a basic frame and then build onto this framework with a variant of a truss-wall system developed here at Earthaven. This system is basically a nonstructural box or form added to a structural post-and-beam frame as a cavity for insulation and a surface for interior and exterior finishes.

Truss-wall system. This end-on view of a truss system like the one Chuck used shows a truss partially stuffed with an insulating clay-slip straw mixture. Scrap wood lath is attached to both sides of the truss. At the bottom is the beginning of an attached cob wall.

There are a couple of basic advantages to the truss-wall system. First, it uses wood that would otherwise be wasted in the milling process. We have our own wood mill, and most of the truss-wall materials are 1x3 and 1x4 sawn lumber salvaged from the edges of milled logs. Second, you can build walls of whatever thickness you desire, with excellent thermal performance and minimal thermal breaks. This lets you use natural insulation materials such as clay slip mixtures, as well as blown cellulose, which is what I used. The clay slip mixtures consist of cellulose in the form of straw

Clay slip/straw infill. An insulating mixture of clay slip and straw fills the space within this wall truss. Scrap-wood lath on each side provides a surface for interior and exterior finishes. Chuck used blown cellulose to insulate the truss walls in his house.

Post-and-truss wall. Round poles mounted on concrete piers form the structural framework for the truss-wall system.

or wood chips coated with clay slip (clay suspended in water) and stuffed into a form, in this case the truss-wall framework. The clay slip mixes are generally less insulative, say R-1.5 to 2.5 per inch on average, than commercial recycled cellulose or fiberglass batts. Thus, thicker walls are needed to provide the same insulation value. This wall system, in combination with a post-and-beam load-bearing frame, can provide the needed wall thickness to make these natural insulating materials effective.

I'm familiar with most natural building approaches, but this building system was evolving at Earthaven, and since it used materials that I had from my site clearing— poles and lumber—I wanted to give it a try. This approach is wood-intensive, but in our case much of the material used is waste from milling. Also, wood can be a bioregionally sustainable resource for residents of the Great Eastern Forest, otherwise known as most of the eastern United States and southeastern Canada. Of course, this is only true if those residents are responsible in their land stewardship choices.

Combining wood with sand, clay, a bit of straw, ingenuity, lots of help, and a careful use of some manufactured materials, I was able to create a simple structure in way *more* time than I ever could've imagined. In my next project, my house, I'll incorporate what I've learned using this building approach to refine both the design and detailing.

Q **What makes up the load-bearing structure of the foundation, walls, and roof of your house?**

The walls' structural posts are supported by poured concrete pads and formed concrete piers. There's a gravel trench foundation around the walls that's linked to 6 inches of gravel below a 5-inch-thick cob subfloor. Actually, it's *the* floor for the foreseeable future. Eventually, I plan to lay some ¾-inch-thick slate slabs on another 2 inches of cob floor base, and grout the joints. I have a foundation stem wall of rammed earthcrete bricks laid with lime mortar. We made the bricks on-site from a mix containing earth and less than 10 percent Portland cement.

The wall structure is a round-pole post-and-beam frame made from trees cleared from my site. We attached the 7- to 8-inch-diameter poles to the foundation by impaling each pole on a piece of rebar that was left protruding from each pier.

Homemade building blocks. Chuck made and used concrete-stabilized rammed-earth blocks to build his house's stem walls. The blocks here have been sitting out in the weather for years without noticeable deterioration.

Installed between the structural posts is an 8- to 10-inch-wide Earthaven truss-wall framework like the one I just described. I used 6-inch poles for sill plates on the north and south walls. On the shorter east and west walls, I installed a pair of 2x6s on edge, spaced to accommodate the width of the trusses. The attached tool shed and porch are of conventional wood frame construction with locust structural posts.

Because I planned to install a trial living roof on my

building, I spaced my roof rafters closer together than usual to accommodate the extra loads. I used milled, full-size 2x6s spaced 12 to 14 inches apart.

Q What creates and maintains the stable temperature within the building?

Around here we have four real seasons encompassing six cool or cold months and six warm or hot months; occasional high humidity; frequent overcast skies; and lots of precipitation. My approach to creating a stable temperature in these conditions was to heavily insulate, seal out air leaks, and build in lots of mass. The mass in the earthen floor and lime-clay plaster wall acts as a thermal flywheel. Put simply, this means that it takes that mass a long time to heat up or cool down, which gives the building a lot of temperature stability. There's cellulose insulation blown fairly densely into the truss framework in the walls, and also between the rafters. I like everything about cellulose but its installation, which is a big pain to get right and needs careful detailing if you're going to use it in the walls. I also used 2 inches of rigid foam to insulate the foundation, and salvaged-foam scraps on top of the roof decking.

Rugged roof. Milled rafters were closely spaced on large round pole beams to create a structure strong enough to bear the weight of living-roof materials and plantings.

I used passive solar design, utilizing south-facing windows, shallow building depth, and the interior mass I just mentioned to accomplish solar gain. Only about 7 percent of my glass faces east; 12 percent faces west, and the rest faces south. I'll be installing insulating curtains soon to reduce heat loss when the sun isn't shining. I have adequate roof overhangs for summer shading and winter sun access. My windows and doors are placed to provide cross-ventilation and to take advantage of predominant summer wind directions for summer cooling. Deciduous trees to the southwest give me shade from the afternoon summer sun, but allow winter sun in. All these factors combine to eliminate the need for any mechanical summer cooling, and greatly reduce winter heating requirements. At present, my only supplement to passive solar heating is a small Ecotherm direct-vented gas heater for occasional winter use as needed. It's clean, efficient, and maintains excellent indoor air quality.

Built-in warmth, and backup too. Natural materials and inviting colors and textures combine to create a welcoming warmth. A direct-vented propane heater provides backup heat on exceptionally cold days. Grouted slate will cover the cob subfloor.

Classic passive solar. South-facing glass, shallow building depth, thermal mass, and insulation combine to keep Chuck's little building warm in winter and cool in summer.

Q **How does the building deal with destructive forces—sun, water, wind, animals, molds, insects, etc.?**

I'll approach this question from the bottom of the building up. I used flashing as a vapor barrier and termite shield between the concrete piers and wooden posts. The gravel trench foundation and gravel bed under my floor should help keep water from condensing or moving by capillary action to places where it could cause damage. So far I've experienced no moisture problems. To make sure this remains the case, I intend to make a few small landscape-drainage corrections to more effectively drain away surface water. My walls are covered with recycled wood scrap lath and covered with a lime-clay plaster both inside and out. I have good overhangs to keep driving rain off my walls. And I have a living roof, with which I'm still experimenting.

I really think that lime-clay plasters are the ticket. They're durable, easily repairable, and vitally important for breathing-wall systems because they wick moisture away from the organic building components. My experience with lime-clay plasters is that they stand up well to moisture, don't support mold growth, are repellant to insects, and provide good rodent protection if close attention is paid to detailing the places where different materials join. If you're going to plaster, it's crucial to design plaster stops into the framing details around doors, windows, and edges.

Because of evidence of powder-post beetles in some of my sawn lumber, and because none of it was kiln-dried, I elected to use a borax-based preservative on all wood used in the building. It deters insects and has antifungal qualities. Wood-eating insects of various kinds, as well as molds and fungi, can be a big problem around here. Kiln-drying is another option because it kills insects living in the green wood, as well as drying it out to make it somewhat less susceptible to mold.

I don't expect the building to need much maintenance for a while. The main upkeep will probably be in protecting the exposed wooden surfaces. I also don't

Useful ooze. When applied, earth plaster oozes between gaps in the wood lath, creating lips that help the plaster grip the wall

Exterior plaster. An earth plaster containing hydrated lime covers the exterior of Chuck's house. This is the rough or "scratch" coat. The finish coat will come later, but there's no hurry; the house is sufficiently protected against the elements for now.

Interior plaster. Chuck used earth plaster for his interior, too. Here you can see the rammed-earth-block stem wall and round-pole sill plate below a south-facing window.

anticipate needing to do much maintenance on the lime-clay plasters for some time, unless I tire of the exterior finishes and decide to do some artistic tinkering.

Q How does the building maintain a nurturing exchange with the outside?

I love that question, because I strongly believe we need to be designing buildings that connect us to the natural world rather than disconnect us from it. Why do you think they call it "thinking outside the box?" The box is the building! I don't want to live in a box, so I'm trying to design my living spaces to keep me connected.

Building small helps. Creating outdoor places to do indoor activities also helps. For instance, we all just love our neighborhood outdoor summer kitchen. Moving work spaces outside also is helpful. My attached workshop is open on one side, next to the garden.

Another factor that I can't say too much about is the use of lime-clay plasters and breathing walls to control interior moisture and therefore create a healthy indoor air quality. The lime-clay walls, plus good daylighting and ventilation, seem to have just about eliminated any summer mildew problems. I chose recycled cellulose insulation over other natural insulation materials, such as straw, because I think it's less prone to mold problems, and I have a high sensitivity to mold. This sensitivity actually is a major factor in many of my design decisions. I think that insufficient attention to mold and moisture issues is a big shortcoming for many natural buildings and amateur builders. It can lead to what I'd call "toxic natural building syndrome." Who cares if you used all natural materials if you end up with a building that's toxic or rotting away beneath your feet?

I don't have indoor plumbing in my little hut, because it's ultimately going to be an office space. I get water from a supply line to my site from the community reservoir. I also can get water from the neighborhood kitchen, which is about 30 yards from my hut. I use the neighborhood composting toilet and will switch to a humanure bucket system during the winter. My lights and electricity come from solar arrays on the neighborhood common building. I designed in daylighting throughout the structure. This is easy to accomplish in tiny buildings, and mine is only 10 feet deep.

Well-lit loft. All too often, sleeping lofts, sufficient light, and good air circulation don't go together. Chuck's bright, cozy little loft is a nice exception.

Q Can you tell me anything else about your home's materials or detailing?

Basically, I used as many materials from my site as possible, but didn't push it where bought materials were the right choice. I took detailing very seriously. Choosing good materials is only half the story. It's just as important that you install them correctly.

When I built my living roof, I laid down a deck of 1x6s and covered it with two layers of roofing felt, or tarpaper. I insulated and vented the ceiling cavity below the decking. Over the layers of tarpaper, I laid in scraps of salvaged polyisocyanurate foam, then a layer of heavy-duty landscape fabric. On top of that, I placed an EPDM rubber roof membrane and then another, double, layer of landscape fabric.

I raised up the roof edges with black locust 2x8s to create a box to hold the living roof materials. Then I draped the EPDM membrane over the edges of the 2x8 box and secured it with aluminum edging designed for the job. I then covered the whole

Living roof. Left: Chuck used 2x8s to raise his roof's perimeter to hold the living roof materials, then draped and secured a waterproof membrane over the edges. Right: A layer of porous, broken-brick aggregate holds enough water to support drought-tolerant succulent plants. Brick and stone pathways connect different areas.

roof with a layer of lightweight aggregate material. I used mostly broken-brick nuggets, which are superior to gravel in both weight and porosity—they hold water in their pores and release it slowly. Porosity is important for living roofs, because you need to be able to store enough water within the thin layer of growth medium to keep plants healthy. I chose a lightweight living roof system, so, even with the porous aggregate, it doesn't have a huge water-holding capacity. That's why I planted hardy, drought-tolerant alpine and Mediterranean plants, such as succulent sedums and sempervivums.

Q Looking back, what would you do differently?

I decided to build a structure that would legally fall outside of local building codes, which meant that the entire building could have no more than a 12-by-12-foot footprint. Here, I probably made a mistake that created unnecessary design constraints. For instance, because we set the posts nearly 12 feet apart on the south wall, I wasn't able to both comply with the 12-foot limitation and set the wall trusses to the outside of the beams. Therefore, the beams ended up partially buried in the walls. This isn't a good idea for many reasons, including completely complicating the detailing of interior and exterior walls. The result was huge additional labor expenditures and lots of unnecessary hassles. This approach also caused me to lose some insulation value, because the insulation-filled trusses are between the structural posts instead of wrapping the entire building.

Also, because I used no plywood in construction, I spent a lot of time and did a lot of chiseling installing 1x4 diagonal bracing everywhere I could fit it in. This complicated the project, because no matter how carefully I placed the braces they affected my options for window placement. So I ended up with a kind of funky window arrangement. I don't think this would present such a problem in a larger structure. This is one area in which tiny size probably worked against me. Looking back, I'd say that this tiny building required an awful lot of work for the small amount of space provided. I probably could've doubled the size of the structure with very little additional work or cost.

I didn't hire an engineer or architect for this small project, but I intend to on my house, just to make sure all the loading details are covered, and that I haven't made any serious design mistakes. Also, getting professionals to sign off on my design will help move any natural building methods through the permitting process without a hassle.

Q What advice do you have for aspiring builders?

If your goal is sustainability, you have to reevaluate the priorities of our modern culture. Take the concept of building maintenance, for example. In my studies of ecosystem dynamics, I've learned that mature ecosystems devote a large portion of their energy budget to system maintenance, not new production. If this is the case for ecosystems, and for little Greek ladies who whitewash a portion of their house each day as a part of their everyday life, then why does maintenance get such a bad rap in our modern world? Maintenance is really loving care manifested. In our relationships, both with our dwellings and other humans, we express our love through the attention and care we give.

In my opinion, the amount of focus put on this attention and care is the essence of the difference between a taker culture and a stewardship-based culture. Which one

Welcome in. Reflecting the owner-builder's spirit and personality, a bright and colorful entry with a sunburst mosaic greets visitors to Chuck's small house.

is the more sustainable in the long haul? The answer is obvious. A part of recreating a culture of caring is to revalue the maintenance function in our daily lives, and an important part of that process is to learn to love our buildings through their maintenance.

What would such a paradigm shift do for someone looking to build a home? For one thing, it would open them up to a variety of building materials shunned by the modern construction world, starting with the very ground beneath their feet. You can dig up a bit of that ground and create an earth plaster, for example. Earth plasters are fun to apply, have an intrinsic beauty, and can help to create a building with healthy indoor air quality. All they require in return is a bit more care and attention than vinyl siding.

DOUG AND NELLE'S POST-AND-BEAM STRAW BALE HOUSE

"A HOUSE STARTS AS A DREAM. YOU NEED TO START WITH A CLEAR DREAM OF WHAT YOU WANT TO DO."

Doug and Nelle's story is a great example of the patient approach, a good path to a good house. Doug had experience as a cabinetmaker when he decided to start working in construction to get the skills needed to build his own home. He spent several years working on various building projects, including houses incorporating straw as a material. During this time, he and Nelle bought property in rural western North Carolina, and got to know it by living there in a trailer. They researched and discussed different construction approaches, and eventually focused on straw bale. Nelle had a solid income as a nurse, which allowed Doug to work full-time on their house once the project started. When Nelle wasn't working for money, she worked on the house too.

From our conversations, I identified two important factors that seem to have helped make Doug and Nelle's house a success: they were clear about their goals, and they went about construction with an attention to detail that only owner-builders can muster. The result is a beautifully crafted, energy-efficient home.

Q Describe your land and building site, and outline what led you to choose it. What did you do to analyze your site?

All we wanted was a decent, sunny house site with some flowing water. Unfortunately, our simple goals were popular. We told one realtor that we wanted south-facing land with a stream and some flat area, and his response was, "You and everybody else; good luck." We spent almost a year looking for land. We ended up buying 6½ acres made up of two-thirds pasture and one-third forest. It has a

Doug and Nelle's house. Inside and out, this handcrafted home reflects its owner-builders' thoughtfulness and attention to detail. Post-and-beam frame, straw bale infill walls, solar water heating, and exterior and interior stucco finishes are among its many features.

southeastern exposure and the prerequisite creek with enough of an elevation drop to have hydroelectric potential.

Before buying the land, we knew that we wanted to build our own house and make it as sustainable as we could afford, and we'd spent time looking at different building techniques. Once we owned something, we pulled a travel trailer onto the property and naively moved into the next phase of our adventure. We spent time siting the house and noting drainage patterns. We ended up facing the house 40 degrees east of south, losing some passive solar efficiency, to take better advantage of the view and to avoid looking directly at a neighbor's house.

Q **What led you to choose your overall building approach? Briefly describe your building and its major characteristics.**

We decided to build a post-and-beam structure with straw bale infill. We appreciated the insulation potential of straw bale and we fell in love with the look and feel of the deep walls. However, not everyone was as excited about straw as we were; we had to get architectural and engineering assistance to satisfy the building code officials. When you tell people you want to build with straw, they immediately conjure up the three little pigs and want lots of proof that the house isn't going to fall down. We chose a simple design, for ease of heating and so the structure would blend in with the local architecture. The white stucco exterior with a tin roof is reminiscent of an old farmhouse. However, the solar panels on the roof do distinguish us from the typical house in this region.

Post-and-beam detail. A post and two homemade laminated beams make up a corner for the first floor.

Q **What makes up the load-bearing structure of the foundation, walls, and roof of your house?**

The foundation is somewhat standard: concrete footer with concrete block stem walls. However, we poured a wide concrete bond beam on the top course of block to accommodate the thickness of the straw bales. We stuck rebar into the bond beam vertically and left about 24 inches sticking out on which to impale the bales after the sill plate was installed. There's also a foundation to support the masonry stove centered in the house. The addition we're completing now is a slab-on-grade with the same use of rebar and sill plate.

The walls of the house are primarily post-and-beam frame with metal diagonal braces and straw infill. Since the building's south side has so much glass, it seemed futile to cut standard-size straw bales and retie them to fit into that small space. So instead, we used conventional 2x6 framing and insulation to fill in the post-and-beam frame on the first-floor south wall, and in the second-floor dormers on the north and south sides of the house. The final look of the house did suffer somewhat, though. We used open-web floor trusses to save wood and to allow a long unsupported span. The subfloor is plywood.

The straw bales are stacked like bricks on the foundation sill plates. The protruding rebar helps to stabilize them. The main house sill plate is pressure-treated wood. In the addition, we used locally milled locust for the sill plate. We wanted to avoid using pressure-treated lumber as much as possible, but cost was a factor.

Rebar ready, bales next. Rebar pins were embedded in the concrete bond beam that was poured on top of the stem wall. The first course of straw bales will be impaled on the pins to tie the straw infill to the foundation.

Metal connectors attach the posts to the sill plates. We used metal diagonal braces attached from the beam to the sill plate. Often people insert window and door frames, or bucks, as independent units into their straw bale walls. Instead, we used standard framing with 2x6 jack and king studs to tie our frames into the sill and beam. This framing is also attached to the metal diagonals. We wanted deep interior window sills and door openings, so the framing was all placed to the exterior of the building.

Our roof is standard wood-frame construction with a combination of trusses and rafters with plywood sheathing. We used a steep, 12/12 (or 45 degree) pitch because we liked the look. We also used shed-roof dormers to add space in the second-floor bedroom and bathroom.

Q **What creates and maintains the stable temperature within the building?**

The straw bales have the greatest impact on creating a very stable and comfortable interior temperature, and the thick plaster and stucco help, too. For the framed south wall, we used conventional fiberglass insulation and attached 1 inch of rigid foam on the outside. We used fiberglass with an attached radiant barrier in the ceilings and floors. The bubble radiant barrier insulates better than the reflective variety. We also insulated our foundation with rigid foam.

Straw infill insulation. Straw bales fill spaces between the framing, creating thick walls with good thermal and acoustic insulation values.

Just add water. These roof-mounted solar panels produce hot water for domestic use, and for the radiant floor heating system.

Masonry wood stove. Doug and Nelle bought a stove kit from Norbert Senf (see page 86) and had it installed by a local mason.

We were lucky to acquire used solar hot-water panels from Nelle's family. As an afterthought, we retrofitted hydronic (radiant) floor heating under the wood floor as a backup heat system. The primary heating comes from the masonry wood stove. This stove produces the most even, comfortable heat we've ever experienced.

There are no hot and cold pockets like you get with other wood stoves. After a quick, hot fire, it evenly radiates heat for 24 hours. For hot water, we ran a heat coil through the firebox and out the back of the masonry stove to a 220-gallon hot-water storage tank. Water is also heated in the solar panels mounted on our roof and stored in the storage tank. If need be, this water is further heated by an on-demand water heater that is plumbed into the loop. Together, these heat sources create all the hot water we need, both for domestic use and the hydronic floor heating system.

Woods and pasture. This is the view of Doug and Nelle's home from the edge of their woods and across the pasture.

The same elements that keep the house warm also work to keep it cool. We kept the floor plan open so air could easily move through the structure, and used windows that open out to direct the air into the house. We open up the house in the cool evenings of the summer months and close the windows in the mornings. The house stays cool and very comfortable, even when the days are hot. Eventually, we'll have plants to the south and west that will shade the house in the hotter seasons. We're planning a trellised patio on the west side of the house to protect us from the hot western sun.

Q How does the building deal with destructive forces—sun, water, wind, animals, molds, insects, etc.?

Any form of cellulose, whether it's wood, straw, or some other organic fiber, is susceptible to rot when in contact with a sufficient amount of water. For that reason, we were careful to make sure that the straw in our house would stay as dry as possible, by paying attention to construction details. The first step was to start out with very dry bales. Farmers were a bit curious when we asked them if their straw had been kept absolutely dry and under cover since its harvest. We installed these bales on a raised foundation that kept them well off the ground. We used a vapor and moisture barrier of asphalt-impregnated 30-pound felt, both under and on top of the sill plate, to keep water from wicking up from the foundation into the bales. We also constructed large roof overhangs to keep rain and the summer sun off the walls.

Perhaps most important, we paid attention to the details of our stucco application. First, before applying the exterior stucco and interior plaster, we covered all the wood in the structure, and in the window and door frames, with tarpaper. We didn't use any additional flashing because we'd heard that aluminum would be degraded through a reaction with the concrete in the stucco. Then we attached stucco mesh to the posts, as well as the window and door frames, and pinned mesh to the adjacent straw bales with 24-inch insulation supports bent in half to form a "bobby pin." We

Exterior stucco. The couple chose a concrete stucco, with perlite added to increase breathability. The finish coat is a white lime wash.

Termite inspection zone. Termites love to tunnel through foam insulation to enter wood framing undetected. Doug left a gap between the foam insulation on the stem wall and the stucco-covered straw and framing above. This allows him to visually inspect for termite tunnels. It's this kind of detailing and attention that separates a durable building from one doomed to premature decay.

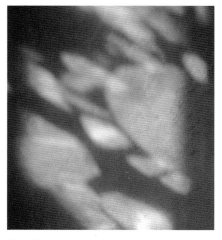

Interior plaster. Inside walls are covered with a gypsum plaster. Here, light reflected from a polished-granite mosaic floor casts beautiful patterns on a wall.

used mesh only in those areas where two different materials met. In those places, the mesh gave the stucco something to adhere to, thus limiting future cracking. Straw bales hold stucco and plaster very nicely without mesh when laid flat, with the rough ends of the cut straw exposed.

We used a type-N cement stucco on the exterior for durability and low maintenance, and applied a lime wash for the finish coat. The lime wash filled in some of the small cracks that appeared in the stucco. The stucco has been on for about four years and seems to be holding up well.

The interior plaster recipe was based on trial and error. We looked at many different recipes and went with a gypsum-based plaster. We applied two coats of gypsum plaster and a finish coat of lime-and-gypsum plaster. Once applied, the results were immediate and very satisfying. We chose not to paint them due to the wonderful variation in colors naturally occurring in the plaster.

We've never had our indoor air quality checked for the presence of mold. Mold growth can occur if the moisture content gets above 19 percent, but if the moisture content was at that level the wood would mold and rot as well. And if that was happening, we'd have seen some signs, such as failure of the plaster or stucco. We did have some rodent problems before the structure was completely closed up, but haven't had any since all the entry points have been sealed.

Although our friends have affectionately called our home "Camp Huff and Puff," our house is actually an environmentally sensitive rewrite of the classic *The Three Little Pigs.* The straw is more fire-retardant than a standard wood structure, because straw walls have no channels of air to help fires gain speed and spread. In fact, the real hassles with this issue haven't come from the house, but from convincing the proper authorities that the building wouldn't rot or burn. The permit process was arduous. We spent six months gathering the most current research. We provided structural-load test information, rodent literature, mildew literature, straw bale code requirements from other states, and a whole notebook of articles and books to prove our point. Finally, with all the required literature, multiple meetings, and much cajoling from the engineer on our project, we received our building permit. After several years, the house has yet to show any evidence of nature's "destructive forces."

Q How does the building maintain a nurturing exchange with the outside?
We feel very connected to the outdoors with the ample amount of light coming in the windows to the south. Actually, all that light can be deceiving when living in a well-insulated house. After looking out the window on a sunny winter day, we've often headed out the door without a jacket only to turn back to find more clothing when hit with the reality of the outdoor temperature.

Breathability is an important factor to consider when planning to build a straw bale house. Since we get more rain here than in the Southwest, where most of the straw bale building codes have been written, we chose a more water-resistant stucco, and added perlite to gain some breathability. This stucco, in combination with our breathable interior plaster, allows air exchange through the wall.

The house breathes in other ways as well. The easy flow of air through the house in the summer and the warm, radiant heat in the winter certainly create a nurturing and comfortable environment. A straw bale house simply has a different feel than a conventional house. You feel embraced by the structure. The undulating plaster and stucco walls have curves and niches that seem to allow energy to move easily around the space. We also were careful to use natural, nontoxic materials as much as possible. That's something that's difficult to do in the conventional building world.

Cozy daylighting. The house is bathed in warm light on a cold winter afternoon.

We'd hoped to install a photovoltaic system, but we just couldn't afford it. We'd love to explore hydroelectric power as well, but with our low electric bill, we have other expenses that must come first. As for water and sewage, we drilled a well and have a conventional septic system.

Q Can you tell me anything else about your home's materials or detailing?

The preliminary foundation preparation seemed to take forever; then the walls went up in just a day and a half. The straw infill went very quickly, too. We had a bale-raising and enlisted the help of our friends, all of whom were intrigued by our odd choice of insulation. The bales were notched to fit around the posts, braces, window, and door bucks. We had to retie a lot of bales to make the custom lengths needed to fit between the posts and bucks.

The flooring, which was shortleaf pine from Nelle's father's land, turned out very nice, and we saved money there even after paying someone else to kiln-dry and mill it.

In our new addition, we installed a simple radon-mitigation system. It consists of conduit, drilled with holes, attached to the foundation under the slab. The conduit comes through the slab and up through the roof, where any collected radon gas can harmlessly escape.

Curves and niches. Deep, contoured window openings created by the thick walls lend a unique coziness to straw bale homes.

Homemade windows. Doug built many of the house's windows himself, using salvaged, double-pane glass.

Q Looking back, what would you do differently?

We spent a lot of time cutting the wood for the frame and flooring from Nelle's family land. Although we saved some money, it was a huge amount of time and effort. I think we'd just buy that wood next time.

Also, we reclaimed double-pane, low-e window glass recycled from a fast food chain. We actually constructed the house around the windows! Doug built the window frames out of Douglas fir using the salvage glass, and the dimensions of the house followed. This took a lot of time. When we built the addition, we didn't hesitate to pay for well-insulated, low-e windows. They're well worth the money.

Q What advice do you have for aspiring builders?

A house starts as a dream. You need to start with a clear dream of what you want to do. Once you have that, it's basically a leap of faith. For us, the difference between the dream and the reality has been a difficult journey that required vision, perseverance, and courage. If you'd told us when we started that we'd be living in a dilapidated travel trailer for close to three years, we probably never would've had the courage to move forward. From our experience, it's important to have a good support network of friends and family. Our excitement about and dedication to our dream was contagious, so it seemed that everyone wanted to assist us in any way they could. In our case, all the work and hardship has really been worth it. In our rewrite of *The Three Little Pigs*, the folks in the straw house live happily ever after, with lower energy bills and a comfortable, safe structure to call home.

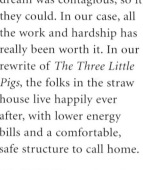

Built-in warmth. The bedrooms feature mosaic floors with radiant hydronic heating.

Floral floor. This lovely granite mosaic flower design is in the sunroom/foyer leading to the living room.

Truth window. It's a tradition among straw bale builders to leave a portion of one wall unplastered. The area is called a "truth window" because it proves the walls really are made of straw. Doug created this beautiful niche for his home's truth window. The small cabinet's doors open to reveal the straw wall behind.

CINDY MEEHAN-PATTON'S HEALTH-CONSCIOUS HOME

"FIND GOOD PEOPLE TO WORK WITH. YOU NEED SOMEONE WHO WANTS TO DO A GOOD JOB AND WHO'S OPEN TO NEW IDEAS."

Q Describe your land and building site, and outline what led you to choose it. What did you do to analyze your site?

My mother owned the lot next to her house, and sold it to me. It's in a fairly densely populated neighborhood in Asheville, North Carolina, sort of on the fringe between suburban and rural. I was concerned about privacy, so I analyzed the immediate neighborhood to determine how much of the surrounding woods would eventually be developed. Because the lot was small, I had to decide if there was enough room to build what I wanted. I didn't want to take down any trees in the construction process, so the location of trees on the lot was important. I also wanted solar access, and had

Meehan-Patton house. Commercial alternatives to conventional, and sometimes health-threatening, modern materials characterize this cozy, healthful home.

Cindy Meehan-Patton has been researching indoor air quality, and its relationship to health and well-being, for a number of years. She's the owner and president of Shelter Ecology, a supplier of products and services intended to assist clients in creating environmentally healthy designs and buildings.

Cindy's desire to build her own home was driven by her chemical sensitivity. She simply couldn't find a place to live that didn't make her sick. She started by building a tiny, chemically safe "pod," as she calls it, on the lot next to her mother's house. Later, she and her husband renovated her "pod" into a small home that also serves as her office and as a demonstration of the products she sells.

to analyze how much sun I'd get, given the existing trees. Because the lot was below the road, I knew drainage could be a problem. I had to figure what to do about that before deciding to build.

Q What led you to choose your overall building approach? Briefly describe your building and its major characteristics.

My decision to build came out of a long history of chemical sensitivity. I kept moving into an apartment, getting sick, moving to another apartment, and getting sick again. I'd struggled for nine years to find a healthy place to live when some friends who were also chemically sensitive let me stay in their home, which had been built with chemical sensitivity in mind. I'd finally found a place that didn't make me sick. Soon afterward I bought the lot from my mother and built a simple 380-square-foot rectangular room, using the safe materials that were available at the time. I lived there safe and sound for six years; then, when I got married, we decided to remodel the "pod" to become our home.

Our house has a compact, open-plan design that includes my home office and a loft that functions as a guest sleeping area as well as a meditation and reading space. With no children at home, we were able to limit the size to 900 square feet. One of my mottos is to be efficient by building only what you require. If people truly did this, most homes would be smaller.

I designed the structure myself with the help of an architect, who was great with things like load issues and stair layout. I went through eight designs before I was satisfied. Aesthetically, I wanted a contemporary but timeless home using exterior materials that would be maintenance-free, durable, and of quality, since they endure the most wear and tear over time. I chose interior materials on the basis of seven criteria; in order of their importance to me, they are absence of toxins, renewability, recyclability, recycled content, energy efficiency, cost, and regional availability.

Form and function. This attractive stone retaining wall separates the site from the road above and, along with the gravel drain bed, helps keep water away from the house.

"De-scrapped" lumber. These framing studs are made from recycled scrap lumber pieces finger-jointed and glued together.

Q What makes up the load-bearing structure of the foundation, walls, and roof of your house?

My foundation is conventional concrete block poured solid. Fly ash was added to the slab to reduce the amount of Portland cement used.

The walls are conventionally framed with finger-jointed studs, which

Raising the roof. A crane was used to lift and place the structural insulated panels that form the addition's roof.

Spray-in insulation. This foam insulation creates a tight thermal barrier and is safe for the environment and humans.

are made of scrap pieces of lumber that are jointed and glued together with a superstrong adhesive. They cost about the same as conventional studs, but are recycled. We used standard plywood sheathing because it was the only thing locally available.

The original little pod has conventional dimensional-lumber roof rafters. On the addition we used structural insulated panels (SIPs), sometimes also called stress skin panels. These are large structural units consisting of a layer of foam insulation sandwiched between two layers of oriented strand board, or OSB, sheathing.

Q What creates and maintains the stable temperature within the building?

Our walls are insulated with Icynene, a spray-in foam that contains no CFCs, HCFCs, or formaldehyde. It's certified environmentally safe and healthy for humans and creates a very tight, superinsulated envelope. The roof rafters in the original pod are also sprayed with this foam insulation. The stress skin panels in the addition's roof have integrated foam insulation. We also insulated under the slab. We used double-pane, argon-filled, low-e windows for energy efficiency.

The temperature in the house is stabilized by radiant floor heat and a wood stove in the winter, and a window-unit air conditioner during the rest of the year.

Q How does the building deal with destructive forces—sun, water, wind, animals, molds, insects, etc.?

Our walls are covered with a combination of plank siding and stucco. We chose a smooth-lap, fiber cement siding called Hardi-Plank because of its durability, partial recycled content, and low to no maintenance. This siding was covered with E-Coat recycled paint. The majority of the exterior sheathing is finished with a three-coat cementitious stucco with low-toxic paint integrated into the final coat. We chose it because of its clean, contemporary aesthetic, zero maintenance, and durability. Our roof is covered with metal roofing.

All the doors in our house are recycled, old wooden doors. We had them stripped down to their original wood. While this is not an energy-efficient

Cement siding and stucco. The plank siding behind the large potted plant is made of reinforced concrete. The stucco is a cement mix with pigment added to the final coat.

Foundation waterproofing. The green coating is a spray-on, vulcanized rubber waterproofing. The black, flat columns on the wall at left are part of a foundation drain system that replaces gravel and perforated pipe

choice, we did weatherstrip them well, and they really add so much architectural beauty to the home. This choice was also part of my commitment not to cut down any hardwood trees to supply my building materials.

We used ACQ-treated instead of CCA (arsenic salt-treated) sills. ACQ stands for Ammonium Copper Quat. Quat takes the place of arsenic. It's a swimming pool preservative that's supposed to be safe for human consumption. In any case, I know it's safer than arsenic!

There are vapor barriers under the slab, and tarpaper behind the stucco. I don't believe that vapor barriers are always the proper solution for creating a moisture-free home. If they're put with the wrong or incompatible building material, they can cause condensation.

Since my house site is situated below the road, drainage was a big issue. I had to form a gravel drain bed around the house to divert the water away from the foundation. I did this rather than using gutters. I think they require too much maintenance, and when you forget about them they back up on you; then you can really have water problems. I also think they're very unattractive. We also used large overhangs, which help keep water away from the building too. In addition, we used Rub-R-Wall, a spray-on rubber waterproofing, and DynoSeal, a low-odor sealer, to coat the outside of the foundation, so no water can penetrate the block.

Q How does the building maintain a nurturing exchange with the outside?

Since I was diagnosed with Multiple Chemical Sensitivity (MCS) 12 years ago, I've become very educated on indoor air quality issues. Creating healthy homes has become my passion, and also my business. I built my house not only to live in, but as a sort of demonstration project and showroom of the kinds of renewable, natural, recycled, and toxin-free materials you need to create a healing home. I believe that this approach to building isn't only for those with MCS. If we all chose to build healthy homes, there would be less illness in the world. Why wait until you're sick? Treat your home as a preventive health care package. In my climate, people who have sensitivities to mold and fungi, which in my opinion is everyone, need to be conscious of indoor humidity levels. For example, although I think water-vapor-breathable, or hygroscopic, walls will work in many climates, I don't think it's a suitable approach in my humid climate. The reason? We have 80 to 100 percent humidity during all the summer months, most spring months, and on some fall days—in other words, most of the time. Whenever you have that level of humidity it's virtually impossible for a breathable wall to do its job effectively in terms of re-releasing moisture. Moisture constantly moves into the structure of the wall, and into the interior air, and creates mold. In my opinion, the same holds true for natural ventilation in a humid climate. Allowing very humid outside air into your home through open windows will most certainly cause mold where I live.

Mold is not only bad for the structural integrity of your home; it's also a subtle energy sucker for the human body. It can degrade the immune system's ability to fight off infection, too. It can also be a hormone disrupter.

In my humid climate, then, I needed to find other strategies for creating good indoor air quality. I started by creating an energy-efficient, air-sealed insulated envelope in the walls and ceiling as I've already described. This insures that there's no moisture infiltration. I then installed a mechanical air exchanger to breathe for the house. It brings in fresh outside air and exhausts stale inside air. Filters and dehumidification are integrated into this system. A window-unit air conditioner helps keeps the humidity down in the summer, and a dehumidifier runs in the most humid months. The only time we let windows do the breathing is when the humidity is below 50 percent outside, which is rare.

All the hot water for our radiant floor, showers, laundry, and sinks is heated by a superefficient, propane-powered tankless heater that's mounted on the outside of the house. We installed the heater outside so that no propane would be brought inside the house. In my opinion, combustible fuels such as natural gas, oil, and propane are very detrimental to your health because of the potential for carbon monoxide and mercaptin poisoning. Mercaptin is a pesticide. It's also what they add to natural gas fuels, including propane, to detect leakage. It was and still is one of the main culprits for my becoming chemically sensitive. I don't care how sealed the combustion chamber is in a gas system, you still get some mercaptin leakage if the furnace, and therefore the pilot light, is in the house.

We recently constructed an adjacent building that houses my husband's chiropractic office, shipping and storage for my business, and our master bedroom. In this building, we chose to experiment with using a ducted HVAC system that's energy-efficient and tightly and properly installed. The system also has a fresh air exchanger, as in the little house. We have a humidistat on the outside of the house that shuts the air exchanger off if the humidity is 100 percent outside; i.e., when it's raining. The heat pump is electric because of the issues with combustible fuels I just mentioned.

I enjoy the air in the little house more. It's more consistent, due to the radiant floor heat and the window-unit air conditioner. The air exchanger also does an excellent job of keeping the air fresh. The bigger building with the HVAC unit is much more difficult to keep at a consistent temperature throughout. One reason is that it has three levels to heat and cool. The small house is all on one level.

As for other issues of connection to the outside, my house was aesthetically designed to maximize the views of the land surrounding us. My office has windows that I look out of all the time. One window has a 100-year-old oak tree just outside. It speaks to me every day.

I also considered the future when I designed the house and chose the metal roof and other materials so that, when my gardens and deck are done, we can install a rainwater catchment system. I'll use this system to water my raised-bed vegetable gardens.

Window-unit air conditioning. Cindy's strategy for good indoor air quality in her humid climate includes the window-mounted air conditioner in this comfortable room's far corner.

Q **Can you tell me anything else about your home's materials or detailing?**

As I've said, my house is a showroom for all the products I sell that work as a system. That's what sustainable, green, or environmental building is all about: creating a working, harmonious system that does not degrade the environment in any way. To accomplish this goal, I put each product I used through a life cycle analysis. I asked several questions: 1) Is this product made of synthetic or naturally occurring materials? 2) What is the embodied energy and pollution impact of the products' manufacture? 3) How much pollution will be generated in transporting the product? 4) What is the recycled content of the installed product, and can the product be recycled or reused when it wears out or the building is renovated?

The answers to these questions are not black and white. For example, in my area, recycled barn boards score very high in a life cycle analysis, so we decided to use some as exterior trim. I got the boards and cleaned them up, but they were too warped and wouldn't lie flat on the subfascia of the house. We had to switch to new southern yellow pine, the most renewable tree in my area next to locust.

Also, you can't always find a local source for products that are otherwise "green" and highly desirable. Many of the materials used in the interior fit this description. Among them were bamboo flooring, a renewable and

Kitchen cabinetry improved. The crown molding and doors for these kitchen cabinets are made of wheat-straw panels. The mold- and moisture-resistant countertops are 100 percent recycled plastic.

uniquely beautiful material used in most of the house; cork-tile bathroom flooring, also renewable and beautiful; 100 percent recycled-plastic kitchen countertops; 100 percent wheat-straw panels, which we used for our kitchen cabinet doors and crown molding for their earthy aesthetic; lumber engineered from 100 percent compressed sunflower hulls, for cabinetry; formaldehyde-free, medium-density fiberboard (MDF) for shelving; and ceramic tile made from 60 percent recycled automobile windshield glass. They're all excellent materials, but they also all had to be shipped to us.

Fortunately, we were able to find local sources for recycled lumber, including some great old oak, redwood, heart pine, and cypress that we used for all the interior trim details, loft framing, and more.

Sometimes you have to compromise and problem solve. For instance, we had to use plywood with toxic glues because it was the only thing locally available. However, we sprayed it with three coats of a product called Safe Seal, a sealer that locks out up to 80 percent of formaldehyde off-gassing.

We used only water-based, environmentally safe, low-toxic finishes throughout the house. These included an adhesive used under tile and flooring; a sealant to prevent off-gassing from plywood; an exterior trim sealant; a masonry sealer; interior paints; a furniture stain; a polyurethane used on the bamboo flooring, recycled doors and wheat-board cabinets; and a grout sealer used on the shower tile.

Q Looking back, what would you do differently?

I would've incorporated solar lighting and water heating, but we ran out of money!

Q What advice do you have for aspiring builders?

Don't be afraid to get involved in the building process. For my original pod, for example, I dug all the water and sewage lines myself, and helped grade the land. I researched and purchased all the materials and did all the finish work myself.

Also, it's important to find good people to work with. My builder was a master craftsman who took a lot of pride in his work. He was on the site everyday, overseeing and helping with the building process and any questions that came up. He built only one job at a time. I think these characteristics can be of great benefit when constructing a green-built home. You need someone who wants to do a good job and who's open to new ideas. In addition, it takes good communication skills from both the contractor/builder and yourself.

Most importantly, you need to understand the "green" concepts that you're trying to implement, or you need to hire a consultant who can speak for you. If there isn't a clear advocate, problems will undoubtedly occur with builders and subcontractors who are unfamiliar with what you're trying to accomplish. Building green can be a paradigm shift for many who attempt it. If you're not ready, wait until you are. If you can't afford it, wait until you can.

Wood and grass. A salvaged door, recycled cypress trim, and bamboo flooring combine nicely in this inviting hallway.

Can you find the car in this picture? The ceramic tile around the wood stove is made from 60 percent recycled automobile windshield glass.

Recycled lumber aloft. Recycled oak, redwood, and heart pine were used in the loft and ladder.

MARC AND AMY'S CONVENTIONALLY CONSTRUCTED "ALTERNATIVE" HOUSE

"ALWAYS KEEP TWO CASES OF BEER CHILLING IN THE CREEK. MOST PEOPLE WHO DROP BY ARE WILLING TO WORK FOR BEER."

To some people, Marc and Amy's house wouldn't qualify as "alternative" because it's basically conventionally constructed: slab-on-grade with commercially manufactured stud framing and fiberglass insulation. However, just as much as anyone in this chapter, Marc and Amy made the most of what they had and, using locally available materials, built a house that fits their needs. They considered other approaches, such as an Earthship or straw bale house, but were concerned that these techniques might not work on their very wet site in their very wet climate. In the end, they built a conventionally framed, energy-efficient, passive solar home with PV electricity, greywater system, solar hot water, and other alternative features. In fact, they're the rare realization of a common fantasy: with little practical knowledge or experience, they built a house with their own hands, in a reasonable amount of time, that was inexpensive, practical, and beautiful. I almost hesitate to include them here, because I think they're the exception, not the rule. You can get yourself into trouble trying to do what they accomplished. It also remains to be seen if their inexperience will show up in how the building ages, how it stands the test of time.

More than anything, though, I think Marc and Amy are examples of how lifestyle choices are the real central issue for would-be alternative builders. They don't mind living at the end of a rough, boulder-studded, rut-filled road. They don't mind walking through the woods to their toilet. They don't mind doing without electricity sometimes, or switching sources of water when one dries up seasonally. One reward for these lifestyle choices is something that almost anyone can relate to: Marc and Amy's house was incredibly inexpensive to build. As a result, they own a house and plenty of land. They own their water source, all the firewood they'll ever need, plenty of room to grow food, and clear access to their main source of heat and electricity: the sun. They have all of this without debt and practically zero shelter-related monthly expenses. If that's not alternative building, I don't know what is.

Marc and Amy's house. Although built using mostly conventional structural materials and techniques, this passive solar, off-the-grid home incorporates a variety of "alternative" features and reflects its builders' independent spirits.

Q **Describe your land and building site, and outline what led you to choose it. What did you do to analyze your site?**

Some friends of ours found the property and were rebuilding a 150-year-old cabin on it. They were interested in having people they knew become land partners with them. When we looked at the property, we fell in love with it. We liked the idea of living in the woods on a mountain, and also the idea of sharing the land with friends. This made buying a big piece of property more affordable, and we have great neighbors we can depend on.

We looked around the property for a building site with a southern exposure for a passive solar house. We also made sure there were springs uphill of the site to provide us with gravity-fed water. We chose to build near the one road that entered the property, for convenience and to reduce the clearing necessary to building. We cleared only enough area for our driveway, house, and a garden, so the house would blend in well with the surrounding woods.

Q **What led you to choose your overall building approach? Briefly describe your building and its major characteristics.**

We knew we wanted to build a passive solar house and be off the grid. We designed and built everything ourselves, without the aid of professionals, because we wanted to do our own thing. We have friends with construction experience who gave us technical advice when we needed it. We also referred to a high school carpentry textbook that a friend loaned us. Other than that, we had no construction experience or expertise going into the project.

The first thing we did was get a book about solar design and read it three times. When we had a good sense of the basics, we started designing the house, drawing up plans on notebook paper. We measured the rooms in our apartment and in other people's houses to get an idea of the size the rooms should be. Then we added special details that we'd always wanted, such as loft bedrooms, a catwalk, and a Dutch door. We played around with different designs until we found something that we liked and that seemed practical.

Blending in and out-sides. This porch creates a pleasant transition between inside and outside, helping the house blend into its surroundings.

Indoor footbridge. This suspended hallway over the downstairs leads to a loft bedroom.

Cozy loft. Here's the bedroom, complete with handmade furnishings, on the other side of the footbridge.

Open floor plan. Only the bathroom and a few closets are enclosed. At left is some milled lumber solar-drying for a future project.

Thinking on dry feet. Marc and Amy intended to berm the concrete block north wall (at left), but water seeping from the hill after grading changed their minds. They installed drainage pipe instead. Thinking on your feet is an important attribute of successful house building.

We looked at a few alternatives, such as Earthships and straw bale construction, but felt our climate might be too wet for those approaches. We ended up using a combination of stick-framing and posts. We used some materials from the land, such as stones and black locust posts. We wanted a lot of light and an open feeling to the house. The house has cathedral ceilings and there aren't any hallways. Other than closets and the bathroom, none of the rooms are completely walled off. This openness allows heat and light to travel freely. We considered earth-berming the north side of the house, but when the site was graded we saw there was too much spring water seeping out of that slope. So we raised the level of the house and put in more drainage pipes instead.

Tin foresight. If you've ever walked on a slick metal roof, you'll agree that this integrated roof ladder is a good idea.

Q What makes up the load-bearing structure of the foundation, walls, and roof of your house?

Our foundation consists of concrete block stem walls. The concrete slab first floor rests on foamboard insulation that sits on a plastic vapor barrier on top of gravel on top of the soil. The slab was supposed to go to the level of the cinder blocks on the south side, but we couldn't convince a concrete company to deliver concrete up our driveway. So we mixed our concrete by hand and chose to pour to a lower level. The slab supports several stone walls inside the house. Under these walls the slab is 6 inches thick to give more support. Otherwise the slab is 4 inches thick in the northern two-thirds of the house, and 6 inches thick on the sunny southern side, for more thermal mass.

The exterior walls are made of 2x6s framed on 2-foot centers resting on top of the cinder block walls. There are some structural black locust posts in the interior that rest on footers we poured before the slab was poured.

Our roof is conventionally framed with 2x12 rafters on 2-foot centers. The 2x12s gave us a deeper space for insulation. We used purlins, boards nailed perpendicular to the rafters, instead of plywood sheathing, then nailed tin roofing to the purlins.

Q What creates and maintains the stable temperature within the building?

Our house is based on passive solar principles. We have no windows or doors on the north side, a lot of glass on the south side, and not too much on the east or west side.

The house is well-sealed and insulated. Our walls are R-26 with a combination of fiberglass batts and foamboard insulation; the ceiling is R-39, and the floor is R-7.5. The foamboard sheathing extends down at least 3 feet below grade. We finished the inside walls with pine boards at a 45 degree angle so that it acts like diagonal bracing. This allowed us to forgo plywood corner boards on the exterior walls and use foamboard insulation to sheath even the exterior corners. The concrete slab floor serves as a thermal mass. This absorbs heat from the sun when the sun is out, keeping the house from overheating during

Windows to winter warmth. In winter, the high south-facing glass lets the sun penetrate all the way to the back of the house.

the day, and releases heat at night to keep the house from getting too cool. We also insulated the slab on the sides with 2 inches of foamboard to keep from losing heat laterally through the foundation. We use a metal wood stove to supplement the passive solar heat.

Our windows are mostly old casement windows that we either hinged like a door or installed as fixed glass. All of these we double-paned ourselves, mostly just by sticking a pane of glass on the outside of the wood window with silicone caulk. Our larger windows are salvaged single-pane sliding glass doors that we sandwiched together in pairs, with ¾-by-¾-inch wood strips between them and on either side, to create double-pane fixed-glass units. We tried to position the working, operable windows so that we'd get a good cross breeze through the house. For that reason, we put windows up in the loft, where the summer heat would rise, and down on the main floor to draw in cooler air. We've found, though, that windows on the south side in the summer draw in only the hot air rising up the southern slope. The windows on the east side also tend to bring in hot air, as this is where our driveway is. The west side is wooded, so the air coming in those windows is cool.

The house stays comfortably cool in the summertime. The tin roof's silver finish deflects a good deal of heat, and the insulation keeps heat out as well. Our roof has a 2-foot overhang, which keeps out direct sunlight until late August. In winter, the sun is lower in the sky and comes through the southern windows just fine. The only time the house gets too much solar heat is on warm, sunny days in late fall.

Homemade double-pane. Adding a second sheet of glass to an old wooden window is a good idea, but in retrospect Marc suggests doing so only for fixed windows.

Local lumber. The builders found that their local sawmill, which provided this wood lap siding, was willing to accommodate special orders and gave them good prices.

Q How does the building deal with destructive forces—sun, water, wind, animals, molds, insects, etc.?

The concrete block foundation walls extend as far up as the floor level or higher, as needed to ensure that the wood walls would be at least 18 inches above grade for preventing decay. We bought rough-cut lap siding from a local mill and treated it with linseed oil before installing. Our roof extends 2 feet out on all sides to keep rain water off the siding.

On the inside, we used vapor barriers under the slab, on the walls, and on the ceiling to prevent condensation in the insulation. The spaces between the sheets of foamboard sheathing should let the walls breathe. The siding we used doesn't seal very tightly, and wasps regularly make their home under it. Mice also can get under the siding, and the foamboard doesn't put up much of a defense to things that chew. The siding is also prone to getting covered with mold. We could either treat it every couple of years or just let it be. Around here, exposed, untreated wood siding on a typical barn probably lasts 50 years.

We chose a tin roof to fit in with the local architecture and because it's durable and reflects heat away from the house. We also like the looks.

Q How does the building maintain a nurturing exchange with the outside?

The first thing we did was tap a spring above our house to provide our water. We've had to develop a second spring to take over when the first spring dries out in the fall. The second thing we did was build an outhouse, which we still use. It's actually quite enjoyable to take a stroll in the woods to the outhouse to do our business.

Homemade solar water heater. This collector in front of the first-floor deck is plumbed to a storage tank in the second-story loft, creating a convective loop or thermosiphon (see page 138).

Simple PV. These little photovoltaic arrays supply all of Marc and Amy's electricity needs.

We have a fairly normal plumbing system in terms of shower, washing machine, and sinks. We use a homemade solar water heater when the outside temperature is above freezing. Copper tubing coiled around our wood stove chimney heats water when we have a fire. Otherwise we use a propane hot-water heater, which also serves as the storage tank for the solar and wood stove heating loops. Our greywater drainage system consists of a single ditch with a slotted drainpipe surrounded by perlite buried 2 feet underground.

We chose to produce our own electricity. It would cost a lot to have power lines brought in, and the lines would be ugly. We also wanted to be part of a cleaner technology than nuclear power or burning coal. We chose photovoltaics because there really isn't anything to break, and our climate is good for solar. Photovoltaics also allowed us to enlarge our system as our demands increased. This kept the initial cost down. We do have a limited amount of power compared to buying electricity off the grid, but by using energy-saving appliances, such as a dorm refrigerator, compact fluorescent light bulbs, and a superefficient washing machine, we're able to go four days without sun before we run out of power. That might happen once in a winter, and when it does we can always use our gas-powered generator for backup. We also run our TV, computer, scanner, printer, stereo, and any shop tools under 8 amps off our little PV system.

We keep quite a few plants in the house, which helps to improve air quality. In the winter, they help keep the air from becoming too dry. Although the house is fairly tight, the pets help with the air exchange every time they use the pet door. We also go out more frequently than people who have indoor toilets. Sometimes in the summer we do get a teensy-weensy bit of mold indoors; like when it rains every day for three weeks and half of the county is flooded.

Solar furniture. Marc made this table and chairs with lumber cut from their land. Solar power, with occasional generator backup, runs all his power tools. Marc even made the wicker seat!

Q Can you tell me anything else about your home's materials or detailing?

Most of our wood came from a local sawmill. This gave us the rough finish we wanted for the inside of the house, and saved us money too. We found the local mills were willing to work with us if we needed anything special, as long as we could tell them which dimensions were important and which could be variable. For

Air fresheners. Plants thrive in the sunny interior, helping to keep the air moist and providing oxygen for their human caretakers.

Bathroom hallway. This is the pleasant path to Marc and Amy's facilities, otherwise known as an outhouse.

example, we might say we needed a certain number of board feet that had to be exactly 6 inches wide but that could vary from ¾ to 1¼ inches thick and be 8, 10, or 12 feet long.

We built our own doors, which, to our surprise, do work. We insulated them with 1½-inch foamboard and added colored glass and other goodies. They ended up taking a considerable amount of time, though. We also chose to build our own windows. This entailed taking old casement windows and trimming them to size, reglazing, stripping the old paint and repainting. As I mentioned earlier, we also double-paned them ourselves. The result is windows that fog up and don't open very conveniently. But if you want to get creative with window shapes, making them yourself is fun. I suggest buying good windows for places where you want them to open and close, and making your own picture windows out of old sliding glass doors that still have their double-paning intact.

We got a lot of stuff from friends and by shopping the classified ads. Having a house made from partially used materials was nice, because it had an immediate cozy feel. Some of our interior walls are made of stone from the property, with a variety of other objects placed in the mortar—bowling balls, pottery, car parts, bottles, even a potbelly stove.

Q Looking back, what would you do differently?

I would've used a structural stucco on the concrete block stem wall. Structural stuccos—Shurwall is one brand—are applied to drystacked block. They allow you to avoid the time-consuming skilled labor of laying block with mortar, something I ended up doing a lot in the rain.

Q What advice do you have for aspiring builders?

Well, I can tell you some things that worked for us. Living on-site helped to push things forward. If we'd had a cozy house to go home to, we wouldn't have been as motivated to get done. Also, it was good to get all materials from the same mill. Once they realized that we were building an entire house, they started giving us good prices. And, always keep two cases of beer chilling in the creek. Most people who drop by are willing to work for beer.

Two-sided stone. This interior stone wall serves on one side (left) as part of the bathtub/shower, and on the other side (right) as a kitchen wall and shelving unit.

SIX APPROACHES TO A GOOD HOUSE

	DAN'S HOUSE	GEORGE'S HOUSE	CHUCK'S HOUSE	DOUG & NELLE'S HOUSE	CINDY'S HOUSE	MARC & AMY'S HOUSE
MATERIALS	Tires, earth, straw, wood, metal, concrete, glass, plants	Wood-chip blocks, earth, concrete, straw, cotton, wood chips, wood, glass	Wood, earth, cellulose, gravel, concrete, metal, glass, plants	Straw, wood, concrete, metal, fiberglass, granite, glass	Wood, concrete, gravel, metal, foam, glass, many commercial "eco" materials	Wood, concrete, gravel, metal, fiberglass, lots of salvage (including glass)
STRUCTURE	Foundation: continuous (packed tires; concrete under rest of house)	Foundation: continuous (concrete tied into limestone)	Foundation: hybrid (gravel trench with concrete piers)	Foundation: continuous (concrete with concrete block and bond beam)	Foundation: continuous (concrete slab-on-grade)	Foundation: continuous (concrete with concrete block)
	Walls: monolithic (packed tires) and skeletal (wood framing)	Walls: monolithic (wood-chip blocks filled with earth/concrete and rebar)	Walls: skeletal (post-and-beam with ladder truss)	Walls: skeletal (post-and-beam with some conventional framing)	Walls: skeletal (conventional wood framing)	Walls: skeletal (wood framing with interior diagonal siding)
	Roof: skeletal (wood framing)	Roof: Skeletal (wood framing)	Roof: skeletal (wood framing)	Roof: skeletal (wood rafters and trusses)	Roof: skeletal (conventional wood framing and stress-skin panels)	Roof: skeletal (conventional wood framing)
TEMPERATURE	Passive solar with earth berming; radiant floor	Combination of thermal mass and insulation; hot-water radiant heat, swamp cooler, cooling tower, large overhangs, concrete tile roof	Passive solar with thermal mass in floor and walls; propane backup heat, natural ventilation and shading	Passive solar with open floor plan; masonry wood stove, hydronic floor heating, "southern AC" (windows open at night, closed in morning)	Heavy insulation with efficient heating; propane radiant floor heat with wood stove backup, mechanical A/C	Passive solar with open floor plan; wood stove backup
	Insulation: earth, straw, rigid foam, cellulose	Insulation: cotton, straw, wood chips	Insulation: blown cellulose, rigid foam	Insulation: straw, fiberglass, rigid foam, radiant barrier	Insulation: Icynene spray foam	Insulation: fiberglass with rigid foam external sheathing
SEPARATION			Foundation: raised to keep wood off ground	Foundation: raised to keep wood and straw off ground; radon mitigation under slab	Foundation: water- and radon-proofing; no arsenic-treated sills	Foundation: raised to keep wood off ground
	Walls: earth with 6-mil plastic; cement stucco	Walls: "breathable" stucco	Walls: "breathable" earth plaster	Walls: exterior concrete stucco with perlite; interior gypsum-based plaster	Walls: concrete plank siding and concrete stucco with integrated recycled paint	Walls: local milled lap siding
	Roof: part living, part metal	Roof: concrete tile, large overhangs	Roof: living roof with large overhangs	Roof: metal with large overhangs	Roof: metal with large overhangs	Roof: metal with good overhangs
	Other: overhangs, metal-clad windows	Other: wood windows; non-pest-attracting materials				Other: conventional vapor barrier on walls
CONNECTION	Conscious daylighting design, indoor plant "jungle," PV and wind system	Breathable wall strategy, PV system with grid intertie, rain catchment, constructed wetlands wastewater treatment	Daylighting, breathable stuccos and insulation, PV system, community water and composting toilet	Daylighting, some solar hot water, breathable stucco and plaster, well water, conventional septic	"Airtight" wall envelope with mechanical air exchanger, air-quality-oriented materials and installation; municipal electric, water, sewage	Daylighting, gravity-fed spring water, outhouse, PV system for all electrical, thermosiphon hot water with propane backup, natural ventilation, interior plants

CHAPTER 8

REALITY CHECK

I'VE NEVER TALKED TO anyone who had realistic expectations about building their own house. We alternative building types are usually worst of all, because our goals are so high. We don't want just to build a good house; we want to transform our lives and save the planet in the process. These are wonderful aspirations, and I have no desire to denigrate them. My goal in this chapter is to nurture them by inoculating them with realism. To that end, I'll start with my own real-life building story.

"Building a house is a selfish act."

Evolution of a House

I grew up mostly in a small town outside of Austin, Texas. I spent my high school years playing tennis and avoiding getting beaten up. By the time I entered college at the University of Texas, I had a dim feeling that the world was a strange place, and was bewildered over my role in the whole setup. In college, I learned to call this feeling existential angst and was introduced to my country's checkered past, the concept of human oppression, and the tenuous environmental precipice on which we all stood.

After college, I moved to Baltimore, partly to follow my girlfriend and partly in search of a place that was already ruined, that had no pretense of not being a bleak urban expanse of humanity. Strangely, it was here that I became a vegetarian, studied yoga, and began reading about alternatives to modern urban life—including alternative building. I was basically happy. I had good friends and an interesting creative life. But every day, the flush toilet, the supermarkets, the urban lifestyle in general reminded me with recrimination that I wasn't taking care of the basics: I soiled clean water with my bodily waste, didn't grow any food, lived in and contributed to polluted air, and was uninvolved in my housing. Slowly, I began to wonder if I couldn't regain some control over my life.

Eventually, after moving back to Austin, I quit my job working in a law library and became a construction worker for a mad scientist eco-guru involved in alternative building. (Among our projects was a "green building" demonstration home, a showcase of alternative building techniques funded by the state of Texas.) My plan was to gain the knowledge I needed to build my own house. Five years later, I'd worked professionally on various conventional and alternative house-building projects, all the while continuing my research on various building approaches. Also, for three years of that time, my home was a log cabin in the woods, giving me a crash course in country living. Finally, I was ready. I set out with my wife to build a house in the mountains of western North Carolina.

Our rented cabin. We'd never even started a fire in a wood stove before we moved into this cozy little cabin.

Well, to make a long story short, I built that house. But here's the long part of it: What I had hoped would take eight months stretched into *two and a half years*. Even with all of my preparation, I was completely broadsided by my house project. I made many mistakes that wasted materials, time, and money.

At some point near the end of my odyssey, I experienced something of an epiphany, in which the three forces that had combined to make my house a reality were revealed to me. They were Idealism, Stupidity, and Tenacity. Idealism had allowed me to listen to the crazy idea of building my own house when it popped into my head.

Our house. Not even lots of planning and construction job experience prepared me for the reality of building our own home. Was it worth the trials, the hard lessons, the two and a half years? Yes, definitely.

Stupidity had led me to attempt to carry it out. And Tenacity had taken hold like a rabid dog, cajoling me to finish this thing I'd started.

The upside of the story is that, after dedicating a considerable portion of my life to the idea of regaining a bit of self-sufficiency, I find myself living in a small "intentional community" on an old 100-acre farm; I have control over my water source, a spring on the ridge above my house; I have access to fuel for my masonry wood stove; I have plenty of room to grow food; and I have an energy-efficient home that, for the most part, I feel good about.

But that happy list doesn't tell the *whole* story of what I've gained from this long journey. More than anything, I've come away with an intense feeling of humility. And I've also come to understand that building a house is a selfish act. If my goal truly was, as I thought at the time, to become a more responsible citizen of this sweet little planet, then building a house was probably the wrong strategy. Digging holes, diverting water, pouring concrete, cutting roads, clearing land, and trucking in materials are just a few of the things you might find yourself doing. Basically, convening and focusing

Digging nature. Photos of alternative homes often have captions such as, "This house works with nature to create a comfortable living environment." Well, in most cases the first way you work with nature when you build a house is to rip a big hole in the ground. Most buildings require destructive site work such as digging, clearing, and/or road grading.

your complicated human existence on a single piece of earth is not a positive experience for your building site. My family and I now have a wonderful place to live, but it will be many years, if ever, before I can repay the planet for the materials I've used and repair the scar I've left on this poor, defenseless little plot of land.

This story clearly isn't designed to sell books. I share it because, more than anything else, I want to give you a real feeling for what you're getting into. I spent years preparing to build a house, taking on grungy, low-paying construction jobs, reading books, saving money. In many ways my setup was perfect: I had no children, so I had the freedom to focus and could safely take chances. My wife made money while I built, which bought me time. I'm loved and hated as an obsessive hard worker with a one-track mind, so the concept of a daunting project was old hat.

Still, my house pushed me beyond limits I'd never hoped to see. Now, wounded yet safe on the other side, I've come away with a lot of knowledge that I hope I've successfully shared with you in earlier chapters of this book. Perhaps most importantly, I've taken the trip from high-minded novice to realist owner-builder, experiencing a transformation in perspective and an accumulation of practical experience that I also hope to pass on to you in this chapter. My sincere wish is that I can spare you some of the pitfalls that so many of us have had to face in our search for a good house.

Save the World?

As you know by now, this book's core concept is that a good house is specific, the harmonious intersection of a specific spot and specific people. In order to build such a house, you have to know who you are, not who you want to be. Some people confuse house building with personal transformation. They imagine building a house for the person they think they should be. Perhaps it's a rural subsistence farmer from the nineteenth century or the friendly woodland hermit from a children's story. In a related malady, people put the burden of their desire to save the world on their poor little eco-house. They demand that their home absolve them of complicity with modern life's environmental and social problems. Their house will be pure, a temple to the world, containing only the natural and the wholesome.

Is this really you? The fantasy of a self-sufficient life in the country is a wonderful motivator—but make sure you're ready for the reality, too.

These fantasies often manifest themselves in several-year detours to the country. The house constructed, if finished, proves to be of little use to the real people who built it. They'd hoped that the fantasy world and people for whom it was designed would materialize and inhabit their lives. In the end, the real people return to the real world and the house is sold, taking its place among the impersonal, commercial transactions of modern life. The reality can be even worse. I know people who built their own home only to have it bulldozed after they were foreclosed on by the bank. The bank decided to subdivide their property and the house was simply in the way.

Save the planet? Toss the car keys. Left: This mode of transportation is good for you and the planet. Right: This one isn't.

Let's get right down to it. If we were into saving the world, the first thing we'd do is have no children, or perhaps just one if we were feeling really extravagant. Most of the world's ills stem from our crowded planet's exponentially exploding population. I don't care how faithfully 10 or 20 billion people recycle, or how many energy-efficient houses we build; there's only so much humanity this planet can support.

Next on the list would be renouncing all ties to the internal combustion engine. That machine is the flagship of a lifestyle that's choking our planet. Of course, to extricate ourselves from its grasp would mean removing ourselves from the economy,

How you get here is as important as how it's made. If you create an eco-friendly house, but then drive a polluting auto two hours every day from your house to your job and back, what's the point? (The owners of this beautifully crafted home made mostly of indigenous materials don't do that, by the way.)

because virtually every product bought and sold, at least in the U.S. and other industrial nations, is transported by such machines, as are most of the people doing the making, buying, and selling.

Of course, I'm not suggesting that we stop having children or that eternal damnation awaits every owner of a driver's license. I'm simply pointing out that our human problems are complex and paradoxical. I don't know the solutions to our world's woes. I do know that building a house of any kind is not a direct approach to solving these problems. Building a house is a luxurious gift to yourself. It's an exciting, difficult journey that's all about your needs, your abilities, and how well you can recognize the blessings and snares that your chosen site offers up to you. If our good houses have a positive effect on the world, and they well might, they need to be built, loved, and lived in first. A good house will convince you to stay put, to take care of it, to repair the damage done by your descent on that poor little plot of dirt. It can do that only if it fulfills your needs, and it can truly fulfill your needs only if it connects you to your local environment. Perhaps that will lead to a healthier lifestyle, less traveling, more self-reliance, and a deepening partnership between you and your particular place. If that is accomplished, then 30, 40, or 50 years down the road you can sit back in your rocker and contemplate the effect you've had on the planet. Indulging in such abstraction any earlier is simply theorizing, and that won't get a good house built.

Building a house is a process of constant compromise. There are going to be times, perhaps many times, when modern materials are the only choice for a certain goal. For example, as far as I know there are no real alternatives to plastic pipe. The stuff is easy to use and lasts a long time. If you want running water in your house, you're probably going to have to use it. Remember, you're practicing a form of magic: protecting your house from sun, water, wind, and life while cajoling those same elements to fill your space. Such alchemy doesn't come without compromise, at least not in the modern world. If you admit to yourself that your house is a gift to you and your family and not a salve for the planet, you'll be more prepared for the downsides, the times when you're obviously scarring your building site, or choosing materials for the good of your house that might add to the planet's environmental woes.

In my house, I see these things as sins for which I'll work to atone. I did the best I could, but I'd never claim that my house did the planet any favors. I focused on building the sturdiest house I could. It should last long after my lifetime. I think it's a good balance between utilizing my local environment and being protected from it. Perhaps best of all, my life is intertwined with the life of my house. I have a love for it, and for the little piece of land that I've battered with my presence. I plan to care for and nurture them both for the rest of my life. I hope that when I die, I'll leave this spot better than I found it. I have a lot of work to do to reach that goal, and I accept the gamble I made in starting the whole process. Perhaps, after a lifetime of enjoyable work and learning, I can pass on this place, and maybe some of my knowledge, to someone else. Maybe I'll learn things of value; maybe I'll have less of a detrimental impact than the average homeowner; maybe I'll set an example and be part of some sort of social change; or maybe I'll just have had the best life I could muster. In any case, I know that I have a good house, and that's a very good start.

Plastic pipe. This handmade rainwater cistern is plumbed with PVC plastic pipe. PVC is bad for the environment, but because there are no comparable alternatives you'll probably use it anyway. I sure did!

Be Prepared

If you do decide to build a house, the single best thing you can do for yourself, your house, your community, and your planet is to take your time. The world is dispassionate and unconcerned with your desires and needs. Your best intentions mean nothing. Only careful study, planning, and execution will produce a good house. There's no point, for example, in seriously conceptualizing your house until you know exactly where it'll be built. The worst thing you can do is move to a new part of the country and immediately build a house. Direct experience of your exact building site is your most powerful tool.

On the other hand, you don't have to know yet where you might build in order to start preparing. Reading books about alternative building is a good start, an important way to learn the basic concepts. But most of all you need to open your eyes and apply your basic knowledge in the real world. When spending time in a room—any room—ask yourself how it makes you feel. Try to identify what aspect of the space you're responding to, whether positively or negatively. Start noticing structure: how is the building put together? Be conscious of natural light, window size and placement, ceiling height, wall thickness, roof overhangs, entrances, connection to the outside. In the world of good buildings, feeling is the main unit of measure. Buildings are amazing, powerful creations. Usually, they almost force you to feel a certain way; they thrust a view of the world onto you. It may be oppressive, liberating, or anything in between, but it's there and you're experiencing it. Checking out buildings and how they make you feel is instructive and fun, but be careful, or you might get carried away like I did. I once started measuring the lobby of a bank because I liked its proportions. A bank official quickly intervened, and my explanation seemed absurd even to me. I hope that bank never gets robbed, because I'm a prime suspect.

Above all else, avoid packaged ideas. Materials, whether straw bales or vinyl flooring, are impartial; they're tools. Avoid the temptation to latch onto them as complete concepts, as saviors. Likewise for any other aspect of building, whether a particular structural approach, construction technique, or whatever. The tendency to overgeneralize is just your understandable modern desire to hurry, to get an answer and move on. If you aren't prepared to let things take the time that they need, to learn a lot and have fun in the process, no material or eco-guru can save you.

"In the world of good buildings, feeling is the main unit of measure."

Sizing up costs. Left: Big houses come with big price tags. Right: Small houses, such as this little well-planned home, don't.

Cost Factors

Of course, you can't get far into a reality check without talking about money. There are lots of books out there that provide cost estimates and comparisons between different alternative building systems. I won't even go there, because so many variables go into cost. A basic book like this is simply no place for calculating complex cost estimates. However, general advice *is* in order. Fortunately, there are some basic concepts that can help you manage costs, or at least maintain a healthy perspective on them.

MORE, ALWAYS MORE

First and foremost, realize this fundamental truth about building a house: It's going to cost more than you think. If anyone uses words such as "inexpensive" or "easy" to describe a housing approach, check their pupils for dilation. There are many wonderful reasons for building a house, but saving money in the short term isn't one of them.

LESS COSTS LESS

It's an obvious but often-overlooked concept: The best strategy for saving money is to build a small, simple house. A wonderful, well-planned little owner-built cob cottage will be relatively inexpensive. So will the same little building framed in wood. Big houses come with big price tags. Small houses don't.

SWEAT EQUITY

A great way to write fewer checks is to do a lot of the work yourself. However, contrary to many claims I've read, no particular building technique has a corner on this market. Whether of clay, straw, wood, tires, masonry, or whatever, all buildings offer many tasks that the guided novice can perform. With most building techniques, how much you can do yourself will depend on your experience, preparation, determination, and schedule (see the Doing It Yourself section starting on page 203).

MATERIALS CHOICES

Of course, the cost of materials is a huge factor. Local materials, or better yet those gathered from your site, are a great option if they're available. The fact is, though, that most houses, regardless of construction technique, require a fair amount of mass-produced materials. For instance, the most common roofs on alternative buildings are framed with commercial dimensional lumber and covered with mass-manufactured metal.

It's important to be aware that a particular building approach doesn't necessarily translate into saving money on materials. Your lifestyle, rather than whether you build using conventional or alternative methods, will be the major factor influencing your total materials costs. If, for example, you can do without electricity and plumbing, you'll avoid using a lot of expensive (and environmentally questionable) materials. But you can do without water and plumbing as easily in a conventionally constructed house as in an alternative one, so the savings aren't specific to a housing technique. Roads, foundations, roofs, plumbing, electricity, and accessing drinkable water will make up the lion's share of your house's materials consumption and, therefore, expense. Interestingly, these are the elements that are the most independent of your housing approach. Most are identical, or nearly so, regardless of whether you build a conventional or alternative home

FIGURE 1

Conventional vs. Alternative Materials

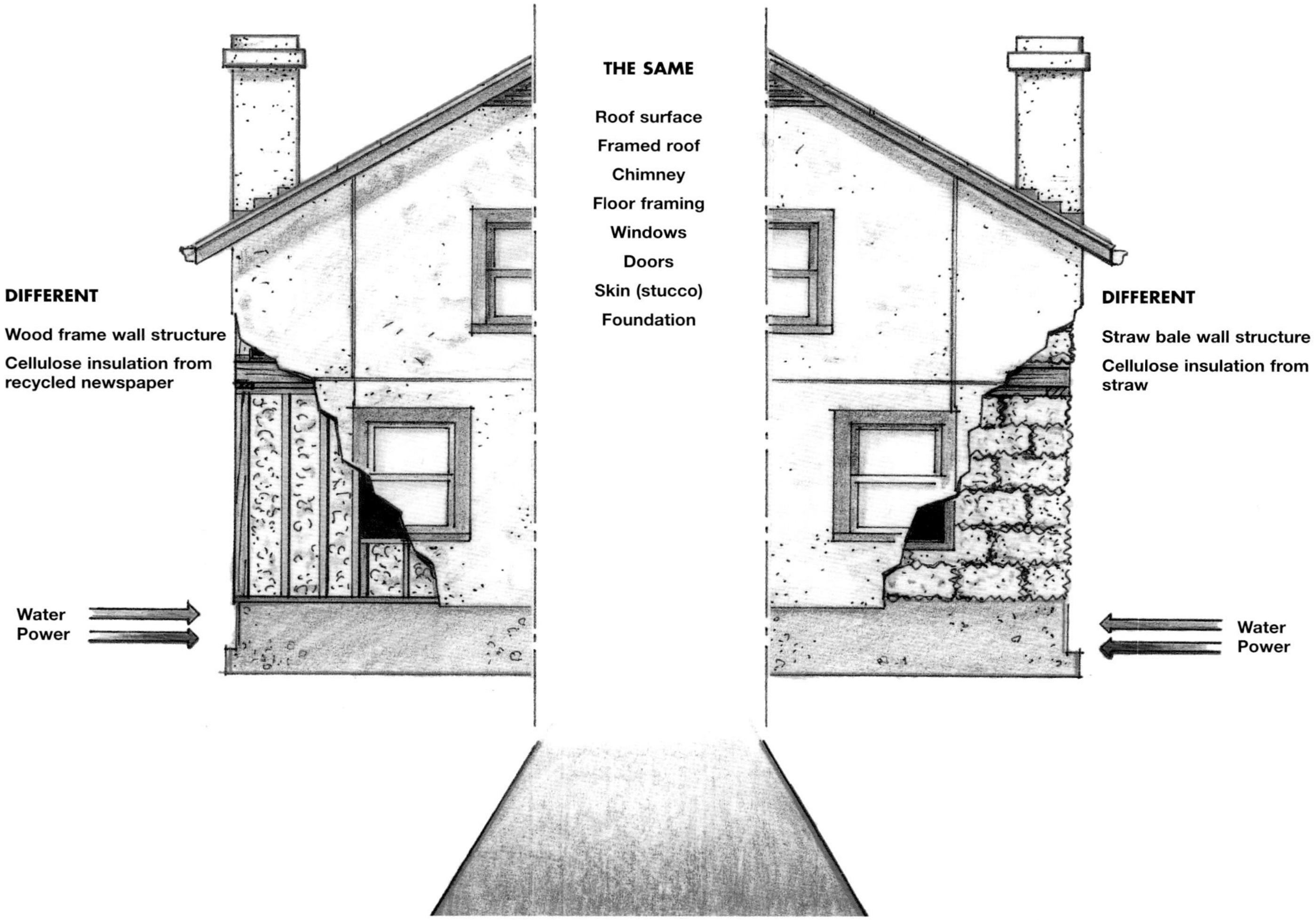

THE SAME

Roof surface
Framed roof
Chimney
Floor framing
Windows
Doors
Skin (stucco)
Foundation

DIFFERENT

Wood frame wall structure

Cellulose insulation from recycled newspaper

Water
Power

DIFFERENT

Straw bale wall structure

Cellulose insulation from straw

Water
Power

These two houses have identical designs and square footages. In many circles, the one on the right would be called "alternative" and the one on the left disdained as a lowly "conventional" house. But as you can see, the only real difference between the two is in the wall systems. The one on the right uses cellulose in the form of straw for structural walls and insulation. The one on the left uses cellulose in the form of wood framing and recycled newspaper insulation for structural walls and insulation. The lion's share of materials for these two buildings is identical.

Salvaging is often mentioned as a way to obtain inexpensive or free materials. That's definitely true, but keep in mind that, from a cost perspective, using salvaged materials can produce a net loss. Old doors and single-pane glass windows are beautiful, but require a lot of time and work, much of it skilled, to be utilized in a house. And they're usually less energy-efficient than their modern counterparts, so exterior applications can create an added cost throughout the life of the building. Comparing strictly in terms of cost, a brand-new, insulated steel door purchased from a megahardware store, complete with frame, hinges, exterior trim, threshold, and weather stripping, is impossible to beat. However, money isn't everything. Working with salvaged materials can be a great education about the past. In addition, older materials are often of higher quality, and using them saves virgin resources. Most of all, salvaged materials can be aesthetically wonderful. Remember, that house you're building isn't just an insane project you want to be finished; it's the place where you're going to live. The environment you create will have a huge effect on your daily psyche. Using salvaged materials can make a shiny new building feel immediately lived in and give it character.

Salvaged charm. Top: We got this cool old sink and the window above it from our friends Robert and Jane's barn. Details such as this make the house feel lived in and cozy. However, I had to rebuild the plumbing fixture, a process that required lots of phone calls and running around for parts. Bottom: These shingles, made from metal roof cut-off scraps, add a bit of whimsy to this conical roof.

Interior old door. Salvaged doors and windows are an especially good choice for interior use because they don't need to be energy-efficient. This means they can be hung less tightly, and thus more easily than exterior doors and windows.

MAINTENANCE AND ENERGY EXPENSES

The cost of a house only begins with its construction. Repair and daily overhead costs, such as water and space heating, cooking, and any other activities requiring some sort of collected energy, are a major part of the equation. Of course, those expenses will come later, but they'll be determined largely by choices you make now, while planning and building.

There are many ways of creating an energy-efficient structure, and most alternative approaches incorporate a consciousness of this issue. Again, success here requires appropriate site-specific design, careful construction, and a sensible lifestyle. Without these factors, the house, no matter how "hip," will be an energy hog. My best advice: don't cut corners. Our masonry stove, for example, cost a bundle even though we did much of the work ourselves. However, gas prices tripled our first winter in the house. It sure felt good to be efficiently burning wood that I'd gathered free.

As for maintenance costs, it's difficult to make general statements. No matter what kind of house you build, the quality of materials you use and the care with which they're installed will make the biggest difference. Inferior windows and doors will drive you crazy. A good roof, large overhangs, a dry foundation, and persnickety attention to flashing and other water-excluding detailing are money in the bank.

On the other hand, the regular maintenance built into some housing styles can really just be a thinly veiled excuse for a party. The "job" of adding a coat of earth plaster every few years to a cob building, for example, entails inviting some friends over to have a few beers and play in the mud. Remember, work (even muddy work) isn't always a dirty word.

Water detailing, bad and good.
Right: This outbuilding isn't lifted off the ground sufficiently, doesn't have adequate overhangs or gutters, and is situated so that rainwater flows downhill toward it. Above: This bermed wall has a large overhang, the ground slopes away from it, plants are kept back, and the gutter downspout routes water away from the building through a pipe.

WILL YOU LOVE IT?

In my opinion, probably the biggest influence on cost, and your perspective on that cost, will be whether you love your house enough to stay there the rest of your life. Dragging ourselves, our families, and our stuff around the country in a continuous search for the right life is incredibly inefficient and expensive. If you build a house and sell it, then the new occupants have to come in and change things around to make it their own. You have to do the same at your new place, or perhaps build another new house. I say if you aren't going to stay there, don't bother building a house. Some people who build knowing they'll be moving in a few years focus more on

resale value, which usually means cutting corners, than on creating a quality building. A good house is better measured in value than cost. As with an oak tree, you'll only truly reap the benefits of a good house after many years. When humans nurture things, those things become beautiful and bountiful. It takes a long time to create good soil for a garden. What's the cash value of a beautiful shade tree next to an old porch? What would you pay to have a place that your children really call home?

How much is a good life worth? If your house helps you to cultivate the things in life that are really important to you, and is part of the package that convinces you to stay put long enough to allow those things to bloom, it'll be worth every penny. Top: a group house at Earthaven eco-village. Above and left: A comfortable living room and child's bedroom, respectively, in the house.

BORROW OR PAY-AS-YOU-GO?

You'll often hear the argument that you can avoid the financial worries of house ownership by building only what you can pay for with cash. The idea is to start small, using only the money you've been able to save, and then add on over the years as more cash becomes available. You avoid paying interest, which makes your house less expensive. I'm no lover of banks, so this idea sounds good. But there are other factors to consider.

First, many of us wouldn't be able to build a birdhouse with what we've saved. If the choice is between borrowing to build or renting, then the idealistic cash-only stance doesn't hold up. Chances are that you've been paying interest on housing all your life. If you're renting, a good portion of your monthly rent check probably is paying interest on your landlord's mortgage. So why not pay off your own interest instead? The only difference is that at some point, after making payments month after month for a number of years, the building you live in will be yours and not someone else's.

Even if you've saved some money to get started, borrowing enough additional money to build your entire house at once might make sense, because building in stages can be problematic. It's often inefficient, since adding on usually means tearing down an exterior wall or transforming it into an interior wall. Either action usually requires demolition. Extending or joining roofs also requires some backtracking, as well as more carpentry skill than building from scratch. In addition, planning to add on sometimes simply means putting off decisions. When the time for the addition comes, you may find that your ideas don't integrate well with your existing building, or that construction details are unnecessarily difficult because of lack of forethought, or that adding on would simply be too disruptive.

Also, whether doing it yourself or just paying for it, building involves a specific mindset, and elements of momentum and inertia. Decisions have to be made, materials have to be collected, the order of tasks to be accomplished must be planned and carried out. Once construction has begun, a certain amount of stress is inevitable because materials are exposed to the weather and costly actions have been set in motion that require timely conclusion. Building in stages usually means doing things over many years during the evening and on weekends. I can't imagine efficiently constructing a house in that manner. Often, by the time you get your tools together on Saturday, it's already Sunday and you need to start putting them up. Personally, I don't like the idea of construction stretching indefinitely into the distant future of my life. On the other hand, I'm sure there are situations where it's the best way to go. For example, a grouping of small buildings constructed one or two at a time—a studio or office, a teenager's bedroom, a guest room, a live-in relative's quarters—might be just what you need. I'm only suggesting that you consider all of this carefully before you commit to a plan of action.

Adding on "someday". Adding on sounds like a good game plan for pay-as-you-go, a-little-at-a-time building—but will it happen? The boarded-up openings to "someday" additions tell a common tale. After you've moved into your home and commenced a busy daily routine, will you really be willing to disrupt it all to tear out walls or open up roofs for the next add-on? Only you know the answer.

Doing It Yourself

If you accept this book's premise that good houses are a symbiosis between specific people and a specific hunk of earth, then you have no choice but to get involved in the creation of your house. The only question is, how far should you go? Like everything in this process, that'll depend completely on who you are. The only real imperative is that the house come from you. As long as that holds true, how many people you get to help actualize the building is unimportant. Even the most rugged individualist with only a few hand tools and some nails in the bed of his pickup has already enlisted the help of hundreds, if not thousands, of people. He didn't design and build his truck, manufacture his tools, or forge those nails. Enlisting the help of architects and carpenters is no different. The important issue is how you utilize that help.

MAKE YOUR OWN DECISIONS

If you're like me, you have trouble deciding what movie to watch, so making really big decisions sends you bowing at the shrines of experts. However, if you've ever seriously researched anything, the one thing you've learned is that experts disagree. And in housing, experts don't just disagree; they seem to live in alternate universes. Now, this may sound like an exaggeration, but I can't think of a single basic house construction issue on which I haven't read credible, diametrically opposed opinions. Venting, vapor barriers, materials, insulation values, air exchange—and on and on. These things are debated hotly. So-called "accepted" practices are in a constant state of flux. Debate is one thing that the alternative and conventional building worlds have in common.

I believe that the main explanation for this phenomenon is that experts are expected to have general knowledge applicable to a wide variety of situations. That simply isn't the way the world works, especially in housing. To me, a housing expert is someone with access to generations of experience about a way of building in a specific location. Only this kind of experience can speak with meaning about any particular detail of building. Everything else is theorizing. How many experts out there have even a minimum, let's say 30 years, of personal experience with a single building? In our society, people build, consult, or install—and then move on.

Now, I'm not saying that there aren't lots of competent, highly knowledgeable people out there. These people and their ideas and experiences comprise an invaluable knowledge base. But you're the one best suited to decide how that knowledge should be applied to your specific situation. As I've said, I prepared for years to build my house. In the end, the worst mistakes I made came from following advice that went against my better judgment because it came from people who I assumed knew more than me. Whenever I took the road of least resistance and abdicated my role as decision maker, I paid a price.

DISTRUST NUMBERS AND STATISTICS

I studied astronomy in college at a time when new calculations suddenly increased the size of our universe tenfold. One day we had the universe, and the next day it was 10 times larger. Of course, the universe hadn't changed; only the numbers and, therefore, our perception had been altered. Here and there throughout this book I've used

> *"Debate is one thing that the alternative and conventional building worlds have in common."*
>
>

a smattering of statistics to underscore points. I've taken these numbers from various websites or books. And although I've been careful to use reliable sources, the fact is I can't personally vouch for their accuracy. Statistics are psychologically powerful. They often quantify abstractions, making them more real in our minds. But your house won't be a statistic; it will be real, existing in a specific time and place. Be vigilant not to let a certain statistic or theoretical number get lodged in your head. What's the R-value of a straw bale wall; the embodied energy of concrete; the cost comparison between thatch and metal roofs based on construction costs, maintenance, and longevity? The accepted answers to questions such as these change all the time, so don't get too dependent on any of it. If you make major decisions based on numbers you've read in books, I have a perpetual-motion machine I'll sell you—and just because I like you, if you act now I'll throw in the Fountain of Youth.

IF IT SOUNDS TOO GOOD TO BE TRUE, IT PROBABLY IS

One Sunday morning while building my house, I was digging a trench for a retaining wall footer and listening to public radio. A show about straw bale building came on. It was produced by a well-known homesteading magazine. The announcer, in a voice that a three-year-old would find patronizing, explained how easy it is to build with straw. Beginners could do it; almost any shape could be made; and the whole thing would cost almost nothing. Plus, our little homemade straw building would be better in every way than some conventionally built monster.

Well, I've done some straw bale building, I've dabbled in cob, I've been around rammed earth, I've used concrete, I've laid a variety of masonry materials, and I've worked with wood. Never, while working with any of these materials, did the word "easy" come to mind. And if there's a way to use them to build a fully functional house for next to nothing, it's a closely guarded secret. I e-mailed the producer and asked him, in so many words, what planet he was from. He could offer no corroboration for his claims, and simply said that his goal was to get people interested in the alternatives.

This story illustrates one of the real dangers of educating yourself about alternative building. Many well-meaning people in the field see it as a crusade, a battle of good versus evil. In struggling to get people to listen, they fall prey to painting too rosy a picture. The unfortunate result is that even in the ostensibly altruistic world of alternative building, you have to take everything with a big grain of salt.

Take, for example, the phenomenon of the construction workshop. Taking a day or two, or even a week, to help someone stack straw bales or dabble in cob on a real building project is a great way to meet people, get some information, and gain a little perspective on what it's like to use these materials in construction. If that's all that you expect, and all that is being promised, then these workshops are fun, helpful, and enlightening. However, saying that you can learn much about building a house by stacking bales is like claiming that you can learn to be a lion tamer at a petting zoo. With the same preparation that's typically done before these workshops begin—the foundation is already completed and the wall materials are laid out and ready to assemble—I could run a workshop on conventional stick-built wall raising that would be as easy and fun as the straw bale version.

Now, don't get me wrong. Workshops and other avenues encouraging a do-it-yourself mentality are an important part of the alternative building world. Many wonderful and knowledgeable people run workshops, do seminars, consult, and in other ways help people help themselves. These people are worth their weight in gold and well worth listening to. All I'm really saying is that it's up to you to judge whether someone is an expert or a charlatan.

I've tried to point out in this book that the struggles of housing have always been the same. Housing, like life, is a balancing act between embracing nature and defending against it. Building something that will withstand nature's onslaughts while welcoming it with open arms has never been and cannot be easy. It takes a lot of thought, hard physical labor, and careful attention to detail. It's an art form of the highest sort. Truly good buildings are sublime human achievements. In this real world of ours, almost every undertaking of any meaning is difficult, both physically and mentally. Life is and will continue to be a struggle, and there's nothing wrong with that.

The high art of building. A work of art if there ever was one, this is the Grand Mosque in Djenne, Mali. How do people take mud and sticks and create a building of such haunting beauty? The answer is the story of a culture written slowly over centuries.

TRUST PRACTICAL EXPERIENCE AND LOCAL KNOWLEDGE

I used to live in Austin, Texas, a hotbed of the alternative or "green" building movement. Once, when I was at a meeting of the local Green Builders Association, a well-known alternative building architect from up North gave a talk, explaining the concept behind a house he'd designed for an Austin client. It involved using thermal mass to absorb heat during the incredibly hot days, and accessing cool evening air, through natural ventilation and other strategies, to allow this heat to dissipate at night. An audience member pointed out that it didn't cool down in Austin at night in the summer, a fact that I can definitely vouch for personally. After some hemming and hawing, the architect simply said, "It should work," and quickly moved on to another topic. In my opinion, that client had made a big mistake. This architect was knowledgeable and competent, but he knew nothing about our climate. There is no substitute for practical local experience.

Remember that alternative building isn't really about materials or making political statements; it's the creation of a building that fits specific people in a specific environment. In that quest, all information is good information. When looking for guidance, it's much more important to find someone with solid, practical, locally based experience than a card-carrying alternative builder. If there are any surviving indigenous building practices in your area, learn about them first. Find out what the

"There is no substitute for practical local experience."

old-timers are doing. Keep in mind, too, that there are more similarities than differences between alternative and conventional buildings. Therefore, local experience, even if it's staunchly conventional, is often very valuable. Stuccoing is a good example. How different stucco mixes will perform in your area can be determined only through experience. I'd rather discuss stucco formulas with a local conventional veteran than with an alternative builder from another climate.

Remember, you're educating yourself about the basics. Armed with that knowledge, you should be able to listen to all sources of information and make the best decision for your situation. Only you can do that.

"CAN I BUILD IT MYSELF?"

Your house may be the single largest financial investment of your life. In addition to being a financial weight, it's a physical weight—poised directly over the top of your head. We all know that practice makes perfect. Unfortunately, the novice owner-builder gets only one chance to assemble this expensive pile of materials, and then moves in underneath them. Many factors go into how sensible or crazy such a plan might be.

First, childhood backgrounds play a big role. Many people come away from childhood with few or no basic tool skills. They weren't around people who fixed cars or did projects around the house. Others, who don't consider themselves carpenters or even especially handy, may have learned as children all the basic skills necessary to at least be a helper on most aspects of house building. There is a feel you get for building things, a general understanding of how to deal with materials, that can cross over between many different activities and approaches to building. Will the force exerted by this thing cause that thing to fall over? Does this stuff seem like a good consistency to set up the way I'm expecting? Do I need to step back, take a break, and maybe call someone who knows what they're doing? Without this basic experience, this quasi-intuitive knowledge of tools and materials and problem-solving, I advise thinking long and hard before attempting to build your own house, regardless of design or materials.

A load over your mind. The uneven, rough-cut lumber in this overhead floor framing adds to the room's beauty. But how can a first-time, novice builder know if it'll be strong enough?

Remember, the success of your house will be measured in the details. We could build two houses side by side that look identical. One might be drafty, moldy, and suffer structural damage in just a few years. The other could be warm and cozy, withstanding the elements for many, many years without damage. The difference would be in the details. Is the flashing correctly installed around the roof, chimney, doors, windows, and at the base of the walls? How was the slab prepared before pouring? Was caulking used or abused? Is there a foundation drain? Was it properly installed? Has the site been graded to shed water? Have local insects been taken into account? The answers to these questions and many more can't easily be determined after the fact. Planning and careful attention to detail are required during installation. I once worked on a house in a fancy country club development. Only 10 or 15 years old, the house had serious structural rot in several areas because of poor flashing installation. It happens all the time.

This is boring stuff, seemingly far removed from the dream of a wonderful, cozy, socially responsible house. However, these details are really the core of your dream. If your house doesn't last, its hip design is completely irrelevant. It's a failure, plain and simple. Many crucial details aren't conceptually difficult, but they need to be executed skillfully. When you're dealing with water, small imperfections in detailing can cause big problems. Identifying and performing these tasks on your precious house for the first time ever, without guidance and supervision, would probably be a mistake.

Detailing is a potential downside to choosing some alternative building techniques because these approaches haven't yet become part of the construction vernacular. Who do you turn to when you have technical difficulties attaching wood roof framing to a monolithic cob wall, or are confused about flashing details for a straw bale building? Books can give you only general information, and there will be many situations not covered in those simple diagrams. Text that seems clear while reading it on the couch can be frustratingly incomplete when you're actually trying to carry out the operation described. Inexperience and trailblazing don't go well together. If you don't know what you're doing, choose alternative building techniques that have a history in your area. You'll want to have an experienced ear to turn to in times of need.

"Inexperience and trailblazing don't go well together."

Having said all that, I think you probably can build or be deeply involved in building your own house. But the decision is yours, and the only way to make it is to soul-search and be honest with yourself about your limits and your strengths. You have to look yourself square in the face. If you do that and still want to build a house, you can accomplish it without a doubt no matter what your childhood was like or how completely clueless you may be. The key is simply to get experience before starting your precious dream house. And the less experience you have, the more preparation you'll have to do.

The ideal approach is to get involved in a project similar to your own with an experienced person in your area. If you plan to build with wood and straw, for example, look for a project using those materials. It usually isn't difficult to get a job as a lowly construction-site helper. Getting paid to gain experience in a building project similar to what you envision for your own home would be a terrific deal. If this isn't possible, try to spend some time working on any construction project. If you can't make the time for that, but will have the time to work on your building, then find the most experienced person you can and see if they're willing to let you work with them while building your house. They might be very wary of this prospect, so you may need to convince them. I'm reminded of a sign I once saw: "I charge 20 an hour to do the work, 25 an hour if you watch, and 30 an hour if you help."

A shed for learning. If you're inexperienced, cut your teeth by building a small, simple version of your house as a shed. You'll need the storage space, and it won't be a disaster if it leaks or doesn't last forever. Doug and Nelle, whose post-and-beam straw bale house was featured in the previous chapter, built this little straw bale shed to house their well pump before they built their home.

As I said earlier, I had book learning but no practical experience when I quit my job to become a construction worker. After several years of making a living in the building trades, I started building my house and found myself overwhelmed by the task. It all turned out fine in the end, but I wouldn't want to go through it again. Remembering those oblivious days of renting, when I never worried about my housing, I sometimes think ignorance really is bliss. On the other hand, my house is my biggest achievement. I know its strengths and weaknesses; I know how everything went together. Building my own house has given me skills, muscles, and a perspective that I didn't have before. From that point of view, I really recommend it. If you're inexperienced and decide to build yourself, please get some practical experience first. Get a construction job, help a friend, or even just cut your teeth by building a shed. No matter how much you prepare, I predict that you won't feel you prepared too much.

"WHAT IF I DON'T BUILD IT MYSELF?"

You've done all your research, you know what you want, but you don't want to build it yourself. You need a builder. How do you find the right one? This is a difficult question, because you aren't going to be a typical client. You want to be very much involved in the decision-making process. There are things you've read about that you'd like to try, and other things you're unsure about but want to discuss before making a final decision. Many builders will balk at this level of involvement, and often for good reason.

House building is a difficult profession. In a recently published book of job ratings, carpentry came in 237th out of 250 listed jobs, falling well below cashier, security guard, janitor, and maid. House building is physically demanding while requiring considerable skill and careful thought. It doesn't pay especially well and has low job security. On top of all that, as a professional builder you must spend huge amounts of someone else's money to buy materials, pay subcontractors, and more. The fact that the client asked you to spend that money, that this whole thing was their idea, is often conveniently forgotten, leaving you open to all sorts of accusations and disputes. Every builder has a grab bag of jerk client stories that will set your hair on end. Approaching someone with this job history and saying you want your house to be a team effort can be tricky.

The problem of finding good people to work with is exacerbated by our mobile society. Probably the worst time to build a house is right after you move to a new area. Not only will you be unfamiliar with the specific local climate, and thus unable to make intelligent decisions about your house, but you'll have no social network to help you. Remember, we're social animals. Not until you become a part of the local culture, start to make friends, and give something to your community, can you expect to develop relationships that will lead to the creation of a good house. People work for money, yes, but good builders also work to build good houses for reasons of personal satisfaction and pride. If things are going to go well, your builder needs to be your friend, or at least someone who respects you as a part of the community. You can't fake that and you can't hurry it.

Once you do find someone who you trust and who's willing to work with you, make it your mantra that you're going to be the best client they ever had. Put yourself in their shoes and it won't be difficult to calm down at frustrating moments. On the other hand, you have to hold firm to making your own decisions. This is your house and having someone else build it is a compromise that to some degree waters down its specific nature. Maintaining a balance between not getting in the way and remaining the decision maker is a delicate dance. Take your time when choosing a builder. Try to really get to know them, and be completely straightforward about how you see things getting done. Picking a builder will be one of the most important decisions you'll make.

My hero. This is Gary. He saved my butt when I ran into problems building my house. I never could've done it without him. Being blessed with good people like Gary will make or break your project. Look long and hard. When you find them, don't let go.

MISTAKES

No matter how much you prepare, you're going to make mistakes on your house. Probably the best way to minimize them is to see your project as two distinct phases. The first phase is planning your home's design. People tend to be anxious and rush through this period. On the contrary, this is your opportunity to spend some time dreaming, exploring the possibilities, and getting things the way you want them. Take your time and do it right. When I was planning my house, I was paranoid about spending too much money on architects and engineers. If I was building my house again, I'd take my basic design to two or three different architects and get their take on my plans. All those different perspectives would help me tweak my design for the better. In addition, it's a good way to pick up detailing advice or other little tidbits from people who do this stuff all the time. Of course, I'm not saying that you always need architects and engineers to build a house. My main point is, don't be penny wise and pound foolish. Ask for help, take your time, and have fun. Remember, even if you're spending money, until you actually break ground, you haven't made any commitments. That's a freedom you should cherish, because you won't see it again throughout your project.

Once you're completely satisfied with phase one, then start thinking about phase two: the actual construction. Before you do any site prep or collect any materials, all major decisions about your home's construction should be made, and many minor ones should be pretty clear, too. Now, look hard at your available funds, do a budget, and see if you can build what you've planned.

Of course, you're still going to make mistakes, probably some pretty big ones. At least you did your best, and, hey, we all make mistakes. As in life, the grace with which you bounce back will say more about you than pretty much anything else. And none of this means that you can't take an organic approach to building. There are good arguments for making many decisions as you build, for remaining open and responsive to the building process. (The most beautiful description of this concept that I know of is in Christopher Alexander's book, *The Timeless Way of Building*, listed on page 216.) All I'm saying is to be clear about your approach. If you start building before you're ready, you're going to make more mistakes, plain and simple.

Printed planning. Blueprints are called "plans" because they're the printed version of your thoughts, your intentions, your wishes—your planning. Printed plans communicate to everyone involved the numerous decisions you've made about your house. The more people working on the construction of your building, the more important it is to materialize your dreams in tangible, printed-on-paper plans.

"When you think you're almost done, you're probably about halfway there."

❧

HOW LONG WILL IT TAKE?

There's a strange phenomenon in the building world: people always think their house will be finished long before it actually is. You'll do the same thing, so I don't know why I'm even writing this. You may want to take a novel approach and be realistic. Even better, make no predictions at all, moving along day to day and taking on each new task as it comes up. Sure, right! Or you can pick some baseless, absurd, and arbitrary deadline like the rest of us do, as if by sheer force of will we could simplify the world. It's truly mind-boggling how many steps go into creating even a modest well-built house. Just remember that when you think you're almost done, you're probably about halfway there.

It really does end, though, and all of those time-consuming tasks fade into fuzzy memory. Sometimes I'll just sit and stare at a part of my house, and memories of everything I did there come flooding back. If I'm in a good mood, I'll laugh at the hilarious person who thought he could control this bucking bronco of a building with the simple declaration of a finishing date.

Point of no return. Once this machine shows up, there's no turning back—so make sure you're ready. You may not actually use a bulldozer for your project, but you get the idea: prepare as best you can before you start construction!

Codes

You don't have to hang out around the alternative-building water cooler for long before you learn that codes are the big whipping boy: "The pea-brained government has done it again with some closed-minded, outdated blah-de-blah that doesn't apply to the environmentally conscious owner-builder" . . . and so forth and so on, and on and on.

I have a love/hate relationship with codes. Where I lived in Texas, there were no building codes or zoning outside the city limits. This is a great situation for your greywater-recycling, composting-toileted, straw-bale-dome paradise—until someone puts a radioactive medical waste landfill next door. Codes are designed to protect us from each other first, and from ourselves second. Codes are the unsuspecting home buyer's main defense against unscrupulous builders. As a house is being built, codes give local authorities their only opportunity to assure the quality of that building. Unfortunately, this all seems to have little to do with the owner-builder who has every intention of constructing the best possible building. In our case, codes are often outdated barriers to our forward-thinking ways.

In retrospect, however, I can think of instances when I cussed a code only to later see its purpose. Where I live, for example, owner-builders doing much of their own work can get their own permits, thus foregoing the expense of a contractor. Plumbing and electricity, however, must be done by licensed tradespeople. Without that code, I probably would've tried to run my own electric. Instead, I found a contractor who would supervise me, letting me do most of the work without the worries. To be honest, that turned out to be the best approach. I've been involved in a job where someone did their own wiring, and it was a real mess.

Depending on where you live, choosing alternative building techniques can create considerable code hassles. There are several ways to deal with this problem. The most direct way is to take the time to educate and convince your inspector that the approaches you're planning are safe. Inspectors generally have a lot of discretion to award permits if they decide that the plans fit the intent of the law. They also usually have the power to issue experimental permits for building approaches that have yet to make it into local code books. Most of the popular alternative building approaches now have considerable code histories somewhere. Inspectors from areas where they're familiar with your chosen technique might be willing to talk with your inspector about their experiences. Also, advocates for various techniques have amassed code information that you can access and pass on to your inspector. Or you may be able to hire an engineer or architect with experience in alternative building to discuss your project with the inspector.

I live in a large, mountainous rural county where there's only one building inspector. The poor guy is running around constantly trying to keep up with permit applications. He's a nice guy, but he doesn't have much time for chitchat. Consequently, you have to be totally prepared when you talk with him. Chances are, your inspector will require the same level of preparedness. Be sure you're ready when it's time to discuss matters. Also, here's some general advice: don't tell your inspector how things ought to be. You're going to be working with this official for quite a while, and the fact is that he or she has a lot of legal say over what you can do.

Compromise is another approach. I wanted a greywater system and composting toilet, but found that in my area greywater must, by code, be routed to a septic

Shocking shortcut? This electric wire is rigged to supply power to an outbuilding. It extends from the house's main circuit breaker through a wall, along some siding, and down into a six-inch-deep trench, where it runs buried for 100 feet before emerging at a barn. Every inch is an accident waiting to happen. If someone clips the protective insulation with a lawn trimmer or while digging with a shovel, they could receive a painful, possibly fatal, shock. Obviously, this is—and should be—a code violation. Is the time and money saved circumventing the code worth the risk?

system. Around here, a lot of people straight-pipe sewage directly into creeks and waterways, so this code is probably a good idea. I decided to put in both a septic system and a composting toilet and greywater system. Art Ludwig, a knowledgeable greywater systems advocate, recommends having a septic system in place for overflow and for those rare times when you might need to wash something noxious down the drain. It was expensive, but now I have all bases covered. I met the code; any squeamish relatives or friends have a comforting flush toilet to use; and I have the system I wanted for my needs. When the in-laws aren't around, the flush toilet makes a nice plant holder.

Some people opt to find ways around codes. For example, I've heard of people setting things up one way for an inspection, and then changing them around after the inspector leaves. Others go all the way and build their homes without official inspection or approval. Where I live, as far as I can tell, the only real clout the inspector has if you haven't met the code requirements is to refuse to allow power to be hooked up to your house. I know people who've built houses off the grid who never applied for a permit and had no problems. Of course, I'm not suggesting any of these options, because they're illegal. The fact is that some people do it that way.

If you're patient, don't lose your temper, and work with your inspector to address any concerns about a particular approach, chances are you can get official approval to do what you want. You'll be doing a real community service, too, by opening the doors for others in your area who may have similar building plans.

Other Considerations

Of course, the realities of planning, designing, paying for, and building a house aren't the only things you need to think about before you start your project. Alternative building isn't just about building, after all. All sorts of other considerations go with it. I've listed a couple here. Undoubtedly you'll encounter others unique to your own situation.

LIFESTYLE

To a large degree, alternative building is about lifestyle. Most concepts and approaches labeled "alternative" in this book share a common trait: they're only loosely controllable. For example, to live in a house dependent to some degree on the sun for heat, you have to be willing to sometimes put on an extra sweater. If you have solar hot water, you have to learn to adjust your need for hot water to fit the sun's habits. If you have solar electricity, you learn to conserve when it's cloudy, to spare your batteries. If you have a sawdust toilet, the bucket determines when it's time for a walk to the compost pile.

In short, most alternative buildings have a different standard of comfort than the modern pushbutton house. For me, the differences are mostly positive. For instance, I don't like being in forced-air heating and cooling. I don't mind splitting and stacking firewood. I'd rather climb around in the woods checking a spring than drink chlorinated water. Still, all these involved lifestyle changes for me just the same. Be honest with yourself about your willingness and ability to make similar changes.

Just add water. There are many good reasons to put ponds near buildings. The water can be used for vegetable gardens, swimming, attracting wildlife, or just gazing into. However, a pond needs to be planned along with the building, not as an afterthought. Remember, the same machines that you may need to clear land, dig foundation trenches, etc., can also build your pond.

Good thinking. Putting a vegetable garden along the path to this little straw bale house is a great idea. Plants thrive in the open, sunny area created when the house site was cleared. And humans passing by each day will be drawn to take care of the plants.

OUTDOOR SPACE

If you're interested in alternative building, chances are that a house isn't the only part of your vision. You're probably thinking about food gardens, outdoor rooms, and the like. So don't forget to squirrel away some money for the outside before you spend it all on the inside. A house has a tendency to expand to engulf all available funds. I've never heard anyone being surprised at how much money they had left over after building.

In fact, you may want to do some of that outdoor work early. In retrospect, I wish that I'd slowed down and done as much landscaping and planting as would've been logistically possible *before* building. We're in serious need of trees around our house, but I still haven't recouped the money or found the time to complete our landscaping plans. It would've been a real comfort to have had vegetable gardens established and trees planted and growing while the house building was going on. After planting and with a little care, trees and vegetables do most of their own work—so why not let them have at it from the get-go?

Hammering It Home

This has been a reality check, but the fact is that I know very little about your reality. My primary goal in this chapter has been, as usual, to get you thinking. For me, alternative building isn't about fads, right way versus wrong way, how things ought to be, or how you wish things were. It's about how things *are*: How you are, how your land is, and how the two can come together. It doesn't get more real than that.

Yet the true reason most people are drawn to thoughts of housing is to dream. You dream about your "dream house," that place where you can relax, where all the pieces of your life come together in a harmonious whole. The paradox of building a house is that you have to remain grounded in reality while dreaming. To do that you have to understand and deal honestly with the realities of your specific situation —your skills, your finances, your site conditions, your time constraints, your personal likes and dislikes, your social network, and so much more—while allowing yourself to push the envelope of your perceived limitations. It's the dance between these two poles that ultimately will lead to what will truly be your good house.

Outdoor details. A salvaged-granite-and-marble path (above) and patio (below), a log bridge, a handmade garden gate—these are the kinds of expressive, personal details that make the outdoors around your good house good, too.

Chapter 9

AFTER THIS BOOK

We all live in some kind of shelter, so, whether you rent, remodel, or build, learning about the way housing works, about the buildings that surround you, makes sense. Likewise, as you start out on the road to the house that's right for you, it makes sense to explore as many possibilties as you can. I've repeatedly returned to the idea that a good house is specific to the people and environment with which it's involved. Alternative building approaches emphasize such concepts as self-sufficiency, local solutions, and minimizing environmental impact, so to my mind they're especially valuable to anyone searching for a good house.

But once you have a basic understanding of housing, all knowledge is good knowledge in your quest to learn more. Limiting yourself to alternative building literature, or focusing on a single style of or approach to housing, is a mistake, plain and simple. There is always something more to learn. You can understand, then, why I believe a bibliography to be a somewhat limited tool. No bibliography can be truly complete.

Going Deeper

Still, whatever road you take, you're going to want to delve deeper, always deeper into the fascinating labyrinth that is the world of housing. This book is only an introduction, a starting point. To really understand and use many of the concepts that we've touched on here, you'll need to go into more depth. I can't tell you what you'll need to know for your particular situation, but I can help you start to identify what to look for and where to look for it.

To my mind, there are three important, even essential, sources of information you'll need to tap: hard-copy printed materials (books and magazines), the Internet, and buildings themselves. Each source offers things that the others don't.

Books and magazines can be valuable not only as sources of information for you, but as references, to show to others when you need to illustrate a point, or to keep with you to refer to—for formulas, calculation tables, concepts, whatever—when your house is actually being built. One tip: When evaluating books or magazines, beware of publications—I don't know how else to say this—that are too positive, that make things sound too easy. People who are excited and passionate about a concept sometimes paint too rosy a picture. In the world of building, a realistic, honest book or article by someone with a depth of practical experience is far more useful.

Of course, you'll want to consult the Internet because it has such a broad reach, is continually updated, and is highly interactive: you'll find not only a wealth of information-laden websites, but also many experienced builders and other experts who are willing to answer questions from strangers like you or me. Our modern world often seems like it's all about money, so it's refreshing to find how many people are simply passionate about something and willing to help with their expertise. Internet bulletin boards and discussion groups also are great places to post questions and share answers. And the Internet can be a good source for hard-to-find alternative or "green" products.

Finally, and in some ways most importantly if only because people tend not to do it, you'll want to study actual buildings. Would it make sense to be interested in trees, but spend all your time indoors reading books about them? Of course not. The same holds true for buildings. You have to get out and look at buildings; crawl in, around, on top of, and under buildings. Each building is an open book with a story to tell.

So, as our last act together, let's go back through the chapters of this book and look at some of the ways you can delve deeper into the concepts introduced.

CHAPTER 1: WHAT IS A HOUSE?

I'm a firm believer in intention and focus. If you don't know what you're looking for, how can you find it? In the context of looking for a good house, that means you have to begin at the beginning, by trying to get a feel for housing itself.

HARD COPY

Christopher Alexander, *The Timeless Way of Building* (New York: Oxford University Press, 1979).

Alexander, Ishikawa, Silverstein, Jacobson, King, and Angel, *A Pattern Language* (New York: Oxford University Press, 1977).

These are simply the best books that I know of to create a context for our present situation as modern people in search of meaningful shelter. In fact, they're the only two books that I uncategorically recommend for everyone to read.

The authors call these volumes two halves of a single work. *A Pattern Language* lays out a language for building and planning. *The Timeless Way of Building* explains the theory and instructions for using that language, and is probably the most perfect book I've ever read. It's well-presented, inspirational, and truly mind-blowing. Read it first. *A Pattern Language* is equally powerful and definitely worth reading cover to cover, even though only about a third of it applies to individual housing.

THE INTERNET

Pattern Language (www.patternlanguage.com/index.htm). Created by the originators of the pattern language design concept.

Great Buildings (www.greatbuildings.com). Fun, searchable site where you can see and read about some of the world's architectural wonders, from ancient times to the present.

BUILDINGS

Much of what the two books I just mentioned are about is learning from the buildings around you. If you take the books to heart, you'll start an ongoing dialogue with the buildings with which you share your life. In fact, you can begin right now simply by trying to identify what it is that you like and don't like about the buildings you encounter. Don't use any theory or preconceived notions of what you think you ought

to look for. Look at buildings through the eyes of a child. Experience the outside, the inside, and all the details that make up a building, and try to be conscious of how you react to any given aspect. How do you feel? It sounds overly simple, even childish, but I think you'll be surprised at the places this little game can take you.

CHAPTER 2: MATERIALS

The world of materials is so huge and ever-changing that I hesitate to mention any sources at all. You'll really just have to dive in and see what's out there. Here are some places to start.

HARD COPY

Steve Chappell, ed., *The Alternative Building Sourcebook* (Brownfield, Maine: Fox Maple Press, 1998). A resource guide for the professional and novice builder, with sources for materials as well as contact information for designers, architects, builders, schools, publications, and more.

Daniel D. Chiras, *The Natural House: A Complete Guide to Healthy, Energy-Efficient, Environmental Homes* (White River Junction, Vt.: Chelsea Green, 2000). An overview of all aspects of "natural" housing, including an introduction to most popular materials and how they can come together to create a house. Dan's own Earthship hybrid is featured in the Applications chapter of this book.

THE INTERNET

GENERAL INFORMATION

Building Green: Publishers of Environmental Building News (www.buildinggreen.com). Go to the products section for reviews of a variety of commercial alternative materials.

Oikos: Green Building Source (www.oikos.com/products). This site has a wide variety of information, including product reviews and in-depth articles.

Sustainable Building Sourcebook (www.greenbuilder.com/sourcebook). Great site with a solid section on building materials.

Center for Building Performance Research: Embodied Energy (http://www.arch.vuw.ac.nz/cbpr/index_embodied_energy.html). Embodied energy discussion, with statistics for many materials.

Roman Concrete (www.romanconcrete.com). All about the amazing concrete used by the ancient Romans to create buildings that still stand today. A great read for a healthy perspective on materials past and present.

PRODUCTS AND COMPANIES

There are tons of websites for this category. Here are just a few.

Durisol (www.durisol.com). Permanent insulative concrete form made of recycled wood chips bonded with Portland cement.

Faswall (www.faswall.com). Faswall is permanent form similar to Durisol.

Rastra (www.rastra.com). Permanent insulative concrete forms made from recycled plastic.

Enviroshake (www.enviroshake.com). Recycled rubber, plastic, and cellulose used to make roofing shingles that look like cedar shakes.

Plastic Lumber Company (www.plasticlumber.com). Decking made from recycled plastic milk jugs.

Carefree Xteriors Decking Systems (www.carefreexteriors.com). Recycled milk jug decking and structural lumber made from milk jugs reinforced with fiberglass.

J-Drain: Prefabricated Drainage Composites (www.j-drain.com). A number of interesting products designed to deal with unwanted water around buildings. Among these is the modular foundation drain mentioned in the Structure chapter.

BUILDINGS

Find out what kinds of materials are being used in alternative buildings in your area, then go and visit as many different examples as possible. Use what you've learned in this book to evaluate how each building seems to be faring in your climate. Ask questions about materials-related problems involved in construction, and try to learn what owners and builders would do differently if they had the chance.

CHAPTER 3: STRUCTURE

Here's where you address the serious goal of creating a safe, lasting, load-supporting building. You can't learn too much on this subject.

HARD COPY

No matter what you build, it's going to follow tried-and-true structural principles. It's a good idea to get a few "conventional" texts on building that cover basic structural configurations, loads, framing details and the like. Here are two good ones that I've used.

Francis D.K. Ching, *Building Construction Illustrated* (Hoboken, N.J.: John Wiley & Sons, 2000).

Rob Thallon, *Graphic Guide to Frame Construction: Details for Builders and Designers* (Newtown, Ct.: Taunton Press, 2000).

THE INTERNET

Building Big (www.pbs.org/wgbh/buildingbig). A fun site with lots of basic, interactive information on loads, forces, materials, and much more. The site focuses on large structures—bridges, domes, skyscrapers, dams, and tunnels—and is designed for kids, but there's good information here for adults seriously interested in housing.

History of Domes (www.takenaka.co.jp/takenaka_e/dome_e/history/hisindex.html). A review of the history of major architectural domes through photos, with a good timeline.

Straw Bale Arch (www.strawbuilding.org/tech/archtest.htm). Interesting page describing the results of testing a structural arch made of straw bales. Demonstrates that straw is more versatile than you might expect.

Red Sky Shelters (www.redskyshelters.com) Red Sky Shelters is the maker of the Yome, a portable canvas-covered semipermanent shelter that combines the almost straight walls of a yurt with the triangular structural strength and openness of a dome.

Grand Shelters, Inc. (www.grandshelters.com). This company manufactures the IceBox, an inexpensive, lightweight portable tool for building a snow shelter.

BUILDINGS

Get in the habit of noticing the structural characteristics of the buildings you encounter. Start with where you live. Crawl under, around, and on top of your present abode and learn as much as you can about the foundation, walls, and roof. One interesting and revealing exercise is to look for weaknesses and then try to explain them. What caused that crack in the foundation? Is the floor sagging? If so, why? Cracked drywall? What's the source of the problem? When you're standing in line at the bank, visiting friends, buying groceries, or whatever, take a moment to notice what's holding things up.

CHAPTER 4: TEMPERATURE

The logical place to start learning more about creating a stable indoor temperature, regardless of the climate or the building approach you choose, is to study passive solar design. If you live where it's hot, you'll want to build your house so that the space inside is protected from the sun. If you live where it's cold, you'll want to use the sun to help heat your building. Chances are that your particular real world situation will be some fuzzy combination of the above and you'll want to both utilize and protect yourself from the sun. In any case, you'll need to understand the theory and practice of passive solar design. From there you can apply whatever information on materials, insulation, windows, heat sources, cooling, and the like is relevant to your site, your climate, your specific situation.

HARD COPY

There are tons of books on passive solar; new ones come out all the time. The basic theory doesn't change, so new isn't necessarily better. Whichever book you choose, make sure that it's not overly technical, and that it covers the basics such as how the Sun moves across the sky and how to calculate and plot the Sun's movement at your particular latitude. It should also have plenty of practical information on thermal mass, window placement, window-area-to-thermal-mass ratios, and the like.

A very thorough book on the topic that I've often referred to is:

Edward Mazria, *The Passive Solar Energy Book, Expanded Professional Edition* (Emmaus, Pa.: Rodale Press, 1979).

Also, here are some other good books dealing with temperature. All three are now out of print, but are well worth looking for at used book stores or your library.

Donald A. Watson and Kenneth Labs, *Climatic Design: Energy-Efficient Building Principles and Practice* (New York: McGraw-Hill, 1983). A well-organized book covering the theory and application of a variety of strategies for creating a stable indoor temperature.

Bill Langdon, *Movable Insulation* (Emmaus, Pa.: Rodale Press, 1980). More than 350 pages covering designs for creating insulation for your windows.

Albert A. Barden, *Finnish Fireplaces: Heart of the Home* (Norridgewock, Maine: Maine Wood Heat, 1984). A great book on the history, concept, performance, and design of the contraflow masonry heater.

THE INTERNET

PASSIVE SOLAR
North Carolina Solar Center (www.ncsc.ncsu.edu). A good site about all aspects of solar building from North Carolina State University. Includes in-depth downloadable fact sheets.

Cool Roofing Materials Database (http://eetd.lbl.gov/CoolRoof/). Solar and thermal data on different roofing surfaces.

Thermal Mass and R-Value (www.buildinggreen.com/features/tm/thermal.cfm). Good article on the relation of thermal mass to R-value.

SunAngle (www.susdesign.com/sunangle). Free online sun angle calculations for use in passive solar design.

INSULATION
Cellulose Insulation Manufacturers Association (www.cellulose.org). Lots of information on cellulose.

MWB-R-Pro Corporation (www.mwbrpro.com). A cellulose insulation installer site with good general information.

Bonded Logic, Inc. (www.bondedlogic.com/UltraTouchMain.htm). Insulation made from recycled cotton fibers.

R-Value of Straw Bales Lower than Previously Reported
(www.buildinggreen.com/news/r-value.html). Short history of
tests done to evaluate straw as insulation and the different conclusions that have been reached.

MISCELLANEOUS

Efficient Windows Collaborative (www.efficientwindows.org).
Tons of info on windows, from theory to choosing the right
windows for your needs.

Masonry Heater Association of North America (www.mha-
net.org). This site can help you find a stove mason in your area.

Masonry Stove Builders (www.heatkit.com). This is the site of
stove designer and builder Norbert Senf, featured in the
Temperature chapter. The site includes a downloadable planning guide.

BUILDINGS

Different kinds of heat and cool create completely different
interior environments. Forced-air (convective) systems feel different than metal wood stove radiant heat, which feels different
than masonry wood stove radiant heat, and so on. Also, different insulation types create different interior environments. The
spaces created by the thick, rounded walls of a house insulated
with straw feel and sound
different than those of a
bermed house, such as an
Earthship, which in turn are
different than those of a dry-
walled, fiberglass-insulated
building. When you're in a
building, try to discern what
is heating and cooling it and
what kind of insulation it
has. Visit as many kinds of
different alternative buildings
as possible and pay attention
to the quality of the heat/cool
and to the feeling that the
nature of the insulation
materials gives the space. Try
to identify what buildings
around you are using the sun
for temperature stability and
which are fighting it.

CHAPTER 5: SEPARATION

If I've been successful, you're sick by now of hearing the sentiment that it doesn't matter how wonderful, natural, hip, and
yada-yada your house is if you don't build it to last. If your
building can't protect itself from pesky nature, then it's doomed
to a short, moldy, parasite-ridden life. The little details of construction will determine your success or failure on this front.
Once you start getting a clearer idea of the overall nature of
your house project, the materials used, and how and where
they'll be connected, then it'll be time to educate yourself about
the specific protective construction details appropriate for your
situation and climate. Those decisions are yet to be made, so I
can't tell you what to read or who to talk to. I can only say to
keep this topic locked away until the right moment, and then
dive into it with a passion.

HARD COPY

Separation issues and methods for dealing with them depend
largely on the particular building approach involved, so books
that focus on building with specific materials are often the best
places to learn more. There are a number of such books listed
under the Applications section of this chapter on page 224.

When you're buying books on building with a particular
material, such as straw bale or cob, check to make sure that
the real details of construction, such as flashing, are covered
thoroughly. Also, make
sure that issues of decay
are taken seriously and will
apply to your climate. For
example, if a book on
straw bale has information
based only on buildings in
the dry climate of New
Mexico, it will be a limited
resource for you if you're
thinking about building in
humid Florida.

THE INTERNET

WEATHERIZATION

The Weatherization Pages (www.weatherization.com). The website of Fred Lugano, a weatherization pioneer who's part of a movement that is questioning conventional, code-required approaches to weatherization.

PLASTER/STUCCO

Limebase Products, Ltd. (www.limebase.co.uk/guidetolime.htm). Information on the use of lime in plaster.

ROOF SURFACES

McGhee and Company Roof Thatchers (www.thatching.com). Master thatcher Colin McGhee's website on thatch and thatching. Photos of Colin's work are featured in the Separation chapter.

Roofscapes, Inc. (www.roofmeadow.com). Tons of information on green, or "living," roofs.

INSECTS

Carpenter Ants (www.uky.edu/Agriculture/Entomology/ent-facts/struct/ef603.htm). Fact sheet on carpenter ants.

Carpenter Bees (www.ces.ncsu.edu/depts/ent/notes/Urban/carp-bee.htm). Fact sheet on carpenter bees.

Termites (www.labyrinth.net.au/~dewart/index.html). A humorous and informative site about these common pests.

BUILDINGS

Start noticing the construction details of buildings around you. How are the transitions between exterior materials handled? Do the windows and doors have flashing? Are the chimneys and other roof punctures "sealed" with a sloppy glop of tar or caulk, or are they correctly flashed? Find examples of water, sun, wind, and insect damage and see if you can imagine ways that the decay could've been averted. Try to find out about the different stucco and plaster mixes on the buildings that you come across, especially on the alternative houses that you visit. Are there any living roofs in your area?

CHAPTER 6: CONNECTION

For the modern alternative house, connection to the outside mostly means access to sunlight, the exchange of water and air, and creation of electrical power. All, of course, are important topics to research.

HARD COPY

In many cases you'll need to seek out chapters within more general works to find information on a specific connection-related topic. Daylighting and ventilation is one example.

DAYLIGHTING AND VENTILATION

It's a good idea to have at least one book in your resource library that discusses things like window placement, planting to encourage or discourage air movement, and strategies for shading out and letting in the sun's light. One such book is:

Ken Kern, *The Owner-Built Home* (New York: Macmillan Reference USA, 1975). An inspirational book by a free-thinking pioneer, with interesting information on many topics, including natural ventilation and daylighting. Out of print, but often available in libraries.

WATER

Most people get water from their municipal government or from wells, so information on alternatives is in less demand—and therefore sometimes harder to find—than info on other aspects of alternative building.

Springs

If you're lucky enough to have access to a clean source of gravity-fed spring water, you need to talk with folks in your area about how to tap it. There's not a lot of printed material out there on the topic.

Carolina Water Tank, Box 75, Marr Creek Road, Bryson City, NC 28713, (828) 488-3077. This is the company that made my "spring collection system" (a flexible-plastic dam with pipe and fittings), spring box, and plastic reservoir. They have basic literature to help you plan how to tap your spring using their products.

American Association for Vocational Instructional Materials, *Planning for an Individual Water System* (New York: American Association for Vocational Instruction, 1982). Although this book focuses mainly on wells, there's also some information on springs.

Rainwater

Banks and Heinichen, *Rainwater Collection for the Mechanically Challenged* (Dripping Springs, Texas: Tank Town, 2002). A humorous and informative book for the owner-builder.

Daniel D. Chiras, *The Natural House* (White River Junction, Vt.: Chelsea Green, 2000). Has a good beginner section on rainwater collection.

"Waste" Water

Art Ludwig, *Create an Oasis with Greywater, Revised and Expanded Fourth Edition* (Santa Barbara, Calif.: Oasis Design, 1994-2002). A great introduction and how-to guide to greywater systems for the private home.

Joseph Jenkins, *The Humanure Handbook: A Guide to Composting Human Manure* (Grove City, Pa.: Jenkins Publishing, 1999). Some people find this an uncomfortable topic of conversation, but Joe Jenkins makes a very entertaining and convincing argument. The book can be ordered at www.jenkinspublishing.com.

Sim Van der Ryn, *The Toilet Papers* (White River Junction, Vt.: Chelsea Green, 2000). An inspirational classic of composting toiletology.

ALTERNATIVE POWER

The subjects of generating electric power through harnessing sun, wind, and water are technology-driven and, therefore, in a constant state of flux. Consequently, although many books are available on these topics, I think periodicals are the better way to educate yourself and keep up with the changes.

Home Power: The Hands-On Journal of Home-Made Power (Home Power, Inc.). A bimonthly magazine geared toward the home owner, and the best I know of on this subject. Articles on theory, fundamentals, new developments, and individual experiences, as well as equipment reviews and much more, all in a lively and opinionated editorial style.

THE INTERNET

GENERAL INFORMATION

Energy Efficiency and Renewable Energy (www.eren.doe.gov). Government website with fact sheets on all sorts of related subjects.

Greenpeace Toxics Archive Site (www.greenpeace.org/~toxics) Scary site from the organization Greenpeace discussing the effects of many modern products on the environment.

DAYLIGHTING

Daylighting Collaborative (www.daylighting.org). An information clearinghouse on daylighting in building design.

Biological Clocks (www.sfn.org/content/Publications/BrainBriefing/bio_clocks.html). Article on the effects of artificial light on humans, from the Society for Neuroscience.

INDOOR AIR QUALITY

Prescriptions for a Healthy House (www.nmbea.org/Consumer/healthy.htm). Site on maintaining healthful indoor air quality.

California Air Resources Board (www.arb.ca.gov/research/indoor/indoor.htm). Information on indoor air quality from the state of California.

Indoor and Outdoor Air Pollution (www.lbl.gov/Education/ELSI/pollution-main.html). Research information from the Lawrence Berkeley National Laboratory.

The Radon Information Center (www.radon.com). This is a commercial site by a company that sells in-home radon test kits online, but it also has lots of good radon information and links to other sources.

Bau-biologie (http://buildingbiology.net/). A quick introduction to the concept of Bau-biologie with information on workshops, books, etc.

Retrotec, Inc. (www.retrotec.com) Makers of blower-door testing equipment, and experts in the field of indoor airflow.

WATER AND WASTEWATER
National Testing Laboratories, Ltd. (www.ntllabs.com). Water-testing services.

Texas Guide to Rainwater Harvesting (www.twdb.state.tx.us/publications/reports/RainHarv.pdf). In-depth document on rainwater harvesting.

Oasis Design (www.oasisdesign.net). Great site on greywater and other water-related topics from pioneer Art Ludwig.

Living Machines, Inc. (www.livingmachines.com). This company designs indoor biological water-treatment systems that mimic natural purification processes.

Sun-Mar Composting Toilets (www.sun-mar.com). Manufacturers of a wide range of composting toilets.

ALTERNATIVE POWER
Florida Solar Energy Center (www.fsec.ucf.edu). Excellent site from the University of Central Florida on photovoltaics and other aspects of solar building.

Power Pal (www.powerpal.com). Innovative microhydro generator with built-in water dam.

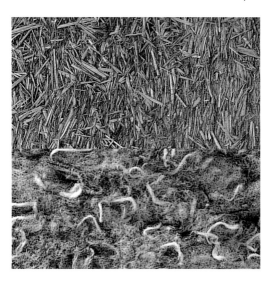

Canyon Industries, Inc. (www.canyonindustriesinc.com). Specialize in custom small-scale hydroelectric turbines and systems.

Energy Systems and Design, Ltd. (www.microhydropower.com). Makers of popular microhydro power generators.

Southwest Windpower (www.windenergy.com). A leader in wind energy and manufacturers of wind turbines and related products.

Real Goods (www.realgoods.com). Real Goods has been around since the 70s. They sell a wide variety of products, from photovoltaics, wind, and hydropower equipment to books and home products.

Controlled Energy Corporation (www.cechot.com). Distributors of tankless water heaters (including mine) and other energy-related equipment, with excellent customer support.

Thermo Technologies (www.thermomax.com). Designers and fabricators of advanced vacuum solar thermal systems.

BUILDINGS
Start noticing how the buildings around you connect to the outside. Use all of your senses, not just sight, for this exercise.

What does an office building or supermarket smell like? Do you notice moldy spaces, places where off-gassing is obvious, or buildings in which the air seems particularly refreshing? Do you encounter spaces that are too dark or that have too much sunlight? Find and visit people near you who have solar electricity, solar hot water, a rain catchment system, greywater system, or a composting toilet.

CHAPTER 7: APPLICATIONS

There are, of course, many sources that describe various applications of the concepts we've discussed. Some focus on a particular material, some on a particular skill or technique, some on a little bit of everything.

HARD COPY

Make sure the alternative housing books you choose discuss climate. No house exists in a vacuum. A practical, how-to book is of little value if it doesn't deal specifically and clearly with different climatic situations. Also, if you're far enough along to be considering actually building something or having something built, make sure the book discusses important construction details and the connection of different kinds of materials. From a construction standpoint, these details are what really set the different approaches apart. If you're not getting clear instructions on detailing, then you're not getting much more than I've already given you here in this general book.

Having said that, I also think it's a good idea to own books on as many different alternative approaches to housing as strike your fancy. Even though a certain approach may not be appropriate to your climate, there will be things to learn from reading about it, and you'll want to be able to refer to these resources at different stages in your process. Most sources that I've come across are at least adequate introductions.

Also, I recommend balancing things out with some reading on more conventional approaches. It'll help keep you on solid ground, not up in the clouds where most of us would rather be. Finally, get a general building reference book or two, something with wood span tables, metric conversion charts, and the like.

MAGAZINES

Fine Homebuilding Magazine (Taunton Press). A monthly magazine dedicated to all aspects of home building. A good place to get a balanced viewpoint on a variety of materials, tools, and techniques, including those from the alternative building world.

Joiners' Quarterly (Fox Maple Press). Quarterly magazine on traditional timber framing and other techniques. Associated with the Fox Maple School of Traditional Building, which offers building workshops.

BOOKS

Robert F. Bailey, *The Pocket Size Carpenter's Helper* (Belfast, Maine: R.S. Wood & Co., 1996). An amazing little book that I always carry with me. It covers everything from estimating volume for concrete pours and computing rafter lengths and angles to R-values for windows and useful trig functions.

Thomas J. Glover, *Pocket Ref* (Columbus, Ohio: Glencoe McGraw-Hill 1999). Another little book I'm never without. This one has basic charts and tables for plumbing, electrical, tools, water, welding, metals, and almost anything else you can think of. Need to know the specific gravity of acanthite? It's in here.

Athena Swentzell Steen, Bill Steen, and David Bainbridge, *The Straw Bale House* (White River Junction, Vt.: Chelsea Green, 1994). This book has introduced many people to building with straw. It has some outdated information, such as an inflated R-value for straw, but it's a good introduction to straw and how to use it in building.

Michel Bergeron and Paul Lacinski, *Serious Straw Bale: A Home Construction Guide for All Climates* (White River Junction, Vt.: Chelsea Green, 2000). Regardless of the title, this book is primarily about cold-climate straw bale construction. Very practical, solid, both-feet-on-the-ground information.

S.O. MacDonald and Matts Myhrman, *Build It With Bales* (White River Junction, Vt.: Chelsea Green, 1998). From two straw-bale-building renaissance pioneers, this book has a lot of information, including many construction detail illustrations.

Michael G. Smith, *The Cobber's Companion: How to Build Your Own Earthen Home* (Cottage Grove, Ore.: The Cob Cottage Company, 1999). A good, thorough how-to introduction to the world of cob building. Includes information on all aspects, from siting to mixes, wiring to plumbing.

Ianto Evans, Michael G. Smith, and Linda Smiley, *The Hand-Sculpted House: A Practical and Philosophical Guide to Building a Cob Cottage* (White River Junction, Vt.: Chelsea Green, 1998). This book is exciting and inspirational and, to my mind, more about paradigm shift than construction. I question some of the construction details and advice for novices, but still recommend it highly.

Michael Reynolds, *Earthship Volume 1: How to Build Your Own* and *Earthship Volume 2: Systems and Components* (Taos, N.Mex.: Solar Survival Press, 1990 and 1991). Michael Reynolds, the pioneer architect behind the Earthship concept, is a passionate advocate for shaking up our modern approach to housing. Both of these books are introductions to the concepts behind and construction methods for building Earthships.

Nader Khalili, *Ceramic Houses and Earth Architecture: How to Build Your Own* (Hesperia, Calif.: Cal-Earth Press, 1999). Khalili is the visionary behind the ceramic housing and superadobe building techniques. This is his book on making a ceramic house, and on superadobe.

Rob Roy, *Complete Book of Cordwood Masonry Housebuilding: The Earthwood Method* (New York: Sterling Publishing, 1992). Rob Roy is a pioneer and popularizer of cordwood construction. This is a thorough look at the topic.

THE INTERNET
STRAW BALE

House of Straw - Straw Bale Construction Comes of Age (www.eere.energy.gov/buildings/documents/strawbale.cfm). U.S. government site on straw bale construction.

The Last Straw (www.strawhomes.com). Website of the magazine of the same name, probably the premier periodical dealing with straw bale building, with many sample articles.

Natural Building Resources (www.strawbalecentral.com). Lots of wonderful, informative photos in the gallery section. The site focuses on straw bale but there's information on all sorts of materials and approaches.

EARTH

Groundworks (www.cpros.com/~sequoia). The website of Becky Bee, author of the popular book, *The Cob Builder's Handbook*.

The Cob Cottage Company (www.deatech.com/cobcottage). The Cob Cottage Company is a pioneer in modern cob construction. They offer workshops and publications.

Kleiworks (www.kleiwerks.com). A great group of people involved in workshops and building projects encompassing stone, timber frame, cob, slipstraw, bamboo, earth plasters, living roofs, built-in fireplaces, ceramic tiles, and other fine details.

California Institute of Earth Art and Architecture (www.calearth.org). Cal-Earth, an organization founded and directed by Nader Khalili, is involved in everything from work for NASA on technical innovations for lunar and Martian construction to UN-funded housing design and development for the world's homeless. Their website has lots of project photos as well as information on workshops, products, and more.

EARTHSHIPS

Earthship Biotecture (www.earthship.org). The website of Earthship founder Michael Reynold's organization.

Earthship Landing (www.earthships.com). A personal site about an Earthship project. Includes a virtual tour.

OTHER

Environmentally Conscious Building Design and Construction (www.geoswan.com). Website of George Swanson, who's featured in chapter 7 and is a consultant and designer of natural housing.

Experiments in Sustainable Urban Living (http://users.easystreet.com/ersson). Wonderful chronicle of Ole and Maitri Ersson's creative approach to urban living. Ole and Maitri are featured in a sidebar in the Connection chapter.

The Center for Maximum Potential Building Systems (www.cmpbs.org). My former employer and the place where I received my official indoctrination into alternative building techniques. The Center is an interesting place to visit either on the Web or in person.

Green Home (www.greenhome.com). A source of green alternatives to the household products you use everyday. Also a great source of information on creating a healthy home, including the Toxipedia (www.greenhome.com/toxipedia/), an alphabetical listing of definitions for and explanations of environmental terms.

Shelter Ecology (www.shelterecology.com). Cindy Meehan-Patton's company website offering a variety of building materials and household products geared toward a healthy, environmentally friendly home. Cindy's house is featured in chapter 7.

Ecovillage Training Center (www.thefarm.org/etc). The Ecovillage Training Center at the Farm, an intentional community in Tennessee, is "a whole systems immersion experience of ecovillage living." ETC founder Albert Bates contributed a number of photos for this book.

Earthaven Ecovillage (www.earthaven.org). If you've read this book you're familiar with Earthaven, because I've featured Earthaven buildings throughout, as well as member Chuck Marsh, in the Applications chapter. Among other things, Earthaven offers workshops on a wide variety of community, horticulture, and building topics. They are also actively soliciting new members. The Earthaven folks are into all sorts of things; check out their website to get a taste.

Earthaven Forestry Cooperative (www.earthaven.org/fc/fc.htm). A cooperatively owned business with a fresh approach to building houses using wood.

BUILDINGS

Once you get comfortable with what you've learned in this book and have done some of the building observation exercises I've suggested in this chapter and throughout the book, you should be ready to talk intelligently with anyone about housing. All you have to do now is keep your eyes open, and ask questions. Once you start to formulate ideas of what your own building might be like, seek out buildings that will be sources of inspiration and information for your personal situation. If you're interested in using straw, look for people and projects in your area that incorporate straw. Start trying to at least observe all the different stages of the construction of a house. Watch some site work, and a foundation being poured. Try some workshops. If you can swing it, sign onto a construction crew for a few months. If not, build a dog house or a shed or some other practice project.

This all may sound obvious, but for many people the first house building they've really paid attention to is the one they're paying for with their life savings and a 30-year mortgage; the first bulldozer they've ever really looked at is the one that pulls up at their house site. Don't wait that long; get involved right now. Observe the process of building. Get your hands on some tools. Get your hands in the mud. Get some sweat on your brow. A house isn't primarily intellectual or monetary. It's mostly a material manifestation of physical action. The more you understand what that means, the more successful your role will be in the process of creating your good house.

CHAPTER 8: REALITY CHECK

Here's where your dreams for a good house meet the realities of actually building that house. Learning about, understanding, and dealing with those realities is the key to making the dreams come true.

HARD COPY

I guarantee that much of the material I recommend below is reading that you *can* put down—but that you probably shouldn't if you want a full picture of the realities of building a house.

MONEY MATTERS

Most of the books dealing with alternative or natural building, including many I've listed in this chapter, lean toward the "banks bad, cash good" view, and have sections on building without a mortgage. Central to this strategy is the necessity for investing your own physical labor. There are also a number of books devoted entirely to the subject of debt-free building. One, which I admit I haven't read, is:

Rob Roy, *Mortgage-Free!: Radical Strategies for Home Ownership* (White River Junction, Vt.: Chelsea Green, 1998).

If you're considering the mortgage approach, there are literally hundreds of books on the subject to choose from. Just be sure you do some exhaustive research beyond reading that little pamphlet handed to you by your friendly bank loan officer.

BUILDING CODES

Even if you don't plan on ever seeing an inspector, buy a copy of your state building code as soon as you decide to build. You don't have to read it cover to cover, but look it over and then keep it close at hand for quick reference. Even if you aren't building within the confines of the code, it has all sorts of good information like span tables and load charts.

PLANNING

Get your hands on a copy of the blueprints for a house and spend some time learning to read them and the various symbols used. Even if your plans will end up being little more than a sketch on a napkin, you'll want to know how to convey important information by using the standard symbols and protocols used on blueprints.

THE INTERNET

Our Earthship (www.earthpower1.com). A website chronicling the real-life trials and tribulations of a determined couple, Jason and Ellen, as they go through the process of building their own Earthship. Be sure to read the amazing saga of their efforts to obtain a building permit!

Also, while you're on the Internet, see if your state's building code is available online; at the least, you can probably order it online. Just do a search for "(your state) building code".

BUILDINGS

Talk to people who've been there. Seek out owner-builders and get their full stories, which most likely will come pouring out as soon as you start asking probing questions: What went wrong? What went right? If you meet a professional builder, describe your plans and ask for an honest reaction. Look for buildings that you really love and try to find out the stories behind them. Is such a project possible for you? Also, keep an eye out for stalled, abandoned, or otherwise unfinished house building attempts. Try to determine what problems the builders may have run into. Are there signs of serious mistakes—a cracked foundation, sagging walls? Use all the buildings around you to help gauge your own limits and abilities.

METRICS CONVERSION CHART

To convert from U.S. units to metric, multiply by the number given in the middle column, then round the resulting number up or down. Example: To convert 10.1 feet to meters, multiply by 0.3048; the answer is 3.078 meters, which can be rounded to 3.08. To convert from metric units to the U.S. system, divide rather than multiply.

	U.S. "INCH-POUND" SYSTEM	MULTIPLY BY	TO DETERMINE METRIC EQUIVALENT
LENGTH	Inch	25.4	Millimeter
	Foot	0.3048	Meter
	Yard	0.9144	Meter
	Mile	1.609344	Kilometer
AREA	Square inch	645.16	Square millimeter
	Square foot	0.09290304	Square meter
	Square yard	0.8361274	Square meter
	Square mile	2.589988	Square kilometer
	Acre	0.40469	Hectare
MASS	Ounce	0.02834952	Kilogram
	Pound	0.45359237	Kilogram
	Ton	0.9071847	Tonne
VOLUME	Fluid ounce	29.57353	Milliliter
	Gallon	3.785412	Liter
	Cubic inch	16.387064	Cubic millimeter
	Cubic foot	0.02831685	Cubic meter
	Cubic yard	0.7645549	Cubic meter

U.S. "INCH-POUND" SYSTEM	MULTIPLY BY	TO DETERMINE METRIC EQUIVALENT
TEMPERATURE		
	Formula:	
Degrees Fahrenheit	Minus 32 times 5 divided by 9	Degrees Celsius
OTHER APPLICATIONS		
	Pressure	
Pounds per square inch (PSI)	6.896	Kilopascals
Feet head of water	2.988	Kilopascals
Feet head of water	0.3048	Meters head of water
	Energy and Heat	
British thermal units (BTU)	1055.06	Joules
R-value	0.176110	RSI
	Velocity	
Miles per hour (mph)	1.6093	Kilometers per hour (km/hr)

ACKNOWLEDGMENTS

An unexpected bonus in writing this book, one that often re-energized me, was meeting, talking with, and receiving help from a lot of wonderful, interesting people. I'd like to specially thank the following:

Don Gurewitz is a photographer and world traveler whose wonderful photos of traditional buildings expanded the breadth of this book tenfold. To learn about his schedule of slide lectures and gallery showings, contact Don at 23A Kelly Rd., Cambridge, MA 02139, 617-354-6266 or dgurewitz@juno.com.

The folks at Earthaven, a community of people building a wonderful little village in the mountains of western North Carolina. Earthaven's buildings are a smorgasbord of approaches to housing construction. You'll find many photos of them in this book. Check Earthaven out at www.earthaven.org.

Chuck Marsh was my Earthaven tour guide, historian, and building sciences consultant. To me, Chuck embodies hope for the future of building: he has the courage to think and act big and outside of the norm, plus a sense of humor that realizes we are all so very small and normal. He's also a permaculture/ecological design teacher and consultant, and a landscape horticulturist. Contact Chuck at 828-669-1759 or chuck@earthaven.org.

Janel Kapoor was both a great networking source for this book and a calming, positive influence on my somewhat jaded sensibilities. She also let me photograph a couple of her building workshops. Contact her through Kleiwerks at www.kleiwerks.com.

Rob Amberg is an amazing photographer and neighbor. When I found myself suddenly cameraless, Rob generously and without trepidation lent me some of his personal equipment. The result was most of the best photos that I took for this book. Thanks, Rob!

A lot of building professionals took time out of their busy lives to answer my questions and, in some cases, to lend me photos. I hope the following is a complete list: **Erik Alm, David Moore, Mollie Curry, Helmut Ziehe, Phillip Van Horn, Norbert Senf, Dan Chiras, George Swanson, Cindy Meehan-Patton, Art Ludwig, Albert Bates, Colin McGhee, Larry Comras, Peter Belt, Fred Lugano, Charlie Miller,** and **Michel Spaan.**

I'm especially indebted to the builders and owner-builders who opened their homes up to my scrutiny and so openly answered my detailed questions about their buildings and the process that brought them into being. Thanks so much **Marc** and **Amy, Nelle** and **Doug, Chuck, George, Cindy,** and **Dan!**

A general thank you to everyone who contributes to creating the incredible library of information that is the Internet. Many strangers answered my queries with nothing to gain but the pleasure of sharing information. Thanks specifically to:

Jason Crow for sharing his story and pictures of an owner-builder's Earthship odyssey.

Ole and **Maitri Ersson** for their inspiring "Experiments in Urban Sustainability."

Allen Stankevitz for supplying photos of the cordwood house that he is building with his family.

Thanks to the following friends and family for their help and/or inspiration:

Greg Jackson for being my first carpentry teacher and helping me to envision a slightly different way to do things.

Pliny Fisk and **Gail Vitorri** for giving me my first hands-on access to the world of building alternatives at the Center for Maximum Potential.

Robert and **Jane Peebles** for babysitting us through our crash course in backwoods living, letting me photograph their reservoir, and giving us all of those salvage doors and windows!

David Reed for loaning me his light table and slide loupe the first time I met him. That little act of kindness saved me many hours of eyestrain.

Ann and **Farley Snell** for everything!

Bill and **Eileen Mandle** for being my favorite parents-in-law.

Of course, I also need to thank everyone at Lark Books who helped make this book a reality:

Carol Taylor, Deborah Morgenthal, and **Rob Pulleyn** for making this project possible and standing behind the book as it changed and grew.

Terry Krautwurst, my editor, for wrestling the beast onto the page.

Kathy Holmes, my art director, for her incredible vision and ability to somehow keep all of those photos in the vicinity of relevant text.

Olivier Rollin for taking my extremely rough sketches and turning them into superb illustrations, featured throughout the book.

Veronika Gunter for patiently hunting down the photos I couldn't find.

Rosemary Kast for cheerily answering what must have been hundreds of phone calls.

Most of all, I want to thank **Lisa** for being my partner in every bizarre scheme of the past 15 years. Does anyone exist who has more skills than this woman? You make it all worthwhile.

Photography Credits

Clarke Snell

Pages 3; 5 (middle bottom); 6 (top); 7; 8; 9 (top, middle left, middle right); 10; 17 (upper left, lower left, lower right); 18 (upper left, lower left); 19 (lower left); 20; 21 (upper right, middle left, middle right); 24 (upper left, lower right); 25 (lower right); 28 (lower right); 29; 32 (upper right); 33; 34 (middle, lower right); 35; 36 (lower right); 37; 39 (bottom); 41 (upper right, lower right); 43 (top, middle left, bottom); 47; 49 (top center, middle left, middle right, bottom center, bottom right); 50; 51 (upper right, lower right); 52 (upper right); 54 (upper left, middle, lower right); 55 (middle, bottom row); 56 (top row, bottom right); 60 (bottom row); 61 (top left); 62 (upper left); 63 (upper right); 67 (middle left, middle right); 71; 73 (lower right); 74; 75 (lower right); 76; 80 (upper left, upper right); 81; 83 (lower right); 84; 85 (lower right); 88 (upper right, middle left, middle right); 89; 90; 91 (right); 92 (upper left); 93; 94 (lower left); 95 (top center, middle center, middle right, bottom left, bottom center); 98; 99; 100; 101; 103 (center, right); 104 (upper left); 105; 106; 107; 114 (upper left, upper right, lower right); 116 (lower left); 117; 120; 122; 123; 124; 126 (bottom center); 128 (upper left, upper right); 130; 132; 134; 136; 139; 141 (upper left); 142; 145 (upper left, middle, lower right); 160–167; 168; 170 (lower left, right); 171; 172; 173; 174; 175; 176 (upper left); 177 (lower right); 179; 181 (left, center); 182–188; 190; 191; 192; 194 (upper right, bottom); 195; 196; 199; 200; 201; 202; 206; 207; 208; 209; 210; 212; 213; 214 (upper right, middle right, bottom); 218; 221; 223; 225; 226; 227

Don Gurewitz

Pages 5 (top); 14;16 (upper left, lower left); 17 (upper right); 18 (upper right, lower right); 19 (upper right); 21 (upper left); 23; 24 (lower left); 25 (lower left, middle right); 27 (upper left, lower right); 28 (lower left); 30; 31 (middle); 32 (upper left, lower left); 39 (upper right); 43 (middle right); 45; 49 (top left, top right); 52 (upper left); 55 (top row); 57 (upper right); 60 (top row, middle row); 72; 88 (bottom); 92 (lower left); 95 (top left, middle left); 96; 97; 103 (left); 104 (lower left); 110-111; 115; 116 (upper left); 119; 121; 131; 194 (upper left); 205; 214 (middle left); 216; 219; 220; 224

Other Individuals

Albert Bates (© 2001 Institute for Appropriate Technology): 63 (top center); 79 (lower right)

Dan Chiras: 9 (bottom); 67 (bottom); 79 (upper right); 82; 109 (middle); 145 (upper right); 147 (left); 148; 149; 150; 151; 152

John Fulker: 26 (lower right)

Greg Jackson: 38 (lower left)

Janel Kapoor: 56 (bottom left); 61 (bottom left); 222

Doug Keefer/Nelle Gregory: 169; 170 (upper left)

Cindy Meehan-Patton: 145 (lower left); 176 (lower left); 177 (upper left, upper right); 178; 214 (upper left)

Norbert Senf: 86; 87

Michel Spaan: 27 (upper right); 51 (bottom center); 57 (middle right); 62 (top center); 85 (upper right)

Alan Stankevitz: 5 (bottom); 40 (lower right)

Linda Stuart: 147 (right)

George Swanson: 56 (bottom center)

Phillip Van Horn: 6 (middle); 25 (upper right); 26 (upper left, lower left); 95 (top right)

J. Weiland: 180; 181 (right)

Other Sources

Asian Phoenix Resources Ltd.: 141 (upper right, lower left)

The California Institute of Earth Art and Architecture: 40 (upper left, lower left); 58; 61 (bottom right); 217

Canyon Industries, Inc.: 141 (lower right)

Durisol Building Systems, Inc.: 54 (upper right); 83 (upper right)

Grand Shelters, Inc.: 59 (lower right)

Image45: 153; 154; 155; 156; 157; 158; 159

J-Drain: 46 (lower right)

Jenkins Publishing (from *The Humanure Handbook*): 127

MWB R-Pro: 80 (lower left, lower right)

National Park Service/photo by Chris Judson: 73 (upper right)

Oasisdesign.net: 114 (middle); 125

Optigrün International AG: 113

The Plastic Lumber Company, Inc.: 38 (upper left)

Rastra Technologies, Inc.: 38 (lower right)

Red Sky Shelters: 65; 66

Roofscapes Inc.: 41 (upper left); 59 (upper left)

Solar Survival Press: 21 (bottom); 36 (upper left); 49 (bottom left); 61 (top right); 67 (top); 75 (upper right)

Southwest Windpower: 114 (lower left); 140

Sun-Mar Corp.: 126 (lower left)

Thatching.com: 5 (top middle); 31 (top); 59 (upper right); 88 (upper left); 94 (upper left, center); 109 (top center, upper right)

Thermomax: 138

USDA-ARS Information Staff: 91 (left)

U.S. Dept. of the Interior, Bureau of Reclamation, Lower Colorado Region: 46 (upper left); 49 (middle center); 128 (lower left)

Users.easystreet.com/ersson: 143; 144

U.S. Fish and Wildlife Service/photo by Steve Hillebrand: 34 (lower left)

Courtesy Village Igloo, Quebec/photo by Bardy-Canet: 16 (upper right)

Wellington Polymer Technology, Inc.: 95 (bottom right); 109 (lower right)

Wichita State University Libraries, Department of Special Collections: 31 (lower right); 36 (lower left); 193

ABOUT THE AUTHOR

Clarke Snell is a builder with experience using a wide variety of materials and techniques, both conventional and alternative. He entered the world of construction with a clear and simple goal: to build his own "good house." His first construction job was at The Center for Maximum Potential in Austin, Texas, where he helped create the Green Builder Demonstration Home, a state-funded showcase of alternative building techniques. Since then, Clarke has been involved in a number of building projects, including the construction of his own partially bermed, passive solar house in the mountains of western North Carolina. He plans to live there for the rest of his life with his wife, Lisa, an ever-increasing array of plants, some cats, and tons of ladybugs. Clarke can be reached by email at alternativebuilding@hotmail.com.

INDEX

A

Acid rain, 122, 134

ACQ, 178

Active solar design, 69, 69 fig. 3.
    See also Passive solar design;
    Photovoltaics

Adding on, to houses, 202

Adobe, 25, 72, 108

Air, composition of, 129, 129 fig. 7

Air circulation, 129

Air conditioning, southern, 78

Air exchanger, mechanical, 132

Air locks, 71

Air movement, heating and cooling
    with, 77–78. *See also* Ventilation

Air pollution, 34–35, 86–87, 96, 130, 222

Air quality
    indoor, 34, 130–32, 133, 178–79,
        222–23
    outdoor, 130

Ammonium Copper Quat (ACQ), 178

Anasazi, passive solar design of, 73

Ancient cultures
    passive solar design of, 72–73
    water systems of, 120

Anemometers, 140

Animal products, as building
    materials, 32

Animals, damage-causing, 91

Applied skins, 93–94, 95

Aquifers, 121

Arbors, solar, 85

Arches, 58, 218

Architecture, Vedic, 153, 154

Arrays, photovoltaic, 135 fig 9, 136

Artesian wells, 123

Artificial light, sunlight vs., 119, 120

Asphalt, 19
    roof shingles made from, 109

Atmosphere, 129

B

Bamboo, as building material, 31, 40, 96
    examples of, 41, 55

Basement walls, 48

Batch water heaters, 138

Batteries, for solar energy storage, 136,
    136 fig. 10

Bau-biologie, 133, 223

Bermed houses, partially, 50, 77, 105

Biological clocks, 119, 222

Biological land treatment, 122

Blackwater, 126

Blueprints, 209, 227

Books. *See* Resources

Breadbox water heaters, 138

Breathable walls, 102–5, 132, 133
    examples of, 153, 154, 157, 158, 173
    in humid climates, 178

Bricks, 25
    veneers of, 93

Builders
    being own, 197, 203–7
    finding, 208
    local, 205–6

Building materials. *See also specific types*
    alternative, 35–41
    choosing, 22, 195
    combining, 82–83, 100, 198 fig. 1
    cost of, 197–99
    criteria for good, 22, 34–35
    local, 39–41, 96, 97
    mass production of, 33, 34–35, 159
    misinformation about, 78
    modern, 33, 96
    natural, 41
    resources on, 217
    salvaged, 177–78, 181, 199
    traditional, 23–32, 39

Buildings, modern, 16–18, 73–74

Building sites
    choosing, 118, 118 fig. 1, 147–48, 153,
        161, 168–69, 183
    using materials from, 39–41, 96, 97

C

Cancer, lung, from radon, 131

Capillary action, 90

Catchment systems, rainwater,
    124 fig. 4, 124–25, 143, 158

Cellulose
    in breathable walls, 102, 133
    insulation from, 37, 80–81, 219

Cement, Portland. *See* Portland cement

Cement stuccos, 104–5, 106

Ceramic construction, 40, 59, 225

Chemical sensitivity, building a
    house for, 175–81

Chimneys, flashing for, 101 fig. 5

China, ancient, passive solar
    design in, 73

Chiras, Dan, house of, 109, 147–52, 189

Chlorine, added to water systems, 117

Circadian rhythms, 119

Cisterns, 124, 124 fig. 4, 125 fig. 5
    examples of, 124, 143, 158

Clay-slip straw construction, 36, 37,
    161–62

Clearcut, 34

Climate, housing as response to, 14, 14
    fig. 2, 15 fig. 3. *See also*
    Environment; Nature

Cob construction, 24, 34, 39, 108, 225
    connections for, 62 fig. 14
    examples of, 24, 56
    mass and insulation in, 82

Codes, building, 210–11, 227

Coliseum (Rome), 28

Color, in cooling and heating, 70 fig. 4,
    71, 78, 85

Composite blocks, 37, 48, 83, 108.
    See also Faswall blocks

Composting toilets, 126, 127, 223

Compression, 44 fig. 1

Concrete, 27–28, 29
    for foundations, 48
    recycled ingredients in, 38
    roller compacted, 29
    Roman, 28, 29, 217

Condensation, 91

Conduction, 71
    preventing heat loss from, 78, 79

Connections, structural, 62 fig. 14, 62–63

Continuous foundations, 47, 47 fig. 6